The Divine Mistress

by SAMUEL EDWARDS

[pseud.]

DAVID McKAY COMPANY, Inc.

New York

THE DIVINE MISTRESS

COPYRIGHT © 1970 BY SAMUEL EDWARDS

Library of Congress Catalog Card Number: 70-112446

MANUFACTURED IN THE UNITED STATES OF AMERICA

VAN REES PRESS • NEW YORK

For

Anne W. Brennan

Émilie, in truth, is the divine mistress, endowed with beauty, wit, compassion and all of the other womanly virtues. Yet I frequently wish she were less learned and her mind less sharp, that her appetites for the making of love were less voracious, and more than all else, that she would acquire both the ability and desire to hold her tongue on occasion.

—VOLTAIRE

The Divine Mistress

I

"Hate me if you must," Émilie, Marquise du Châtelet, wrote to Frederick the Great of Prussia. "*I would not deny you the pleasure that this primitive feeling would give you. But be not indifferent to me, I beg you, as I could not tolerate it. Ridicule my scientific studies and my translations from the classics of antiquity, if it gives you pleasure to treat me with contempt, but do not ignore me.*

"*Judge me for my own merits, or my lack of them, but do not look upon me as a mere appendage to this great general or that renowned scholar, this star that shines at the court of France or that famed author. I am in my own right a whole person, responsible to myself alone for all that I am, all that I say, all that I do. It may be that there are metaphysicians and philosophers whose learning is greater than mine, although I have not met them. Yet, they are but frail humans, too, and have their faults; so, when I add the sum total of my graces, I confess that I am inferior to no one.*"

Frederick, one of the most arrogant men of the overbearingly intellectual eighteenth century, did not take offense at her tone, perhaps because he was trying to coax Émilie and her current lover, Voltaire, the age's giant of letters, to pay a visit to his country-town capital, Berlin. Certainly he was not yet enmeshed in his violent feud with Émilie, when both dipped their pens in acid, and it is possible that he felt genuine admiration for her work. After all, few women of the period could read and write, much less make valid experiments in physics, chemistry, and mathematics, write poetry that was original, if not striking, and translate the Greek of Aristotle and Sophocles and the Latin of Virgil, Ovid, and Horace into French with fluent, fluid ease. Regarded as one of the great beauties of her time, even by her enemies, she had good cause to consider herself out of the ordinary.

In any event, Frederick displayed a sense of tact, a rare quality he seldom utilized, in a reply he sent to both Émilie and Voltaire. *"What admirable and unique people you both are!"* he declared. *"The wonder of all who know you increases day by day."*

It was not accidental that Gabrielle Émilie le Tonnelier de Breteuil du Châtelet was, as Voltaire once called her, a natural phenomenon of the first half of the eighteenth century. Although no one knew it at the time, she was destined from birth to be different, exceptional, and frequently impossible. At first glance neither her heredity nor the environment in which she was reared appear unusual, but her life and personality prove that hasty glances can be deceptive.

Émilie, at times her own most ardent admirer, had to search for clues in order to determine what made her remarkable, and attributed much to her maternal great-grandmother, Mme. de Neuillant, the tutor, counselor, and lifelong friend of an even more remarkable woman, Françoise d'Aubigné. The latter, as the widow of a poet named Scarron, became the governess of the illegitimate children of King Louis XIV and achieved a permanent place in history under the name of Mme. de Maintenon. A curious blend of the devout and the sensual, she reformed a dissolute court, persuaded Louis to marry her in private, and became the most influential woman in France. There is reason to suspect that Émilie, as a child, dreamed of emulating great-grandma's protégé, and she achieved her goal, although her influence was exerted in fields unknown to her as a little girl.

Nothing in Émilie's immediate background indicated the heights to which she would rise. Her father, Louis-Nicolas, Baron de Breteuil, was a minor noble whose whole life was devoted to petty pursuits at the court of Louis XIV, where the inconsequential was magnified beyond the limits of reality, provided it took place at the Versailles court of the self-styled Sun King. Her mother, Alexandra-Elisabeth de Froulay, was the impoverished younger sister of the Baron's mistress, who at the same time was married to his own uncle. When the Baron met Alexandra he transferred his affection to the lovely, frivolous girl, and they were married in 1699, a year to the day after the birth of their first child. René-Alexandre. The coincidence, as the Baron was fond of saying, was an omen.

In 1701 de Breteuil received a juicy royal plum, the appointment to a post as chief of protocol at the court, a position that required him to present all visiting foreign dignitaries to Louis, other members of the royal family, and the principal dignitaries in residence at Versailles. The visitors were expected to pay him for the privilege, which they did, handsomely, bringing him an income equal to $150,000 per year today. Louis-Nicolas's family lived accordingly in sumptuous splendor, and the children were denied no luxury. The youngest of the four children, Émilie, born in 1706, was her father's favorite, so it is not surprising that she developed exorbitantly expensive tastes early in life. It never occurred to her, literally, to want or accept anything other than the best.

"*Émilie*," mourned the Duc de Richelieu, the distinguished soldier-statesman who became her lover for a time, "*has no interest in the cost of anything she desires. It is enough that she wants it.*"

Her own attitude is reflected in her response to Richelieu's complaints of her extravagance. "*Money*," she wrote him, "*bores me almost as much as your carping.*"

When Émilie was one year old, her father received an additional appointment, that of Principal Secretary to the King, which fattened his purse, increased his influence at court, and made him unbearable. A vast majority of the many inveterate letter-writers of the period report that Louis-Nicolas was pompous, opinionated, and empty-headed, qualities that made him a perfect choice for the post he held. His blonde, gray-eyed wife had little to commend her, either, other than her beauty and her insistence that her children acquire impeccable manners.

Versailles was so crowded that no quarters were available for a minor noble's large family, so Louis-Nicolas lodged his wife and children in a three-story Paris town house overlooking the Tuileries gardens. A staff of seventeen servants waited on them, making it unnecessary, as Voltaire later observed, for Émilie to scratch herself when she suffered an itch. By the time the girl was six she had been taught by her mother to eat soft-boiled eggs in any one of eight correct ways, to serve after-dinner liqueur to guests without spilling a drop, and, above all, to reject the standards, attitudes, and customs of the middle class. No de Breteuil was permitted to forget for an instant that he or she was an aristocrat.

By the time Émilie was seven or eight, it appeared that of all the children she alone had been deprived of her mother's good looks. *"My youngest,"* Louis-Nicolas wrote sadly, *"is an odd creature destined to become the homeliest of women. Were it not for the low opinion I hold of several bishops, I would prepare her for a religious life and let her hide in a convent. She stands as tall as a girl twice her years, she has prodigious strength, like that of a wood-cutter, and is clumsy beyond belief. Her feet are huge, but one forgets them the moment one notices her enormous hands. Her skin, alas, is as rough as a nutmeg grater, and altogether she is as ugly as a Gascon peasant recruit in the regiment of royal footguards."*

Perhaps the Baron exaggerated, but several cousins indicated in their correspondence that Émilie was an unattractive child. She herself referred to the situation in her later years, commenting smugly that she did not become beautiful until her fifteenth year, at which time she was forbidden to go into the kitchens when tradesmen were present. It is possible that she was considered ungainly because of her unusual height; she stood almost five feet nine inches tall, which was exceptional in her day, and towered over almost everyone she knew. She looked down at Richelieu, she was the better part of a head taller than Voltaire, and she had to stand on her toes to kiss only one man, Saint-Lambert, the rogue who, half her age, proved her undoing when she was in her forties.

Ignored by her mother, who spent hours primping before a mirror each day, Émilie found a substitute in a half-sister many years her senior, her father's daughter by a previous marriage. Ann-Louise, who died of a mysterious ailment at the age of twenty-two, was passionately devoted to her extensive wardrobe, and Émilie, imitating her, developed an equally intense interest in clothes. *"No queen owns a larger wardrobe,"* Voltaire wrote, *"and no one but a queen could afford so many gowns, shoes, wigs, and other fripperies."*

Louis-Nicolas apparently felt the need to help his clothes-conscious ugly duckling prepare for a life as a spinster. It was taken for granted that young ladies of quality would marry gentlemen of the same station, but it was inconceivable that any man would be interested in someone as homely as little Émilie. So from the age of six or seven the child was surrounded by governesses and tutors of exceptional talent, men and women devoted to learning for its own sake, who worked hard to kindle the same enthusiasm for knowledge in their charge.

Émilie, shunned by all her relatives except Ann-Louise, with whom she spent two or three hours each day, desperately wanted the approval of her tutors, which meant she had to study. By the time she was ten she knew that intellectual self-

5

discipline was the secret of learning, and she had acquired astonishing aptitudes. Voltaire is the authority for the assertion that she had already mastered Latin, and knew by rote long passages from Virgil, Lucretius, and Horace. She was also familiar with all the philosophical works of Cicero and was already showing a persisting interest in metaphysics and mathematics. Her ability to learn foreign languages appeared almost unlimited. By the time she was twelve she could read, write, and speak fluent English, Italian, Spanish, and German. She was translating Aristotle's *Politics* and *Aesthetics* from the original classical Greek for her own edification and amusement, and made her first translation of the *Aeneid* from Latin, a task she would repeat as an adult, thereby winning herself enduring fame.

Her life was not confined to the world of books, however. Hoping to cure her of her clumsiness, her father also hired a fencing master, a riding instructor, and a gymnast to tutor her. By the time she was fourteen she was a superb horsewoman, could beat most gentlemen of the court in a duel, and could climb any tree in Paris or in the woods of St. Denis beyond the old gates of Paris.

The death of Ann-Louise left Émilie lonelier than ever, and she threw herself into her studies, her riding, and her fencing with an energy that would amaze the colleagues with whom she was later associated. The source of that energy is difficult to ascertain, since she inherited it from neither of her parents. There are hints in the letters of the ever perspicacious Voltaire, written after her death, that Émilie incessantly sought and demanded love, which her mother and father had denied her. Seen in modern psychiatric terms, it might be argued that the yearning for love was responsible for her over-abundant, inexhaustible energy. But such speculation serves little purpose, since it is impossible to analyze the inspiration and drives of a genius.

In 1720, when the ugly duckling was fourteen, she began to be transformed into the proverbial swan, a change that her parents noted first with incredulity, then with delight. For five years, since the death of Louis XIV, the Baron's influence at court had been negligible. Louis XV, the Sun King's grandson, was a child, and France was being ruled by a Regency, in which the powers were divided. One of the regents was dissolute, a second was extravagant, and only the third, Cardinal Fleury, the boy monarch's tutor, was a man of ability. It was unfortunate that Fleury had strong despotic tendencies, which he curbed to some slight extent until he could gather power completely into his own hands. In the meantime he managed to dispense with some of the almost innumerable officials whose wages were a drain on the royal treasury.

Among those rendered jobless was Louis-Nicolas, who had saved only a small fraction of his enormous income, but who had no idea how to cut down expenses. His two sons were of little help, the elder going to court and the younger entering the army. His third child, Elisabeth, was a vapidly pretty girl who could not be expected to contract a brilliant marriage because she lacked a sufficient dowry. That left the newly emerging beauty, Émilie, who had so many talents that she might attract as a husband a man of stature willing to overlook the financial pittance she would bring with her.

Louis-Nicolas cannily waited for her beauty to develop, and not until Émilie was sixteen did he take her to court. Her brothers and sister had been familiar with Versailles for years, and took its splendor, its extravagance, its licentiousness, and its corruption for granted. Émilie, lacking the sophistication of her more cosmopolitan siblings, was delighted by this gaudy world. Although a girl of sixteen was considered a woman in the first half of the eighteenth century, her reactions were those of an enthusiastic, somewhat unpredictable child. Isolated by her studies and her outdoor activities, she was lacking in the more worldly attributes of her class. This joyous, sometimes

7

bumptious, delight was a vestigial form of infantilism she retained until she died, and was regarded—by those who liked her, at least—as an integral part of her charm.

Her future enemies were less charitable. Mme. du Deffand, who despised her and made a career of writing nasty letters about her, later commented that *"Mme. du Châtelet displays virginal delight at all the wrong moments. How absurd it is to see a grown woman, herself the mother of an adolescent daughter, behaving like a contemporary of the daughter. I cannot believe these feelings which she parades are genuine."*

King Louis XV was not only more charitable, but proved himself a better judge of character when he remarked, *"Mme. du Châtelet's joy with all things, the pleasure she shows in response to small things, make her attractive. The ladies who cannot conceal their boredom become boring, but one is never bored in her company."*

Certainly the many rakes and profligates of the Regency court were not bored when the young, ripe Émilie made her appearance at Versailles. She was uncommonly tall, to be sure, but her figure was that of a grown woman and fitted the ideal of the era. Her bust was full, her waist tiny, and her hips broad, and although still rather awkward, she carried herself with the refreshing vigor of an outdoor girl. Large quantities of very bad poetry soon were written in her honor, many of these worthless works describing her as a modern Juno. Her hair was blonde, like her mother's, gradually turning somewhat darker as she grew older, and her eyes were described by most who knew her as gray. Voltaire, a more precise observer, called them hazel. Her oval-shaped face was narrower than the fashion of the times dictated, but her lips were provocatively sensual, providing a startling contrast with her innocent eyes, and her nose, unlike that of other members of the de Breteuil family, was straight. Nature, making up for lost time, was also responsible for the clearing of her skin.

It was said that a prince and a marquis made a wager the

day Émilie arrived at Versailles, each vowing he would be the first to seduce her. Other nobles, high-ranking army and navy officers, and a number of government officials also had the same goal in mind. In all, the chances that the girl would remain a virgin were slim.

In spite of the dissolute nature of high society, in which every man had an official mistress as well as a wife, and every married woman had an official lover as well as a husband, the young, unmarried maiden long had been considered taboo. This was not because the gentlemen of the court entertained high scruples, but was a practical matter dictated by necessity. As every father and mother knew, their daughter's chances of contracting a satisfactory marriage declined sharply if she lost her virginity prior to her wedding night.

Louis-Nicolas made it his business to act as a buffer between Émilie and the many who lusted after her, and he obviously had his hands full. The girl was protected far better than he knew, or than she herself realized, however. Her ingenuousness was a wall the lechers of Versailles could not penetrate, and Émilie succeeded in confusing them. Then, one afternoon about three months after her arrival, she donned fencing clothes for a bout with Colonel Jacques de Brun, commander of the royal household guard. She needed the exercise, she said, and most of the ladies and gentlemen of the court appeared in the hall of arms to watch the rare spectacle.

Émilie was no match for the professional soldier, to be sure, but she gave a remarkably good account of herself. Admirers whose intentions were other than honorable became thoughtful, and all but the most intrepid promptly directed their attentions elsewhere. No affair was worth running the risk of being forced to fight a duel in earnest with the lady herself, and any man who might be wounded by her would be laughed out of court.

"The wench is formidable," the Duc de Richelieu wrote years later, when their famous affair was beginning to wane.

"No man can resist her natural beauty, but no man has the courage to admit that she exhausts him. She rides and wields a sword like a hussar, and she becomes so ferocious when a lover vexes her that she would not hesitate to run him through. I hope to arrange the termination of our relationship in such a way that Émilie, not I, will be responsible for our parting. I have no desire to cross swords with her, for I am convinced that her blade would be as deadly as her tongue."

Richelieu, of all men, was able to judge her talents as a duelist. Not only was he commander-in-chief of all French armies in the field, with the rank of full general, but he had won three duels, wounding two opponents and killing the third.

Apparently the young Émilie's tongue was also as sharp as her sword, and her scathing wit held would-be seducers at bay. In later years she would acquire the reputation, richly deserved, of slicing the pompous, the boring, and the pretentious to shreds, utilizing the simple technique of speaking with brutal candor. The many letter-writers of the Regency court give no examples of her humor, but they refer to her frequently, saying that within a short time of her arrival at Versailles, her tongue was feared. She herself had not yet become a letter-writer.

In one way or another, she was her own most effective protectress, and her virtue remained unassailable. But the influence of Versailles was pernicious in many ways, and she quickly acquired habits that complicated her life for the rest of her days.

Primary among these was her love of extravagance. She had been reared in a family that showed a magnificent scorn for money, of course, both of her parents spending recklessly, saving virtually nothing in spite of the huge income her father had earned for many years. Now, at the court, the impressionable young girl saw jewelry, clothing, and furnishings that were sumptuous beyond her wildest dreams. Wanting everything that life had to offer, she developed a craving for the finest, regardless of whether she could afford a gem, a length of silk cloth, or a coach of her own with her crest on the doors. *"Émilie's tastes,"* Voltaire wrote many years later, *"are impeccable, and she is so covetous that not even the wealthiest of kings could afford to grant her desires. What she sees, she wants, and her eyesight is remarkably keen."*

Games of chance fascinated her, and she soon acquired such skill as a card player that other young ladies were reluctant to sit at the same table with her. This suited Émilie, who preferred to play *vingt-et-un* with the men, who gambled for higher stakes. Since her own funds were limited, she could ill afford to play with princes related to the royal family and wealthy dukes, but she refused to be deterred by common sense. Good luck and an instinct for cards enabled her to win consistently, and she spent the money as fast as she acquired it.

"My daughter," Louis-Nicolas wrote to his uncle, *"is mad. Last week she won more than two thousand gold louis at the card tables, and after ordering new gowns that cost about half of that sum, she spent the other half on new books. I argued with her in vain; she would not understand that no great lord will marry a woman who is seen reading every day."*

Émilie, however, didn't care what anyone thought. She had just discovered the works of Descartes, the great seventeenth-century philosopher and mathematician, and when she wasn't playing cards or parading through the palace gardens in her finery, she found a quiet corner in which to read. Descartes's theories of analytical geometry absorbed her, and she was even more interested in his complex discussions of the relationships of mind and matter, soul and body.

It was difficult to find anyone at the frivolous Regency court with whom she could discuss the philosophy of Descartes, but Bishop Louis de Bourbon, a cousin of the boy King, who was one of the few scholars in the royal family, heard of her strange enthusiasms and engaged her in conversations. Soon they were debating so ferociously that they had to call in professors from the Sorbonne to mediate fine points in their disputes that were beyond the grasp of ordinary, nonintellectual mortals.

Émilie's mother was in despair. *"My youngest,"* she lamented, *"flaunts her mind, and frightens away the suitors her other excesses have not driven off. We may be forced to send her to a convent, but no abbess would accept her. We don't know what to do with her."*

Certainly one of her least charming attributes was her recognition of her own worth. *"I do not deny your genius,"* she later wrote to Voltaire during one of their many quarrels, *"so I do not understand why you persist in denying mine. Ah, well, I am bursting with generosity, a quality you sadly lack, but it does not matter. Close your eyes as tightly as you please; the light of my genius will shine through the lids and will dazzle you."*

There was no need for Émilie's parents to have worried. Knowing that her dowry was limited, thereby putting a brilliant marriage beyond her grasp, she began making her own plans. She wanted a husband of higher rank than her father, someone who would be flattered by a union with a girl who was as bright as she was beautiful. She preferred someone older, who would allow her to go her own way and would not interfere in her life, and she was prepared to grant him the same freedom in return. There were few bachelors at the court who fitted her specifications, so she quietly began to search beyond the confines of Versailles. Her family and friends were mildly amused, but she herself never doubted she would find the right man, or so her later, adult correspondence indicated.

II

The Marquis Florent-Claude du Châtelet-Lomont, Comte du Lomont and Seigneur de Cirey, was an eminently successful soldier of the crown. Born in 1695, and therefore ten years older than Émilie, he entered the ranks of the royal musketeers as a cadet in 1712, at the age of seventeen. He served with distinction in the campaigns of Landau and of Freiburg, and achieved renown at the siege of Phillipsburg, where he served as deputy commander of the French forces. When he returned to Paris on furlough early in 1725, he had risen to the rank of major general, and, at the age of thirty, was considered one of the most promising soldiers in France. In time he would fulfill his promise, winning the baton of a field marshal in 1738, and succeeding to the highest post in the realm, that of lieutenant general of France, in 1744.

The Marquis's background was impressive. His family was one of the oldest in Lorraine, and his ancestors had served the kings of Lorraine and of France as soldiers and diplomats for hundreds of years. He owned a number of large estates, as well as a palace, the Hôtel du Châtelet, in Paris. All of them were somewhat run down, unfortunately, because he lacked the funds to repair and maintain them. His grandfather and father had been poor business managers, so their wealth had dissipated. Florent-Claude simply did not care. His passions were wars

13

and the serving wenches, preferably brunettes, whom he took with him into the field as his mistresses, and he had no real interest in building up the family fortunes again.

He was a heavyset man with a florid face, a loud voice, and a prodigious love of good food and drink. Hunting was his principal peacetime avocation, and he hated the frivolous, artificial atmosphere of the royal court so intensely that he spent no more time there than was necessary to further his career. His love affairs with commoners were beneath the notice of noble gossips, and he was considered eminently respectable by everyone who knew him, a dependable, solid soldier lacking in the graces of the court, with a limited sense of humor. If he had ever read anything other than a military treatise, none of the letter-writers of the age considered the feat worthy of comment.

The Marquis made his first appearance in several years at Versailles in January or February, 1725, and was immediately subjected to pressure by his many aunts and cousins, who were squabbling over their rights of succession to his titles and estates. Florent-Claude was annoyed by their presumptiousness, and decided to produce his own heir. First, however, he had to find a wife, and the obvious place, perhaps the only place to conduct his search, was the royal court.

Émilie, on the eve of her twentieth birthday, was husband-hunting with a vengeance, since she would be considered too old for marriage in another year or two. Her second brother, Charles-Auguste, held a military commission as a captain, and had spent a year as the Marquis's personal aide-de-camp, so it is probable that his little sister was one of the first people Florent-Claude met at Versailles. There is no record of their initial reaction to each other, but it soon became evident to everyone at the court that Émilie had found the man she wanted. He not only fitted all of her very precise specifications, but there was an unexpected bonus: he was one of the few men she had ever met who towered above her by at least six inches.

The Marquis was equally impressed. Émilie's credentials were impeccable, he was dazzled by her gorgeous gowns, and he was just shrewd enough to realize that someone as tall as she would give birth to large children. Cautiously, like the leader of a patrol making a reconnaissance in enemy territory, he began to woo her.

The ladies and gentlemen of the court watched the spectacle avidly, and were amused beyond measure. They wrote that the Marquis talked about nothing except his campaigns, Émilie discussed only her evolving metaphysical philosophical concepts, and neither understood or cared to understand a word the other said. If there was a sex attraction on either side, a touch of sentiment, or a romantic feeling, both succeeded admirably in concealing all emotion. And Florent-Claude cared nothing whatever about the infinitesimal dowry that Émilie would bring her husband.

Therefore he made the appropriate addresses to her father, and the delighted Louis-Nicolas immediately gave his blessing. Since he was no longer in high favor at court, the wedding took place at Notre Dame on June 12, 1725, with Bishop de Bourbon officiating. The story to the effect that the bride halted the ceremony in order to correct the clergyman's pronunciation of a Latin phrase may be apocryphal.

The marriage of convenience was consummated that night at the Hôtel du Châtelet, where Émilie accepted her inevitable fate without comment. She made no reference to the occasion in any of her later correspondence, either, making it one of the few incidents in her life that she failed to dissect and analyze. It might be argued that the occasion was too important, but her subsequent conduct indicated that it meant little, if anything. In all probability she accepted the loss of her virginity with quiet resignation, and then put her husband out of her mind.

15

Émilie quickly demonstrated some of the compulsive traits that would deepen as she grew older. The town house of the du Châtelet family was located within a stone's throw of the exquisite royal palace built by Henry IV behind the Louvre, in the most fashionable Right Bank section of the city. Most of the furniture was the better part of a century old, the drapes were crumbling, and the rugs were threadbare. Some wives might have enjoyed the antiques, but Émilie found the condition of the house intolerable.

Displaying the fine disregard for money that she showed throughout her adult life, she had the house redecorated from cellars to attics. General du Châtelet had no funds for the purpose, and Émilie's private fortune was scarcely large enough to pay for her wardrobe, but she refused to permit practical matters to deter her. Within a week of her marriage the Hôtel du Châtelet was swarming with upholsterers and cabinet-makers, carpenters and masons and seamstresses.

The horrified Marquis protested, claiming that he could not pay for such extravagance, but he finally realized he was wasting his breath. When he gave an order in the field, thousands of men hastened to obey him, but his bride seemed deaf to his commands and equally indifferent to his pleas. He was compelled to sell one of his better farms in Lorraine to pay for the redecoration of the town house, and was forced to admit that Émilie accomplished a miracle, transforming the place into a comfortable, handsome home.

All the same, he learned a lesson. Thereafter, whenever she felt the urge to buy furniture, change the decor, or build new gardens, Florent-Claude made it his business to notify all the tradespeople with whom she dealt that he refused to be responsible for any debts she might incur. Émilie found his foresight frustrating, but he had the satisfaction of staying solvent and avoiding debtor's prison. Apparently he bore her no ill will, however. A wife was expected to indulge in spending sprees, and it was a husband's place to protect himself as best he could.

Work on the refurbished house was completed about three months after the wedding, at approximately the time Émilie became pregnant. She was being the perfect wife, and Florent-Claude went off to rejoin his troops in the field, secure in the knowledge that he had chosen the right spouse. In the next year and a half he returned to Paris for occasional brief visits, and Émilie was on her own.

At no time, however, did she neglect her duties. She entertained the Marquis's military superiors, accompanied him on his formal visits to court, and made all of the other small gestures required of a noble French matron in the eighteenth century. More important, she bore her husband three children. Gabrielle-Pauline, who looked like Émilie and developed an intellect of her own, was born on June 30, 1726, a year after her parents were married. Florent-Louis-Marie, the heir to his father's titles and estates, was born on November 20, 1727, and, in spite of his mother's sometimes frenzied efforts, grew up to be as much of an oaf as his father. Victor-Esprit, who was born in 1734, died in infantry, perhaps because Émilie, who had been afraid of putting on too much weight, had been dieting for more than a year, and was painfully undernourished throughout her pregnancy.

According to the aristocratic standards of the day, the marriage was a success. No man had the right to hope for more than several legitimate children and his wife's polite interest in his career.

On a surface level, her days were like those of other aristocratic ladies. She awakened in mid-morning, was served breakfast in bed, and then spent several hours preparing for her afternoons of amiable conversation. At least two chambermaids helped her dress, passed her the innumerable cosmetics she used, and drenched her in perfume. By early afternoon she was rouged, powdered, and ready, and either entertained guests in her own salon or went calling on friends.

Most ladies and gentlemen were content to spend their time

making small talk, but Émilie took her salon life seriously, and from the outset insisted on discussing questions of philosophical importance, sprinkling her conversation with long, accurate quotations from the works of Descartes, Erasmus, and others, all of whom she cited from memory. Most of her friends thought her odd, but suffered her peculiarities, since she was pregnant as well as exceptionally attractive.

Not until the eighth month of her first pregnancy did Émilie change her routine. Then, on the advice of her physicians, she retired to her bed, but she did not give up her social life. Her friends came to her every day, clustering in her bedchamber for the afternoons of chat and light refreshments.

What few of the gentry realized was the Émilie was leading a far more active intellectual life than any of them imagined possible. She was one of those unusual people who require very little sleep, and she made it her habit to read far into the night. In her childhood she had acquired the ability to read quickly, absorbing as she scanned, and she put that talent to good use. She was interested in everything under the sun, and her reading was eclectic, ranging from the classics, which she consumed in the original Greek and Latin, to contemporary works in French, English, German, and Spanish.

In later years, Voltaire, when in a generous mood, enjoyed telling her she loved life so much that she wanted to taste every aspect of it. When they quarreled, however, which happened frequently, he accused her of rank greediness. Perhaps there was something of both in her attitudes. She read with the intensity of a scholar, and she simultaneously played the role of a great lady of fashion to the hilt.

She gave birth without undue difficulty to Gabrielle-Pauline, whom she immediately handed to nursemaids for rearing. Thereafter she saw her child for brief periods each day, a practice she continued to follow when Florent-Louis-Marie was born the following year. According to the standards of the times she was a good enough mother, no worse than other aristocrats, certainly, if not any better.

As soon as Émilie recovered her figure after the birth of her daughter she resumed her normal social life, but there was a change in her approach that soon caught the attention of everyone who knew her. It is difficult to determine whether she was more narcissistic than other spoiled noblewomen of the age, but there was no question that Émilie's vanity was expressed in theatrical terms. She had not yet developed the interest in the drama that later led her to stage and play the principal roles in amateur productions of plays, but her instincts, which developed swiftly, were those of an actress.

Her new wardrobe created a sensation. Others were wearing low-cut gowns, but no lady could match Émilie's daring, and her dresses exposed so much of her breasts that she rouged her nipples, thereby starting a style that lasted for the better part of a hundred years. In the summer of 1726 she had several costumes made in cloth-of-gold and cloth-of-silver, which had been reserved by custom for the exclusive use of royalty. But no one protested; she was the center of attention wherever she went, and the worldly said she was ripe for an affair.

They were right. Word had reached her soon after the Marquis returned to his army duties that he had taken a new mistress, a seventeen-year-old Alsatian peasant girl of exceptional beauty, but the news had left her completely undisturbed and unruffled. She, who could display violent jealousy when her own emotions were involved, simply did not care. What did matter, however, was that Florent-Claude, by engaging openly in an affair, was granting her the right, in effect, to do the same.

There were few ladies of stature in France during the first half of the eighteenth century who refused to take official lovers, and the rules governing the conduct of both sexes were strict. A man was permitted to sleep with as many ladies as he could coax into his bed. That was an ancient custom, and remained unchanged. A lady, however, lived according to another standard. Affairs were forbidden until she was safely married. Thereafter she was allowed one lover at a time, and the man of her choice automatically became her sole protector, sharing her only with her husband on the infrequent occasions when protocol required her to sleep with her spouse. Under no circumstances was it acceptable for her to have two or more lovers during the same period, and any lady who defied this injunction was regarded as a wanton, beyond the pale.

Émilie, who had slept with no man except her husband, soon became the object of a whispering campaign, and it was said that she was successfully juggling several lovers. There is no evidence to indicate there was any truth to these rumors, which may have started because of her outrageously provocative, scanty attire. She herself believed that other women, jealous of her superior intellect, were responsible for spreading the falsehoods. In any event, she regarded the stories as hilarious, and her flirtatiousness in the salons of friends and at Versailles indicated that she was searching for the man with whom to launch a life of sin.

She found him in the person of the Marquis Robert de Guébriant, a vapid fop who had little to commend him except a handsome physique and one of the most expensive wardrobes owned by any man in France. He was a mediocre card player, and Émilie could beat him at *vingt-et-un* with ease. If he possessed an intellect, he was successful in concealing the fact from his contemporaries, and the few letters he wrote reveal him as a semi-literate. He was a nephew of the Marshal de Maillebois, after whom he believed he modeled himself, which is to say that he liked to think of himself as a taciturn realist. He deluded himself as well as Émilie, who was too inexperienced to know better.

It is not easy to imagine any man with whom Émilie could have made a worse match. She soon discovered the fact that she and the handsome young Marquis had nothing in common, although she faithfully followed the prescription of inviting him into her private chamber every afternoon. Whatever there may have been in the way of a mutual sex attraction proved to be an insufficient bond, and Émilie enlivened their relationship by creating scenes. She found she could weep at will, that she had a gift for working herself into an intense, dramatic emotional state, so she indulged her whim for the theatrical.

De Guébriant, to whom histrionics of any sort were anathema, had no desire to maintain the relationship, and, after sharing Émilie's bed for only a few weeks, found himself another mistress. Émilie may have been relieved, but she could not allow any man to jilt her without creating a scene, and she was responsible for an incident that caused excitement throughout France, winning her rather dubious fame abroad, as well.

The version of the incident that won the greatest acceptance was that penned by the Abbé Raynal, one of the premier gossips of the age, who was not one of Émilie's warm admirers. Despising her because of her intellectual friendship with his enemy, the Bishop de Bourbon, Raynal characterized her as an extremist in all things, and went out of his way to make her appear ridiculous. According to his account, Émilie learned that de Guébriant had taken a new mistress, and begged him to call on her so they could say farewell in an appropriate manner.

The reluctant de Guébriant was a gentleman, so he obeyed the summons, knowing that Émilie would treat him to one of her emotional scenes. She did not disappoint him, but he stood firm, refusing to return to her.

She was exhausted by her tears, and, stretching out on a chaise, asked her former lover to hand her a bowl of soup that stood on a sideboard, explaining she needed refreshment. The young Marquis did as he was bidden, and as he took his leave Émilie handed him a farewell note she had already written. Curiosity impelled him to read it when he reached the ground floor of the Hôtel du Châtelet. Life was not worth living without him, Émilie declared, so she had taken poison, and would be dead by the time he read her words.

The Marquis immediately proved he was practical, if un-imaginative. Dashing to the kitchen out-building behind the house, he obtained an antidote from the startled cook, and raced back up to Émilie's bedchamber with it. There he found her in a half-fainting condition which may or may not have been genuine, and forced her to swallow the antidote, which made her violently ill, but nevertheless removed the poison from her system. Then, her life having been duly saved, her former lover took his belated departure.

Other accounts vary only in detail, some of them omitting the farewell scene. According to these stories, de Guébriant received a letter from Émilie, and read enough between the lines to fear that she had harmed herself. So he hurried to her house, found she had drugged herself with an opiate she had poured into a bowl of pea soup, and had hastily administered the antidote that had restored her to good health.

Voltaire, when he became Émilie's champion, told a far differ-ent story. Mme. du Châtelet, he declared, had become so bored by her dull-witted lover that she had sent him a firm letter of farewell, in which she had ordered him not to present himself at her house again. Then, because the breaking off of an affair was always unpleasant, she decided to spend the rest of the day at home, and had ordered the cook to send up one of her favor-ite dishes, pea soup with sausage.

The sausage had been tainted, giving her food poisoning, but she felt strong enough and clear-headed enough to admin-ister her own antidote. Thereafter, while she was resting on her chaise, de Guébriant had burst into the house and had forced his way into Émilie's presence. She had dismissed him at once, and he, stung, had been responsible for making up the vicious lie that she had tried to kill herself.

Regardless of which version was correct, Émilie du Châtelet gained a new measure of notoriety overnight, and malicious hostesses, wanting to see her reaction, delighted in serving her pea soup with sausage. Émilie invariably exclaimed that the peasant dish was one of her favorites, and she always ate several helpings.

In any event, she and de Guébriant had parted company, and any number of other gentlemen were eager to take the young Marquis's place. Émilie did not wait long before selecting a partner who was the opposite of her first lover in every respect. The Comte Pierre de Vincennes was middle-aged, a former abbé who had found the religious life too confining and had returned to the more permissive society of the lay world. The gossips were agreed that Émilie was the first woman who had ever attracted him, other than the harlots he occasionally frequented. Until he formed his liaison with her, his exclusive interests were metaphysics and gourmet dining.

Vincennes was a pudgy, balding little man, and during her brief affair with him Émilie seemed partial to wigs that made her appear even taller. And their relationship, based on what others saw of them, did not conform to any of the accepted lovers' patterns. Even after they acknowledged that they were sleeping together, making no secret of their intimacy, Émilie and the Comte treated each other with rigid, polite formality when they met at the salons of friends or at dinner parties. A stranger, seeing them for the first time, would have assumed that they were casual acquaintances who did not care for each other.

No one enjoyed the affair more than the wits of Paris, who went to great lengths to explain the relationship. "Mme. du Châtelet wanted a dwarf," one humorist declared, "and when she couldn't find one who could appreciate her chef's cooking, she chose Vincennes instead."

"What do you suppose they do together?" was a question asked everywhere in high society. The reply, which invariably caused gales of laughter, was: "They talk each other to death."

There was a germ of truth in the cruel joke. Émilie's previous affair with a handsome nincompoop had taught her there was little or no satisfaction to be found in a romance with an intellectual inferior. This time she went to the other extreme and formed a liaison with a man who, although dismally unattractive by any standard, was an authority in a field of intellectual endeavor that fascinated her. When the current joke about two talkative people was repeated to her, she is said to have replied with dignified asperity, "The Comte and I discuss the nature of man in relation to himself and his universe. What do those who mock us dare to discuss without revealing their abysmal ignorance?"

Vincennes himself is the authority for the disclosure that he appreciated the meals served at the Hôtel du Châtelet. The woodcock prepared by her chef was a delicacy superior to any he had experienced elsewhere, and the mousse of river pike was superb. He boasted so loudly and frequently about the dishes served at her table that a number of nobles tried to hire the chef. This unfortunate situation aroused Émilie's wrath, and she had her only known quarrel with the Comte, blistering him in public at a large dinner party she was giving. Thereafter Vincennes became more discreet, and although his appetite remained voracious, he guarded his tongue.

By the time she indulged in her affair with the Comte, Émilie's personality was formed, and changed very little in the years that followed. She seemed to take her beauty for granted, and wore her daring clothes rather carelessly, almost as though they meant nothing to her. By the same token she frequently lost an expensive earring or dropped a valuable bracelet, disrupting a social occasion while most of the gentlemen present searched for the missing item.

She needed an audience, and required the admiration of the dolts, the applause of the dullards. Apparently incapable of enjoying any relationship with another individual exclusively for its own sake, she felt compelled to live in a spotlight. This love of the theatrical, which Voltaire and others found attractive and amusing, grated on the nerves of most people, who

24

found her so intense that they felt uncomfortable in her presence.

Virtually no one enjoyed or approved of the emotional excesses that had become second nature to her. When she was displeased or disappointed, she usually lost her temper and became an expert in the staging of raging tantrums. Having discovered that she could weep at will, she utilized tears, too, whenever the situation appeared to call for them, throwing herself into her role of the moment with such passion that she became hysterical, and did not grow quiet until she had exhausted herself.

No one, even her greatest admirers, ever said that Émilie was practical. Until the day she died she maintained the splendid disregard for money she had displayed in her youth. When she wanted something, she bought it, and let her lovers worry about paying the bills. She displayed the same streak of recklessness when she gambled that had driven her father to distraction. Her card sense remained sharp, which was fortunate, and her luck rarely deserted her, so her excesses at the gaming table caused her few embarrassments.

A spoiled product of her profligate, luxury-loving age, Émilie had no concept of the meaning of self-discipline, except in matters of the intellect. Her devotion to intellectual pursuits was sincere, and no one was permitted to interrupt her when she studied a philosophical tract or a treatise on the laws that governed physical phenomena. Her mind was obviously so much better than that of most of her contemporaries that she had developed a thoroughly unattractive scorn for her inferiors, which she made no effort to hide. It was this trait that caused other women to avoid her, and she enjoyed very few feminine friendships in her life. She was interested only in her equals, who happened to consist of a small number of men, and to them she devoted her full attention.

It is astonishing that her whole personality was transformed when she opened a book, wrote a paper, or conducted an experiment. She worked hard for long months at a time, spending grueling hours at her labors, without complaint.

It is almost inconceivable that the unstable social butterfly and the serious scholar could have been the same person, yet they were. Émilie's own hard work and intellect were responsible for her achievements, to be sure, but she owed a tremendous debt to two men who influenced her, and the stage was set for their entrance into her life after her affair with Vincennes dwindled and died early in 1727.

In that year the Marquis du Châtelet returned to Paris, and Émilie, following the custom of the time, was faithful to him while he was in the city. She became pregnant again, giving birth to a son later in the year, and had the satisfaction of knowing she had done her duty. She was ready, at last, for the supreme adventures of her life.

III

Louis François Armand du Plessis, Duc de Richelieu, was one of the great soldiers and statesmen of his age, a dashing, brilliant cavalier who stood above the petty politics of his age. His success was assured at his birth, in 1696, as the heir to a powerful duchy and owner of one of the most awe-inspiring names in France. His grand-uncle had been the renowned Cardinal Richelieu, the patriot-statesman who had been the nation's First Minister during the reign of Louis XIII. The Sun King himself, Louis XIV, acted as the baby's godfather, thereby defying the tradition that the monarch could become the godfather of no one but close blood relatives.

The Duc de Richelieu lived a long, useful life, dying at the age of ninety-two, in 1788, and his accomplishments were matched by few of his contemporaries. His preparation for his future life was thorough, and he spent his childhood in the hands of tutors, joining a household regiment at sixteen as a cadet, and thereafter receiving training for the diplomatic corps in addition to his military service.

He first achieved distinction when he was sent as the French Ambassador to Vienna in 1725, and, spending four years there, negotiated the complicated peace treaty between France and Austria, on terms far more favorable to France than anyone in Paris had anticipated. In 1733 he was in uniform again, and served in the Rhine campaign, first as a colonel, then as a major general. In two battles, those of Fontenoy and Dettingen, he not only displayed great personal valor, but so fired his troops that he led them to victory. His reputation was assured, and in 1737 he enhanced it when, as the commander of the forces defending Genoa, he defeated a besieging army several times the size of his own.

In 1756, by this time a Marshal of France, he expelled a strong British garrison from the island of Minorca by finding the one weakness in the defenses and exploiting it to the full. A hard-bitten campaigner, he conducted a ruthless campaign in Germany soon thereafter, winning the hatred of the citizens of Hanover, where he allowed his troops to pillage at will.

Returning to France as a highly respected elder statesman, he was a trusted adviser of Louis XV, and served in the same capacity during the abortive reign of Louis XVI. One of the few high-ranking nobles who foresaw the approach of the French Revolution, he was powerless to push through the reforms that might have preserved the Bourbon monarchy, and died a year before the outbreak of the great upheaval.

In his early days it seemed unlikely that he would become a person of consequence. In 1711, while still in his adolescence, he defied his stepfather, who had him thrown into the Bastille for his insolence. His stay there was brief, but five years later he was incarcerated in the Bastille for a second time after killing an opponent in a duel. The cause of the fight was a girl, and the occasion marked the first time that Richelieu gained prominence because of his attachment to a member of the opposite sex. It would not be the last.

In 1719 the young Richelieu was sent to prison for a third time, and the charges against him were serious. He, along with the representatives of a number of other prominent households, took part in a conspiracy to rid France of the nation's principal Regent, the Duc d'Orléans. The charge was grave, and Richelieu, making no attempt to dissemble, readily admitted his guilt. Had he been older and his family less prominent, he would have

28

faced execution or exile, but a thorough investigation revealed that he and several of his companions had considered the conspiracy a lark.

Orléans was not amused, however, and allowed the young blueblood to languish in the Bastille for the better part of a year. The prisoner was confined to a small cell, where he was permitted few luxuries, and no visitors were allowed to see him. The eleven months he spent in jail were a torment, and marked a turning point in his life.

When he emerged from the Bastille he was a sober, responsible subject of the crown, ready to devote the rest of his life to France. Few of his compatriots better represented the Enlightenment, or the Age of Reason, as the authors and philosophers of the eighteenth century called the period. Richelieu was calm and dispassionate, a man who relied on intellect and eschewed emotional responses to any situation. Always in command of himself, he became wise, learned, and just.

He made no attempt, however, to give the impression that he was perfect. On the contrary, he readily admitted he had an Achilles heel, and his envious friends knew that, if women were his weakness, females of every station, age, and class found him irresistible. The princesses of several nations wrote him love letters, chambermaids threw themselves at him when he visited the homes of friends, and even professional courtesans offered him their beds without charge. The hawk-faced man of medium height, whose only distinguishing features were his magnetic eyes, was endowed with an appeal to all women.

Richelieu became aware of his good fortune while still in his teens, and until the end of his long life he responded with the single-minded ardor of the true gallant. Living in an era when many men were rakes, he was considered the rake of the age, and did his best to live up to his reputation, never deterred by his marriages to two lovely, high-born heiresses.

Charming, quick-witted, and wealthy, he always dressed in the latest fashions, demanding a similar consciousness of style in his mistresses. He had the knack of making a woman feel he was devoting himself to her alone, and even those who knew he was guilty of chicanery were flattered by his attention. His enemies called him a debaucher and misanthrope, but they were unfair to him. Voltaire, who wrote a carefully documented study of his career as a ladies' man, claimed that Richelieu never seduced a virgin, never took an under-aged girl to bed, and never engaged in an affair with an unwilling companion. The cynicism of the period was so great that there were many who claimed, without foundation in fact, that they were his mistresses, hoping that they would acquire some measure of his notoriety.

Two of the most prominent ladies of the court, Mme. de Polignac and the Marquise de Nesle, became embroiled in bitter dispute, each insisting that Richelieu preferred her to all others. The Duke wisely adopted a neutral attitude, withdrawing his favors from both. Each of the ladies accused the other of responsibility for his coldness, and the argument became so intense that it culminated in an exchange of pistol shots in the Bois de Boulogne. Neither duelist was even vaguely familiar with firearms, so no harm was done, but admiring Parisians said Richelieu had achieved a goal that other rakes could not equal, no matter how hard they tried.

At first glance, some of the stories told about the Duke's conquests appear to be wild distortions of the truth. Voltaire, his friend for many years, swears that some of the more spectacular were not exaggerations. It was rumored, for example, that a room in Richelieu's country château was filled to overflowing with mementos of his exploits. Voltaire, reporting as an eye witness, says there were two such rooms, one in the Richelieu château and the other in the Duke's Paris town house, both of them crammed with miniature portraits and locks of hair, love letters, rings, and trinkets. There were so many that no man could remember the identity of more than a few donors.

Most of the letters, Voltaire states, were unopened, and Richelieu had scribbled above the seals, *"Letter I have not had time to read."*

The Duke granted the curious Voltaire the right to open and read any sealed communication that caught his eye, and the bemused author read scores, but soon became bored by the sport. All were alike, he says; without exception the ladies begged Richelieu for the favor of an affair, always naming a time and place for a rendezvous. Voltaire's summary is noteworthy: *"A man of less agility would devote his whole life to the art of conducting affairs, but Richelieu, extraordinary fellow that he is, is too busy, and spends only a small part of his time in dalliance. But he is so skilled that he needs no more time for the purpose."*

With all womankind at his feet, it was natural that Richelieu should exercise great care in selecting his mistresses. His one criterion was beauty, and over the period of more than six decades he bedded some of the loveliest women in Europe. His approval, in fact, automatically gave a woman stature as a reigning beauty.

"He seeks only perfection of face and form," Voltaire writes, *"and any blemish, however slight, is enough to turn him aside from a conquest. He has no other need in a mistress. If he wishes to exercise his mind, he converses with his friends or reads a book. If he seeks adventure, he leads his troops into a new campaign, and if he yearns for solace, his Duchess is at hand to give it to him, always ready to interrupt her own activities for his sake. Venus adores him because he worships so devoutly at her shrine."*

Émilie du Châtelet had known Richelieu most of her life, her mother being distantly related to his wife, who was too busy engaging in her own affairs to pay any attention to his romances. In the spring of 1729 the Duke and his spouse returned to Paris, fresh from his triumph as peacemaker and ambassador in Vienna, and the soldier-diplomat was the lion of the season. So many ladies besieged him that he was unable to accommodate more than a small number. A hostess who could boast that he had attended one of her dinner parties was able to rest on her laurels for the remainder of the year, so Émilie, had it been her nature, could have rested. Richelieu was a frequent dinner guest at the Hôtel du Châtelet.

At the outset, the Duke and Émilie were attracted to each other only on an intellectual basis. He had long been interested in literature and philosophy, and Voltaire had been one of his closest friends for more than eleven years. Émilie, emerging into her own as the one woman in Paris who read every book of consequence and attended the theatre regularly, was one of the very few persons of either sex in the city who could converse with him on his own level. Her insistence on attending theatrical performances was an instance of her daring, a sign of her growing sense of independence, since ladies were expected to avoid the theater, and Richelieu, although no longer a rebel himself, could admire the streak when he found it in another. He and Émilie became good friends.

Voltaire returned to Paris from a long sojourn in England that same year, and he and Richelieu saw a great deal of one another thereafter, frequently dining and spending long evenings together. Both of them enjoyed their debates, and gradually each became acquainted with the friends of the other. By a strange happenstance which was completely accidental, the paths of Émilie and Voltaire were not destined to cross for another four years. In later years Voltaire admitted that the Duke often had mentioned Émilie's name, but he himself had felt no desire to meet her, privately believing that his friend was exaggerating. Taking a dim view of the world and its inhabitants, Voltaire found it difficult to believe that such a creature as an intellectual woman existed anywhere on earth. There were few enough men, in his opinion, who had the brains of a wild hare.

Richelieu's life was complicated, in mid-summer of 1729, by

the sudden death of his wife, who was stricken with a fever one day and by the next was gone. He went into strict mourning for her, and for the next year was far more faithful to her memory than he had ever been to her person. He had no known affairs during that time, he lived very quietly, and attended no formal functions at the court of Versailles or elsewhere. He dined frequently with friends, to be sure, and high on the list was Émilie, who made certain that any parties he attended were small and discreet.

Many ladies of the nobility thought of themselves as the new Duchess, and a number of them consulted their confessors, wanting to find out how they might have their own marriages annulled by the Church. Émilie considered such women fools, and made no secret of her opinion. Richelieu, she said, was no longer a young rascal who spent a part of "every year" in the Bastille, atoning for his latest escapade. He had become a man of standing in France and the world, and obviously was destined to rise much higher. Therefore, when he remarried, he would take a wife befitting his high station. At the very least, Émilie insisted, she would rank as a duchess and in all probability would be a princess, perhaps of royal blood.

Strangely, Voltaire held the same view and lost no time expressing it to the Duke. Conscious of every intricacy, every nuance in the history of France, the great author saw a splendid opportunity for his friend to better himself through a great marriage of state. Eager to play an active role in furthering the Duke's career, Voltaire made and revised list after list of eligible princesses in France and elsewhere, carefully outlining their virtues.

Partly for his friend's sake, in part for his own amusement, Richelieu played Voltaire's little game, but actually had no intention of marrying again for a long time. He, too, felt supremely confident of his own future, and knew that if he exercised enough patience, his rise in stature through his own merits would win him a bride of that much more importance and greater wealth.

According to legend and Émilie du Châtelet's correspondence, the Duc de Richelieu ended his self-imposed celibacy one year to the day after the death of his wife. His mistress was an obscure young noblewoman on whom he had apparently kept an expert eye for some time, and she succumbed promptly to his advances, demonstrating that he had not lost his touch during his year of abstinence. Émilie, in a dispassionate, impersonal letter to her sister, described the girl as exquisite.

Making up for lost time, Richelieu enjoyed three affairs in the next three months and proved that he had not lowered his standards. All three of the ladies were lovely.

Then, suddenly, in the autumn of 1730, aristocratic Paris awakened one day to discover that the Marquise Émilie du Châtelet had become the newest mistress of the Duc de Richelieu. The court was stunned, and so were the gentry outside the Versailles circle. The unyielding, self-styled intellectual who tried to dominate every conversation and who gave in to excesses of emotion on the slightest provocation was the last woman in France they had expected the discriminating Duke to take as his bedmate.

On second thought, however, everyone from King Louis XV down to the most obscure gentleman had to admit that Émilie was beautiful. She was an Amazon, to be sure, and the fastidious disliked the way she often allowed her waist-long hair to hang down her back, unpinned. The elegant said that, no matter how much she spent on clothes, she was sloppy and allowed too much of her bosom to show. In the next breath they were forced to admit, however, that it was a bosom worth showing.

After Paris recovered from the initial shock, it was the consensus of informed opinion that Richelieu had not lowered or altered his standard in any way when he had chosen Émilie as his new mistress.

None of Émilie's and Richelieu's contemporaries knew what

had sparked the liaison and, unfortunately, nothing has been learned of the details down to the present day. Apparently romance came in a rush; one evening in the autumn of 1730 Richelieu was a dinner guest at the Hôtel du Châtelet, as he had been on so many occasions in the past, and a week later he was Émilie's lover. Being a direct man who knew what he wanted and took it, the Duke probably regarded the development as simple and natural.

Émilie's silence on the subject is remarkable. Never reluctant to discuss any other aspect of her life in infinite detail, she maintained a lifelong discretion in referring to her affair with the Duke. The curious, then and later, often wondered what had caused the couple to realize they might be missing something as friends, but no detail of their affair appeared anywhere in Émilie's voluminous correspondence. She avoided the subject in her subsequent letters to the Duke, even though she wrote to him at least once each week until the end of her days.

In that fact lies the clue to her reticence. She and Richelieu were not a man and woman who had loved and parted, but friends who became lovers for a time and then resumed their friendship again on a closer, more intimate level than they had known previously. Émilie's emotional maturation became complete during her affair with the Duke, as will be seen, and it is likely that she had no desire to discuss the most personal matters concerning the man who taught her the true meaning of emotional self-discipline.

In all probability Voltaire wormed the facts of the affair from Émilie at one time or another during the many years they lived together. When his own feelings were aroused, Voltaire was capable of demonstrating violent jealousy, and, although he and Richelieu remained friends until the end of their long lives, Voltaire invariably flared in anger whenever he mentioned his mistress's previous affair.

His reaction contrasts sharply with that of the Marquis du

Châtelet. Florent-Claude knew, of course, that it was his wife's privilege to take anyone she wanted as a lover, and he was in no position to object, since his own mistresses were such vapid nonentities. Nevertheless he felt that Émilie's first two lovers were beneath her, and in letters that he wrote from his tent in the field he frequently chided her for her lack of taste. Richelieu, however, was a man of a far different caliber, and Florent-Claude heartily approved his wife's choice.

Richelieu's regiment had been attached to his command during military maneuvers for several months, and Florent-Claude had found a seemingly kindred spirit in the Duke. Richelieu was chameleon-like, and, able to deal with people on their own level, had been bluff, hearty, and coarse, matching the General drink for drink, telling off-color stories, and, in the main, behaving like a seasoned campaigner.

Florent-Claude left much to be desired as a correspondent, and most of his communications to his wife were brief notes concerned with day-to-day household matters, combined with exhortations urging her to curb her expenses. But word reached Paris through the letters of some of his noble subordinates that he thought Richelieu a "splendid fellow." The gossips, always eager to find the worst in anyone, claimed he was impressed because his wife had become involved with a man who belonged to the top layer of the aristocracy. This was an untruth that did the Marquis an injustice; with all his faults, he was not a snob.

Émilie and Richelieu continued to live in their separate dwellings, which happened to be located within short walking distance of each other, although neither would have dreamed of walking. When the Duke came to the Hôtel du Châtelet, he usually rode, and when Émilie went to the Hôtel de Richelieu she made the short journey in her closed carriage. Both were the products of their class, and certain amenities had to be observed.

From the outset this affair was unlike the others in which

Émilie had engaged. Richelieu, who was a busy man, did not spend all of his waking—much less sleeping—hours with his mistress. Sometimes he dined with friends, Voltaire among them, and he made it his business to cultivate Cardinal Fleury, who had gathered the reigns of power into his delicate but capable hands. It was necessary for a man of ambition to maintain good relations with government ministers and other high-ranking nobles of influence, and Richelieu assiduously sought his own advancement. So, no matter how important a woman might be to him, she necessarily took second place, and it was impossible for him to act as Émilie's constant companion.

Although she and her previous lovers had been inseparable, she accepted this very different sort of affair with astonishing good grace. She made no scenes when the Duke made appearances without her, and she had no tantrums when he left her at home. In fact, she dispensed completely with her histrionics. Richelieu was a quiet, eminently sensible man, and expected a woman to behave as he did, in a civilized, dignified manner.

It did not take Émilie long to discover that he was doing her a great favor, that his demands were forcing her to adopt a completely new mode of conduct, and that, as a consequence, she was becoming a far more attractive and productive person. She still had a sharp tongue, to be sure, and did not hesitate to shred the boor or the banal at a salon gathering or dinner party. But her disposition improved noticeably, and her lack of hysterics gave her greater energy to devote to her work. Those who had called her a "child of nature" were forced to revise their estimate.

Of far greater significance was Émilie's ability to devote herself to meaningful work. She began to develop several mathematical theorems of her own, and, with the Duke's encouragement, began advanced studies with professors of physics and mathematics from the Sorbonne, whom she hired as tutors, and who came to the Hôtel du Châtelet for several hours of instruction and discussion each week. She also started making her first serious translations of poetry from ancient Latin into French, and even if she rightly regarded these efforts as inferior, they provided the groundwork and practice that were essential if she hoped to make definitive translations, currently her goal, and one that she later achieved.

Émilie freely gave her lover full credit for bringing order into her chaotic life, and, above all, for giving her a sense of direction. Until now she had enjoyed scholarship for its own sake, and was so eager to learn that she tried to absorb too much. Richelieu taught her to limit her interests to those subjects which were of primary interest to her, and to bear down harder in those fields.

"If you wish to learn why objects fall down rather than up," he wrote her during a brief absence from Paris, *"you must devote your soul and heart as well as your mind to a sufficient study of physics to enable you to grasp the principles of this indefinable phenomenon. Set yourself the task of climbing a mountain, and if you persevere you will reach the summit."*

The secret of Richelieu's success with women lay in his ability to understand a mistress and to help her realize her ideals. When more was involved in a relationship than sexual attraction, and a great deal more was involved in his affair with Émilie, he developed a genuine interest in the personality and problems of his companion.

Émilie, who wanted to please the Duke, made strenuous efforts to change her approach, principally for his sake. Then, gradually, she recognized the worth, for her own sake, of what she was doing. Her affair with Richelieu marked a period in her life that was unique. Never before had she been so calm, so rational, or so quietly determined. After they went their separate ways she regressed, to an extent, but never became as self-indulgent and undisciplined as she had been.

The life led by Émilie and the Duke, separately and together, during the period of their one-year affair was predictably ordered. They made one major public appearance together each week, driving out to the court at Versailles. The better part of their time at the palace was spent apart, however. There were men with whom the Duke wanted to confer, and he left Émilie to her own devices while he wandered from public room to private chamber, frying whatever fish happened to be in his skillet at the moment.

Émilie, whose flamboyant style of dress had not changed, chatted with friends and acquaintances, observed the latest fashions, and made mental notes she would take back to her dressmaker. She found it impossible to refrain from gambling, of course, and when Richelieu was ready to return to Paris he often found her at the *vingt-et-un* table. But even her card-playing habits had become altered. She no longer risked large sums of money she could not afford, and played cautiously for reasonable stakes. Her card sense had not deserted her, however, and she continued to win consistently. There were some nobles who refused to sit at the same table with her, but others were challenged by her reputation as a constant winner, so she always found opponents.

The couple dined together in Paris two or three times each week, either at the Hôtel du Châtelet or at the homes of friends. On no known occasion did they dine in the presence of others at the Hôtel de Richelieu, since this would have been considered bad taste, and the Duke was a stickler for etiquette.

Custom did not prevent them from sleeping together at his house when they wished, and this they did from time to time. It was considered preferable for a liaison to take place in the home of the lady, however, so Émilie's house was the scene of most of their intimacies. When Richelieu remained overnight, he was always discreet, and even though everyone from young Louis XV to the chimney-sweeps knew of the affair, he made it his business to ride back to his own house soon after dawn. Under no circumstances would he subject himself to the embarrassment of being found in Émilie's bedchamber in mid-morning when some of her friends might call on her.

Émilie did not object to spending the better part of her time without her lover, and there were some who believed she felt freer when she was alone. She continued to receive friends and pay calls, to be sure, but she dined alone when it was necessary, and she began to devote more time to her work. It soon became obvious to everyone who knew her that she was writing a great deal. Her fingers, like those of the most wretched clerk, were invariably ink-stained. Those stains, which grew deeper through the years, became as much a part of Émilie as her remarkable mind, her shockingly low-cut gowns, and the occasional clumsiness that sometimes caused her to smash bric-a-brac and objects of art that were in the path of her sweeping gestures.

To the surprise of all Paris, which had predicted a short-lived affair, the liaison with Richelieu lasted for more than a year and a half. Émilie's fidelity was taken more or less for granted, as she had demonstrated in the past that she was interested in just one man at a time. But the Duke's abiding interest in her caused a great many gossips to raise their eyebrows, and there was serious speculation to the effect that, if she could obtain an annulment of her marriage, she might became the next Duchesse de Richelieu.

There is no evidence to indicate that Émilie, at any time during the affair, entertained any such ambitions. Certainly the Duke said and did nothing that might be interpreted as a hint of his desire to marry her. Rarely in his long life did he show such fidelity to any mistress, and there were rumors to the effect that the Marquise du Châtelet was endowed with sexual appetites so great and talents so extraordinary that she was able to hold Richelieu captive to her charms.

There is no evidence to indicate that there was any truth in these stories, either. Neither of Émilie's first two lovers wrote or said anything that would lead an observer to suspect she was a particularly unusual or sex-hungry bed partner. And Voltaire, who was known to discuss every aspect of their relationship with dispassionate clarity when he was in an objective mood, appeared to consider her a satisfactory but eminently normal partner.

What few people of the age seemed to realize was that the Duc de Richelieu was genuinely fond of Émilie, and enjoyed her company in a salon or at the dinner table as well as in bed. Himself a man of learning and taste, he was fascinated by her mind. Other gentlemen sometimes felt overpowered by Émilie's intellect, but Richelieu was sufficiently sure of himself not to feel a sense of competition with her.

In letters to many of his friends and a few of his relatives he repeatedly referred to her talents for sharp, concise debate. He was unable to beat her in discussions of philosophy and metaphysics, and only when they talked about literature could he emerge the winner of a talk.

Perhaps the most significant aspect of the relationship of Émilie and Richelieu is that they did not go their separate ways when their liaison ended. After a year, more or less, the Duke tired of Émilie as his mistress and began to seek someone else, which wasn't difficult. Émilie, who had known the affair would not last, was neither hurt nor disappointed when they stopped sleeping together, but accepted the inevitable with an equanimity she rarely displayed in any of her other relationships.

Until the time of Émilie's death, almost at mid-century, they corresponded with frequent regularity, even when close enough for personal heart-to-heart talks, in which they also indulged. Their letters were interminably long, after the fashion of all literate products of the Enlightenment. In fact, their correspondence, published a century later, filled four volumes. Every student of the eighteenth century has good cause to wonder how so many men and women, most of them leading incredibly busy, full lives, could have found time for correspondence more voluminous than that of any other age. Letter-writing was more than an exchange of news, opinion, and sentiments; it was a way of life, an integral part of the existence of the educated man and woman.

Émilie and Richelieu carried the custom of the age to extremes. Their friendship was so great and their desire to communicate with one another so intense that, even when madly in love with others, neither allowed a week to pass without sitting down to compose a letter that must have taken hours to write. Émilie thought nothing of turning out letters to the Duke that ran a minimum of twenty pages, even when the romance of her life, with Voltaire, was at its height. The Duke returned the compliment with somewhat shorter letters, even when he was immersed in his military operations on which the fate of France depended.

Émilie, the complete narcissist, concentrated on the subject of the friendship itself and how much it meant to her, why she felt as she did, and how that feeling influenced her thoughts and deeds. Voltaire, although professing to scorn an emotion as base as jealousy, couldn't help feeling dazed by the thick packets of mail he saw being exchanged by his mistress and their mutual friend. Strictly for his own protection, as he put it, he developed elaborate stratagems for steaming open Émilie's incoming and outgoing mail. He trusted Richelieu as much as he trusted any man, which was a form of damning with the faintest of praise, but he made no pretense of having faith in any woman. In spite of his determined detective work, however, he found no foundation for the suspicion that his mistress and his old friend were trying to cuckold him.

The facts of the matter were precisely what they seemed. Two very close friends enjoyed an exceptionally verbose correspondence. It might be argued that Émilie regarded the Duke as something of a father substitute. Her own father had neglected her shamefully, although his attitude was no worse than that of other aristocratic parents of the age, who turned their children over to governesses and tutors, and she knew that Richelieu had been more influential than anyone else in helping her achieve adult attitudes.

The reasons for the Duke's continuing interest in Émilie

are more difficult to fathom. All the women who paraded through his life after his affair with Émilie were beautiful, and some were intelligent. None were her intellectual equals, but her letters conspicuously lacked a cerebral quality, which disproves the theory that her mind was the magnet that continued to draw him to her. It may be that he felt a measure of unique fondness for her because she was the most apt of his many pupils. More than all the others she took his advice to heart, and, changing her personality as well as her habits, became one of the most famous women of her time. After all, Galatea fascinated Pygmalion long after the statue he had fashioned had come to life.

A single excerpt from a letter written by Émilie to Richelieu in 1739, when she was deeply in love with Voltaire, reveals the nature of her friendship with the Duke. In order to obtain an appropriate perspective, it must be remembered that most eighteenth-century letter-writers indulged in extravagant language, and that Émilie was far less restrained than most of her contemporaries. She said:

"It is the privilege of friendship to see one's friend in every condition of his soul. I love you sad, gay, lively, oppressed; I wish that my friendship might increase your pleasures, diminish your troubles and share them. There is no need on that account to have real misfortunes or great pleasures. No events are necessary, and I am as much interested in your moods and flirtations as other people are in the good fortune or bad fortune of the people they call their friends . . .

"I do not know whether it is flattering to you to say that you are as agreeable far off as near by; but I know very well that it is thought to be a great merit by a lonely person, who, in renouncing the world, does not wish to renounce friendship, and who would be very sorry if a necessary absence made a breach between her and you.

"I discover in your mind all the charms and in your society all the delights which the whole world has agreed to find there;

but I am sure that no one has felt more than I have the value of your friendship. Your heart has prepossessed mine. I believed there was none other but myself who knew friendship in a measure so keen, and I was provoked by the proofs I wished to give you of it, sometimes on account of my scruples at other times from fear, always in defiance of myself.

"I could not believe that anyone so amiable, so much sought after, would care to disentangle the sentiments of my heart from all my faults. I believed that I had known you too late to obtain a place in your heart; I believed, also, I confess it, that you were incapable of continuing to love anyone who was not necessary to your pleasures and could not be useful to you —you, unique and incomparable man, understand how to combine everything; delicious friendship, intoxication of love, all is felt by you and spreads the sweetest charm over your fine destiny.

"I confess to you that if, after having made me give myself up to your friendship, you should cease—I do NOT say to love me—but to tell me of it; if you should allow such a breach to appear in your friendship, if the remarks or witticisms of people who find me pleasing today and who will perhaps be displeased with me tomorrow, make the least impression on you, I should be inconsolable. I should be most unfortunate if you do not keep your friendship for me, and if you do not continue to give me proofs of it. You would make me repent of the candor with which I speak, and my heart does not wish to know repentance.

"Until I write again, dear friend, goodbye. There is no perfect happiness for me in the world until I can unite the pleasure of enjoying our friendship with that of loving him to whom I have devoted my life."

What makes the communication remarkable is that there were literally hundreds like it, written over a period of more than sixteen years. Not even Émilie du Châtelet's worst enemies could accuse her of taking her friendships lightly.

IV

François Marie Arouet, who used the pen name of Voltaire, which he eventually adopted for legal purposes, was the most versatile author in the history of French literature. Hailed by himself as a genius beyond compare; among others in his own time he was also the most controversial, contradictory, and perverse figure of importance in eighteenth-century Europe.

He liked to think of himself as a philosopher, a metaphysician, a mathematician, and a physicist, and in all of these realms his achievements were solid, if neither lasting nor original. To the despair of the French foreign ministry, he also thought of himself as a diplomat, and it amused him when his efforts in that field created complications in foreign relations. But he had the satisfaction of seeing most of his efforts justified. "If Louis XV had elected me to act as his foreign minister," he said late in life, "I would have doubled his renown. Even without that employment I made him more important than he was."

The boast was not wide of the mark. To the extent that Voltaire found it necessary to earn a living, he was a professional historian, and his detailed studies of the reigns of Louis XIV and Louis XV are still used as source material by modern historians. Among his many shorter works are superb studies of Peter the Great of Russia and Charles XII of Sweden. Both were his contemporaries, although they died while he was still a young man, and it is surprising that someone who lived in the same era could write about them with such objective clarity.

Voltaire also thought of himself as a poet, and although his verses earned him only tiny sums of money, he was considered a poet by most of Europe. The quantities of verse he wrote are enormous, and it was said he often thought in rhyme rather than in prose. There may be an element of truth to the claim because, when he was rushed, he frequently wrote letters in poetry rather than in prose. No one has ever known, down to the present day, how much poetry he composed. When another cache of eighteenth-century correspondence is found in the attic of a French château or in its cellar box of rubbish, it frequently contains poems penned by Voltaire.

He worked hard in still another field and turned out a number of what he called prose romances, which were ineptly named because they were anything but romantic. Instead they were perfect examples of his style at his best, and no man was his equal in writing bitingly ironic, witty observations of human frailty. *Candide* is often regarded as the best of these works.

Voltaire further demonstrated his versatility by writing extensively for the theater, and here, as elsewhere, his efforts were prodigious. Approximately sixty of his plays, several of them fragments, have been handed down to posterity, and a number of others are believed to have been lost. He himself thought his comedies were the best of his plays, and many of his contemporaries agreed, since he was the supreme master of satire, and his ruthless brand was withering. The ultimate, supremely ironic joke is on Voltaire, however; his tragedies, most of which he wrote for the sole purpose of earning money, have been regarded in later times as his finest theatrical efforts.

Letter-writing was an accepted form of literature in the eighteenth century, and in this field Voltaire has few peers. His energy was seemingly unlimited and inexhaustible, and, no matter what else might be occupying him, scarcely a day of his life passed without the writing of at least a dozen letters. When he spent a full day catching up on his correspondence he was believed capable of writing as many as one hundred, all of which he penned himself. These communications were not short stereotypes, either; each was a carefully composed, well-balanced, and smoothly flowing epistle, usually with a recognizable literary quality.

Voltaire's own life was as fascinating as his vast literary output. Contemptuous of the excesses practiced by the hierarchy of the Roman Catholic Church, he was a Deist who was believed to be violently anti-Catholic. He always maintained that he opposed the men of the Church, not the faith itself; in any event, the iconoclastic French, who traditionally had ignored and defied Rome, were delighted by his attacks.

No author of any age was sponsored by wealthier, more powerful patrons, and no man was at violent odds with them more frequently. For brief periods Voltaire was a close friend of Louis XV, and was one of the few permitted to sit in the King's presence at all times. But for longer periods, equally frequent, his sardonic attacks on monarchy and the house of Bourbon in general, and the ineptitude and moral hypocrisy of Louis and his immediate ancestors in particular, sent Voltaire fleeing into exile before the King's secret police could cast him into prison. Most of the French nobles who befriended him felt the sting of his pen, and he attacked his friend Frederick the Great of Prussia. Only the English escaped unscathed; he flattered Queen Caroline as well as the leading political and literary figures in London. His private opinion of King George II was one of contempt, but he managed to keep his views to himself. He was, after all, an Anglophile, and the English reciprocated his love.

Voltaire's relations with other French authors of the age were turbulent, and on one occasion he himself said, "If there is an author in this country with whom I have not quarreled, his work isn't worth reading."

Although Voltaire towered above the other literary figures of his time, he became embroiled in so many feuds that he was not elected to the French Academy until decades after that election should have taken place. When he was finally admitted, in the spring of 1746, he toyed with the idea of refusing, something that no one had ever done. But his love of mischief-making was too great, his desire to laugh at the whole world too intense, so he accepted membership and thereafter systematically cut down his colleagues, member by member, in a series of brilliantly satiric essays.

Only one of his contemporaries, Rousseau, was considered Voltaire's equal, and Voltaire found the perfect butt for his irony in Rousseau. An incurable romantic, Jean Jacques Rousseau wrote extensively of society being over-civilized, of primitive civilizations being superior to those that were more advanced, and of the necessity that man find true happiness by turning to nature. Voltaire, who enjoyed all the civilized modes of his time, treated him mercilessly in publication after publication. Rousseau knew better than to engage in battle with the greatest word duelist of the century, and remained silent. Only one person ever succeeded in challenging the master, and Émilie du Châtelet relied on weapons other than her pen.

Voltaire did not spare even himself. *"I was destined for immortality from the time of my birth, on November 21, 1694,"* Voltaire wrote, *"because my ancestry made it impossible for me to be less than a genius. My father, the esteemed François Arouet, earned his meager living as a notary, a vocation requiring no skill, and the miserable wretch may have been overpaid. I was the youngest of five children, all conspicuously lacking in talents of any sort, and my mother, who had been Marie Marguerite Daumart, or d'Aumard, as the family began to call itself, was heartbroken when I joined the undistinguished clan. She died a few years later, before I could grow old enough to discover what manner of woman she might have been. Her one contribution of substance, other than my person, was her inheritance from her father. His glorious calling had been that of a tradesman, and I believe, but am not certain, that he sold fabrics from the West Indian Islands. The family was too ashamed of his vocation to discuss it, although they happily spent the money he had earned."*

When Voltaire was seven his mother's good "friend," the Abbé de Châteauneuf, assumed responsibility for his education, and the boy had cause to suspect that he might be the Abbe's illegitimate son. The doubt haunted him all his life. Whatever the true nature of their relationship, the Abbé acted as his tutor, and within a year the child was reading adult essays and composing verses. From the start he demonstrated an extraordinary aptitude for writing poetry.

At the age of ten the boy was sent by the Abbé to the Collège Louis-le-Grand, a school operated by the Jesuits, and although Voltaire later ridiculed the institution, he received the best education available anywhere in Europe at the beginning of the eighteenth century. The school was surprisingly liberal, and its intellectual atmosphere was responsible, at least in part, for his own liberalism. He learned history and the classics, literature and science and mathematics, and no idea was too new or too advanced to be worthy of dissection. No one in Europe could debate philosophy with the skill of the Jesuit fathers, and Voltaire acquired the art from them.

The school was also responsible for his lifelong love of the theater. It had long been the custom there to present a series of plays each year, many of them written by students, and Voltaire soon convinced himself that he was destined to enjoy a career as a playwright. Since his aptitude was astonishing, the Jesuits encouraged him.

Soon after Voltaire entered the Collège, his mentor arranged a meeting between the boy and the celebrated Ninon de Lenclos, for many years the leading courtesan, salon wit, and intellectual in Paris. This encounter made such a lasting impresson on Voltaire that he wrote about it many times throughout his life, each version becoming more extravagant than that which preceded it.

Several basic facts may be deduced. Ninon, although elderly, was still lovely, and became Voltaire's criterion of beauty. He was also impressed by her mind, and it is probable that she was the first educated woman he had ever encountered. As an adult he became interested only in women who had highly developed minds of their own.

Even as a small boy Voltaire was not reticent, and was so precocious, so eager to show off his learning, that Ninon marveled at him. When she died, in 1705, she remembered the child in her will, leaving him the enormous sum of two thousand francs for the purpose of "buying books." Already wise in the ways of scholarship, Voltaire bought most of his books second-hand and soon boasted "the best library of anyone my age in all of France."

When he left the Collège at the age of seventeen, he may have been the best-educated youth in France, too. His capacity for learning having proved itself almost unlimited, the Jesuits had given him tutoring, in depth, that the most learned professors at the Sorbonne could not have matched. The priests had come to know him well, and before he departed they warned him that he was his own worst enemy. He was so facile, they said, that he should concentrate his efforts in one field or he would run the risk of diffusing them too much. And they urged him to curb his quarrelsome disposition, explaining that he would do himself no good if he fought with anyone who disagreed with him on any subject. Then and thereafter, for all his long life, Voltaire chose to disregard the advice.

Notary Arouet wanted his son to become a lawyer, and would not listen to his plan to become a playwright, the professional theater being too dissolute for a member of a respectable family. The Abbé had died, so Voltaire lost his mentor, and he was powerless to protest when his father sent him to The Hague in the suite of the new French Ambassador, the Marquis de Châteauneuf, the Abbé's brother. The foreign climate delighted the youth, and he promptly plunged into his first romance, but his family broke it up. Not only was he too young, but the girl was a Protestant.

Returning to Paris, Voltaire pretended to study for the bar in the offices of an attorney who was a friend of his father's, but he actually spent most of his time writing poems. These verses were of a political nature, and the young idealist attacked the venality and chicanery he saw on all sides, naming names. Not only was his work libelous, but he assaulted persons so high in the government that he was in danger of being imprisoned.

So his worried father sent him, in 1714, to spend a year in the country with an old family friend, Louis de Caumartin, Marquis de St. Ange. Himself a weary cynic, St. Ange told the young man countless stories of chicanery, corruption, and double-dealing in high places, thereby completing his education. He returned to Paris with an introduction from St. Ange to one of the most beautiful, ruthless, and ambitious women in France, Anne-Louise, Duchesse de Maine, in whose veins flowed the royal Bourbon blood and that of the princely house of Condé.

The young man was fascinated by the Duchess, and she, recognizing his rare talents, became his sponsor. Anne-Louise despised the Regent, the Duc d'Orléans, with a deep, abiding hatred, and it wasn't long before Voltaire, quickly sharing that contempt, began to write scaldingly satiric verses about the Regent. These poems, which stung harshly, became enormously popular, and the secret police soon traced them to their source. In 1716 Voltaire was exiled from Paris and was forced to spend several months in rural retreats. The experience would be repeated almost countless times, and a life pattern had been formed.

It did not occur to him to alter his ways, and after two new, vicious attacks on the Regent were published, he was sent to the Bastille, but was treated more like an honored guest than a prisoner. Imprisonment gave him a chance to catch up on his serious work, and he revised a play with which he was dissatisfied, his version of the Oedipus legend, and started a huge project, a history of the reign of Henry IV, one of the few monarchs of France for whom he felt genuine admiration.

After spending eleven months in the Bastille he was released and again exiled from Paris, but he asked for a personal interview with the Regent, and the request was granted. Orléans, treating him with a gracious civility he did not deserve, readmitted him to official good grace, but certainly did not trust him. On November 18, 1718, Voltaire's *Oedipe* opened at the Théâtre Français, and was the biggest hit in decades. Literally overnight the playwright became the most prominent author in the country.

A second play, *Artémire*, was subjected to heavy criticism, but was also a financial success, and a long satire in verse, the *Philippiques*, whose authorship he never admitted, also earned a fortune. It was libelous, the style was unique, and Voltaire voluntarily left Paris again, this time paying a long visit to one of the great soldiers of the reign of Louis XIV, Marshal de Villars, whose reminiscences he put to excellent use in his later history of the era.

The father whose vocation Voltaire had regarded so contemptuously died in 1721, leaving him an income of four thousand gold louis per year, and soon thereafter Voltaire made a deal with the Regent. In return for a lifelong pension of two thousand gold louis per year he undertook a secret diplomatic mission to Brussels and The Hague that required the talents of a writer. Voltaire never fully explained the nature of his mission, and it has been assumed that he performed tasks of espionage for Orléans.

The years 1724 and 1725 were exceptionally busy for the

author whose pen was never still. He completed his history of Henry IV, the *Henriade,* and published it. He formed his close friendship with the Duc de Richelieu, saw his third tragedy, *Mariamne,* become a great success, and had the satisfaction of writing a comedy, *L'Indiscret,* that was also a tremendous hit.

An argument with a hot-headed gentleman, the Chevalier de Rohan, had disastrous consequences, together with blessings it could not have been possible to predict at the time. Voltaire was his usual, scathing self in his quarrel with the Chevalier, and once thereafter, when the author was dining with the Duc de Sully, Rohan obtained his revenge, hiring several thugs who hauled Voltaire outside and beat him up. The amused Duke did not lift a finger in his guest's defense. Voltaire challenged Rohan to a duel, which was against the law, and on the day the fight was to have taken place he was arrested and imprisoned again in the Bastille.

He obtained vengeance in his own way. In poetry, prose, and drama he ridiculed Rohan over a period of many years, often not bothering to disguise his identity and thereby challenging the libel laws. The Chevalier became the laughing-stock of Paris and could not escape his misery. As for Sully, Voltaire removed his renowned ancestor, Henry IV's Minister of Finance, from the new edition of the *Henriade,* no mean feat since the first Duc de Sully had been one of Henry the Great's closest associates and advisers.

"An author," Voltaire said serenely, "always has the last word, the word posterity remembers."

He had no desire to languish in prison again, and proposed that he go off to England in voluntary exile. The offer was accepted, and he departed within two weeks for a stay of more than three years, until the late spring of 1729. The visit to England was the most serene period of Voltaire's life, and his love of England, his unabashed admiration for all things English, particularly freedom of speech and thought, was recipro-

53

cated by a people who considered him the most talented Continental of the age. Queen Caroline became his friend, and he dedicated the English edition of the *Henriade* to her, a gesture that helped make the book a huge success. Congreve, the playwright, and Pope, the poet, were among his closest associates in England, and he numbered cabinet ministers and personages in high society among his good friends. Not the least of them was the formidable Sarah, first Duchess of Marlborough.

No man ever enjoyed a more extraordinary exile. Not only was Voltaire the literary and social lion of London, but he made frequent journeys to Paris to look after his business affairs there. He made no secret of these visits, and the authorities, although well aware of his presence, took care to look the other way. The regime was badly embarrassed by its stern official attitude toward a man who was already regarded as the greatest living Frenchman in England, and Voltaire had ample reason to make slighting references to what he called his "flexible exile."

Returning to Paris in 1729, when the exile came to an official end, Voltaire made up for lost time in a furious flurry of literary activity. He wrote and himself produced three plays, *Brutus, Ériphile* and his great tragedy, *Zaïre*, each more successful than the last. His *Charles XII* was published, even though the official censor had not granted him a license for the purpose, and it, too, was a great critical and financial success.

Voltaire had become a wealthy man, thanks to his own efforts, but he continued to live modestly, at least when he himself was paying the bills. He seldom found it necessary, however, for he had become the lion of French society, too. Every palace door in Paris was open to him; he was welcome at Versailles, and although his presence sometimes made the great and near-great nervous, they continued to cultivate him, hoping they would not unexpectedly find themselves in print.

There was cause for their fears, although they were at first unaware of it. Voltaire had started to work in private on his

54

satiric epic poem, the *Pucelle,* which lacerated every public figure in France, present and past. The *Pucelle* became an avocational pastime he could not put down, and he worked on it over a period of many years, refining it, changing it, and bringing it up to date. Had no one known of the effort while he was working on it, no harm would have been done, but Voltaire could not resist quoting particularly juicy passages to friends, and word of its existence spread. It was quoted so often in high circles that the secret police frequently searched for the manuscript, and he was forced to employ endless tricks and stratagems in order to hide the document.

It was impossible, emotionally, intellectually, and physically, for Voltaire to refrain from writing the truth as he saw it. He felt compelled to puncture the balloons of double dealing, falsehood, and baseless pride, regardless of the consequences. He wanted to avoid the unpleasant, if he could, but was willing to take any risks in order to put his convictions on paper.

The same spirit that impelled him to write the *Pucelle* was responsible for two other works published in 1733. One of these, *Temple du goût,* was a long poem that satirized his most prominent contemporaries on the French literary scene. Most of these gentlemen happened to be members of the Academy, which came in for its share of ridicule, and the verse, which was written in poor taste, to put it charitably, won Voltaire a new host of enemies. It also guaranteed his continuing exclusion from the Academy for some years to come.

His other effort was far more serious. Entitled *Lettres philosophiques sur les Anglais,* it was purportedly a prose study of contemporary English literature. In actuality, however, it was a bitter, specific assault on French censorship in the past half-century, and furiously attacked the government and the attitude of the French Church hierarchy. In this blazing diatribe Voltaire carefully cited chapter and verse, reeling off the names of literary offerings that had been banned and of authors who had been persecuted. Compounding the felony, he quoted

55

liberally from the various banned works, including his own, to show up the absurd attitudes of the lay censors and the Roman Catholic bishops.

The authorities had grown weary of their disputes with the indomitable Voltaire, and were reluctant to prosecute him again, knowing he enjoyed the sympathy of so many prominent Frenchmen as well as that of innumerable civilized men elsewhere. Crown Prince Frederick of Prussia, later to become Frederick the Great, had recently expressed his admiration for the author, and had declared, with heartfelt envy, that he wished this genius were one of his subjects. But the direct challenge to authority could not be ignored without damaging the basic structure of French censorship itself.

Therefore the *Lettres philosophiques* was banned. Voltaire had anticipated the step, and the book promptly disappeared underground, but continued to sell at a merry clip. Scores of freedom-loving Parisians, many of whom had never had any connection with the book business, risked imprisonment themselves by selling copies of the volume.

The authorities, doubly thwarted, issued a warrant for Voltaire's arrest, but took their time inaugurating a search for him. It was their hope that he would take the hint and leave France until the furor subsided. Voltaire, however, had no intention of crossing the border until there was no other choice. It was true that he was no longer in Paris, but he was still very much in France, living under a remarkable arrangement that offered him, like the protagonist of his *Candide,* the best of all possible worlds.

In short, Voltaire had started his long affair with Émilie du Châtelet, and between them they had worked out a seemingly foolproof plan that would guarantee his continuing personal freedom.

V

The Turkish ambassador and the café, a new type of drinking and eating establishment, were of prime importance in the meeting of Émilie du Châtelet and Voltaire, in the development of their brief friendship, and the sudden romantic explosion that resulted in their affair. The café was more than a setting; it was essential to their relationship.

Late in the first decade of the eighteenth century, as the reign of Louis XIV was drawing to a close, coffee was first introduced at Versailles and in Paris by the Turkish envoy. It cost eighty francs per pound, the equivalent of about two hundred fifty dollars in present times, so only the wealthiest nobles could afford the luxury. There were few who wanted to drink the stuff. Gourmets deplored its taste, the sophisticated wouldn't touch the brew because it lacked alcoholic spirits, and physicians were horrified, insisting it was a poisonous substance that would kill a strong man in months if he drank as much as a cup per day.

Meanwhile the Turks were producing coffee at an ever-increasing rate, the drink having become popular in Vienna and, subsequently, in other parts of central Europe. The price declined rapidly, and in 1719 an Armenian named Pascal who was living in Paris opened a public café, a place established for the exclusive purpose of serving the beverage, near the old

57

abbey of St. Germain des Près. Pascal's vision was too limited, and he soon failed, but two other men picked up his idea and expanded it.

A Syrian named d'Alep opened one café on the Right Bank, and a Sicilian named Procope opened another not far from it. Procope's place was the more elaborate, and although coffee was the principal reason for its existence, he also served wine, bread, and sausages and cheese. He was copied by d'Alep, and both places were so successful that, in 1720, three hundred more cafés opened in Paris. That was just the beginning, and Voltaire is the authority for the assertion that, by the following year, the city had become one large café. Every shop kept coffee on hand to serve its customers. Every apothecary brewed coffee and served it on the premises in what was undoubtedly the beginning of the drugstore lunch counter. Even convents installed cafés for the convenience of visitors.

Gradually the cafés became more elaborate as their rivalry grew. The Café d'Alep installed marble-top tables, which soon became the rage, and served ices, which were considered a culinary triumph. The Café Procope became a large, elegant dining establishment by the early 1730s, and hired Italian musicians to entertain the customers. It also had one wing where diners and drinkers could obtain hot, perfumed baths.

In 1733, when Voltaire and Émilie met, the Procope was by far the most famous of the cafés, and had achieved a reputation throughout Europe. It was located across the street from the Comédie Française, so its basic clientele consisted of actors, dramatists, producers, and critics. The wealthier patrons of the theater also went there.

Around the corner was the Café Gradot, which became an informal headquarters for scientists, mathematicians, and philosophers, with a sprinkling the Academy membership thrown in as well. The star of the establishment was Moreau de Maupertuis, a flamboyant explorer, astronomer, and physicist, who achieved a reputation in his day that was equaled only by the swift collapse of his fame.

Also in the same neighborhood was the Veuve Laurent, the third of the great cafés, which catered principally to poets, musicians, and painters. Another, smaller establishment was the Café de la Régence, whose habitués played chess. It was located opposite the Palais Royal in the quarters occupied by one of the great French restaurants of the present day, the Grand Vefour. The highest-ranking aristocrats frequented the Régence, among them the Duc de Richelieu and Marshal de Saxe, the great military hero of the reign of Louis XV. Voltaire frequently went there, too.

In fact, Voltaire could be seen, at one hour or another, in virtually every important café in the city. He was at home with the theatrical people of the Procope, with the scientists and philosophers of the Gradot, and with the poets of the Laurent. He was at home at the Buci, where working journalists gathered and free newspapers were given to the clients. Only at the Bordeaux, where conservative clergymen and their supporters met, was he given a consistently chilly reception.

The cafés of eighteenth-century Paris were typical products of the Enlightenment, and were, in a sense, the precursors of the men's clubs that were formed in London later in the century. Each had its own clientele, with its own social and vocational restrictions, and the "members" of these "clubs" met regularly. Each café had its own distinct atmosphere, and each became the scene of quarrels that developed into duels or feuds of long standing.

Each had its own eccentrics, too, and none boasted more than the Procope, frequented by a customer subsequently immortalized by Voltaire. Colonel Gilbert de St. Foix was an extraordinary, complicated man who had won renown in two fields. Commander of a regiment of musketeers, he had achieved glory on the battlefield, and received a handsome pension from the crown. After his retirement from the army, he developed an interest in the theater, and announcing that anyone could write a play, he proved his dictum correct by scribbling a tragedy that, to the astonishment of the professionals, was a success. St. Foix proved he had not stumbled into the field by accident and wrote two more plays, both of which also were substantial hits.

An aggressive, always angry man with an unlimited capacity for good cognac, St. Foix enjoyed a rousing quarrel, and if there was anything he liked better, it was a duel. Most people gave him a wide berth, and only Voltaire had the temerity to shred him in a poetic satire. St. Foix, who recognized great talent in others, was so amused that he called Voltaire his friend and treated him with consideration at all times.

One day the soldier-dramatist and the great author were sitting together—Voltaire ate and St. Foix drank his dinner—when a captain of the king's guards in full dress uniform swaggered into the place, knocking over several chairs as he threaded his way past the crowded tables. Seating himself near the pair who were discussing the works of other dramatists, the officer loudly demanded a roll and a cup of coffee.

When it was not forthcoming immediately, he shouted, "Damn you, I want my dinner!"

His rude manner had annoyed St. Foix from the moment the man had entered, and the retired colonel could keep quiet no longer. Ostensibly addressing Voltaire, he said in a voice that carried to every corner of the Procope, "What a sorry repast! What manner of man would place an order like that and call it his dinner? Let me tell you. Only an idiot!"

The officer realized he was being baited and wisely remained silent.

St. Foix, working himself into a cold fury, repeated, "What a sorry repast. Never have I seen sorrier. Oh, what a sorry repast."

Voltaire tried in vain to quiet him.

Eventually the captain could tolerate the teasing no more and, rising to his feet, demanded an apology.

St. Foix announced to everyone in the Procope that the time had come to teach a young idiot two things, good manners and how to order dinner. Everyone raced into the street outside, with Voltaire acting as St. Foix's second. The two principals drew their swords and fought the "duel of the roll and coffee" in deadly earnest.

Each inflicted a slight wound on his opponent at approximately the same moment, and, blood having been drawn, that should have been the end of the matter. The captain, observing the amenities, declared that he was satisfied.

St. Foix, however, demanded the last word. "If you had killed me," he said, "I should have died with my opinion completely unaltered. Even when I was an ignorant soldier, my palate knew the difference between food fit for a gentleman and swill. I shall always insist that a roll and a cup of coffee make a very sorry dinner."

A resumption of the fight was prevented by the fortuitous arrival of a colonel of the guard, an old comrade of St. Foix's and the superior officer of the captain. He was required, under the law, to arrest both of the principals, but the Duc de Richelieu wandered into the café with several friends, and was briefed on the situation by Voltaire, so he intervened in his official capacity as lieutenant governor of Paris.

He and the colonel conferred at great length with the duelists at a corner table, wine flowing freely, and it was agreed that the swordsmen would be released on the condition that St. Foix bought the captain a meal he considered appropriate, and further provided that the captain ate it.

Voltaire, who recorded the event in one of his relatively rare excursions into journalism, was delighted to watch the pair consume a meal of nine courses, which included some of Procope's special dishes. They also put away several bottles of wine, as did the Duke, his friends, and a number of other amiable clients of the café who joined the party. Everyone with the exception of Voltaire, who used alcoholic beverages sparingly, became roaring drunk.

"This incident," the reporter concluded, *"proves the worth of the café as an educational institution. A barbarian who could not distinguish between a roll and an epicurean feast will know what to order when he next dines in public with his mistress. An increase in his wages, the pay of the military being distressingly low, would enable him to afford the purchase of a good dinner, and would hasten the civilizing influence exerted by the café."*

Voltaire assumed, as did his readers, that the captain's mistress was not a woman of quality, as the rules governing the appearance of females in cafés was very strict, although it was dictated by custom rather than law. It was carefully observed by the proprietors of the cafés, who had no desire to see their profitable business ruined.

A very few cafés permitted women to dine in one of the establishment's rooms, provided they were escorted by men. A majority of the cafés, however, banned women outright and would not serve them. It was only natural, however, that the professional harlots of Paris should become interested in places where men gathered in large numbers, and they tried repeatedly to gain admittance. A majority of the cafés finally compromised somewhat, each of them setting aside a section in which the streetwalkers were allowed to sit and order light wines. Under no circumstances were they permitted to buy cognac, English or Dutch gin, or other hard liquors, however, because they showed a tendency to become drunk, noisy, and disruptive. Any man who sought the services of a prostitute knew the section of his favorite café in which to seek her.

The better cafés, where the nobles, the gentry, and the intellectuals gathered, did not serve women under any circumstances, and barred them from the premises under a firm but unwritten rule. Ladies were expected to meet their friends in salons, attend the opera and theater, take carriage rides in the Bois, and enliven dinner and supper parties in private homes.

The ladies of Paris, living in what was called a man's world, went through the motions of accepting their fate, but quietly and discreetly nipped at the edges of the dictum in order to weaken it. They developed a charming custom of their own, driving up to a café entrance in their carriages, parking there, and ordering coffee brought to them. It was not long before the service became elaborate, and soon the leading cafés were doing a flourishing curbside trade, serving the ladies their coffee in exquisite china cups and silver saucers. The silver saucer, in fact, became a standard, a hallmark of a café's quality, and ladies were known to refuse the coffee given them if their cups did not rest on a small platter of sterling.

Gentlemen who were dining or drinking at a café always came to the curb to pay their respects to a lady who sat there in her carriage, and it was inevitable that traffic jams should be created in the narrow, cobbled streets of the city. Some café owners protested, but in vain. If women were not allowed inside the sacred precincts of a café, they did the next best thing, and the owner of a place was powerless to halt them.

There was one lady in Paris, only one, who firmly declared that she thought the café ban on women was absurd and that she had no intention of obeying custom. Émilie du Châtelet, somewhat at loose ends socially after the end of her affair with the Duc de Richelieu, became even more active in her intellectual pursuits. Her friendship with the scientist-explorer, Maupertuis, had grown deeper; she was on excellent terms with many of his friends and associates, who treated her as an equal, and she saw no reason why she shouldn't join them for coffee and their stimulating discussions at the Gradot.

That is precisely what she did in the early months of 1733, creating a sensation in the city when she appeared rouged, gowned, and perfumed. Maupertuis and several other scientists were distressed when the management of the café pleasantly but unyieldingly informed Émilie that they could not serve her. In that event, she replied, she had no desire to be served, but would be content with a chair, so she could chat with her friends. The management, with regret, said that could not be permitted either.

Émilie returned home, her head held high, and fashionable Paris snickered.

But anyone who really knew Émilie du Châtelet was ready to wager that she hadn't given up, that she would find a way to break the ban, and she did, enjoying the last laugh. About a week after she had been turned away from the Gradot she returned, emerging from her carriage in man's attire that had been made for her in the interim. She appeared as a male from bicorn hat to buckled shoes, and her white silk stockings did justice to a pair of legs that Voltaire later called "glories and marvels of France." She was rouged and powdered, to be sure, and her eyes were rimmed with kohl, since her vanity would not permit her to appear in public without makeup. But the overall effect, at least from a distance, was enough to gain her admission.

The management of the Gradot was in a dilemma. Émilie's friends, led by Maupertuis, cheered when she approached their table, and other clients of the establishment joined in the applause. In their opinion Émilie had won a great victory, and a cup of coffee, its symbol, was ordered for her at once.

The proprietors of the Gradot, descendants of the original owner, knew that Parisians were fickle, and, if insulted, would go elsewhere for their food, coffee, and conversation. The place would continue to thrive, to be sure, but it would lose much of its luster if its clientele of scientists, philosophers, and mathematicians walked out. It was decided, on the spur of the moment, to pretend that Émilie was a man, to notice nothing out of the ordinary, and to serve her just as any other patron would be served.

Thereafter Émilie became a Gradot "regular," and made a daily appearance at Maupertuis's table.

Voltaire was well acquainted with the scientist and his associates, and felt a grudging respect for Maupertuis's work, although he considered the man something of a poseur. They had one strong bond in common, their mutual interest in the scientific discoveries of Newton, many of whose theories clashed with those of Descartes, who was considered the ultimate authority by most Frenchmen. Both were inclined to be Newtonians, although they sought specific proof of his hypotheses, and Maupertuis, a few years later, went to Lapland on an expedition financed by Louis XV in order to put some of the great Englishman's views to the test.

It seems unlikely that Voltaire, the peripatetic café visitor, could have failed to call at the Gradot when Émilie sat daily with Maupertuis, and it is even less probable that the author would have avoided stopping at the table for a chat. On the other hand, Voltaire was painfully shy, in spite of his sardonic attitude toward the world and his courage, so it may be that he was reluctant to thrust himself into the company of the spectacular woman whose bravado was the talk of Paris.

In any event, they did not meet at the Gradot, and the mystery is compounded by the fact that Voltaire had known her as a child. He had been well acquainted with Louis-Nicolas de Breteuil, and on many occasions had called at the house in which she had been growing up.

Émilie undoubtedly knew Voltaire by reputation, if not by sight. She had seen performances of several of his plays and was familiar with the bulk of his prose work. She also had good reason to know his verse, since he had dedicated a poem, in 1732, to "the charming and sublime Émilie," of whom he had heard much from his good friend, Richelieu, and whose intellect he admired. The poem was his *Ode on Fanaticism,* an attack on several of his colleagues, and the dedication read:

> *Since beautiful, 'twill be your fate,*
> *Émilie, to incur much hate,*
> *Almost one-half of the human race*
> *Will even curse you to your face;*
> *Possessed of genius, noblest fire,*
> *With fear you will each breast inspire;*
> *As you too easily confide,*
> *You'll often be betray'd, belied:*
> *You ne'er of virtue made parade,*
> *To Hypocrites no court you've paid,*
> *Therefore of Calumny beware,*
> *Foe to the virtuous and the fair.*

Emilie had been flattered by the tribute paid to her by the most renowned living French author, but it must be stressed that she considered his praise her due. Modesty was not one of her virtues, and she shared the opinion of those who believed her a genius. All the same, any woman would have been pleased, and her insatiable vanity having been fed, she was eager to thank Voltaire in person.

Perhaps she saw him at the Gradot or elsewhere, and was not impressed when he was pointed out to her. The tall, dashing man was the type who attracted her romantic interest, and Voltaire certainly did not fit that image. Almost painfully thin, he stood only an inch or two taller than Émilie, and although he dressed in the height of fashion, his wig always looked as though it would slip off his head. His face was narrow, his nose was long and thin, and his eyes, his only redeeming feature, invariably expressed his contempt for his surroundings. So, by no stretch of the imagination could he have been considered physically appealing.

Émilie had sent him a brief, polite note to thank him for the dedication, but there had been no other contact between them. It is reasonable to assume that they wanted to meet, and the necessary introductions were performed one day in the spring of 1733 by a man about town and literary hanger-on, Dumas d'Aigueberre. This much is known because Voltaire, in a letter written after Émilie's death in 1749, reminded his friend that he had been responsible for "helping me to renew my acquaintance with that unfortunate lady." It isn't known whether the meeting took place in Paris or the country, nor are any other details available.

Voltaire took it for granted that anyone who met him would make a fuss over him, and Émilie was accustomed to the same treatment, so it would be interesting to learn how they reacted to each other when they met. Whatever may have happened, it is obvious that there was an immediate, mutual attraction.

According to the conventions of the times, a gentleman made it his business to call on a lady after being presented to her and pay his respects to her during her salon visiting hours. Unfortunately, within forty-eight hours of the time Voltaire met Émilie, he went to bed with one of his frequent stomach upsets. Émilie was informed of his illness by mutual acquaintances, and if Mohammed could not make the journey to the mountain, the latter did not hesitate to reverse the normal process. Émilie ordered her cook to poach several chickens, and, packing them in a hamper with a bowl of Italian salad and a few bottles of wine, she went to see the invalid, duly chaperoned by their mutual friends.

He had just moved to new quarters in what he himself called the worst quarter of Paris and was lodged in an apartment located in a dilapidated old building on the Rue de Long-Pont. His rooms were directly across the street from the belfry of the Church of St. Gervais, and the bells, which pealed at length every quarter-hour, made so much noise that they interfered with conversation. Voltaire managed to block out their sound when he was writing and, as he never entertained visitors at home, hadn't been bothered by the bells.

He and Émilie quickly discovered they couldn't talk without shouting, and the situation was so ludicrous they laughed until they wept. Their friends, the Duchesse de St. Pierre and her lover, M. de Fourqualquiers, were not amused, however, and sat in a stiff silence, unwilling to lose their dignity by screaming above the pealing of the bells. Their attitude made the situation all the more absurd, and increased the merriment of the invalid and his lady bountiful, neither of whom hesitated to cast aside any pretense of dignity when they wished.

Voltaire enjoyed himself so much that he suddenly announced, "I am cured." Leaving the chicken, salad, and wine for a later repast, he insisted on taking the trio to a café for dinner. There they ate a sumptuous dinner, and Voltaire, always particular about food and drink, ordered the finest wines.

The party was a great success. Émilie could not stop talking, neither could Voltaire, and they addressed their remarks exclusively to each other. Their chaperones were ignored, and eventually took themselves elsewhere, leaving the verbose couple to amuse themselves. Émilie and Voltaire may not have noticed their departure, and lingered at the table until the establishment closed for the night. By that time it had become evident to both of them that they were in love.

"Everything about her is noble," Voltaire wrote soon thereafter, *"her countenance, her tastes, the style of her letters, her discourses, her politeness. Her words are choice without being affected, her conversation is agreeable and interesting. She has forgotten nothing, and she has seen a great deal. But she always regulates the length of her recitals according to the desire of others. Without omitting any essential circumstances, she makes one regret the brevity of her remarks. If books were written as well as she speaks, love of reading would be the virtue of the world. She has an admirable discernment in the choice of friends, and her friendship is courageous and unassailable. In short, she is a person born to shine in a world wherein few have luster."*

For years it had been his habit to sleep with any lady who made herself available to him, and many did. But his heart had not been involved since his abortive romance with the girl he had met at The Hague in his youth. Now, overnight, the great author was reduced to the level of a schoolboy.

As for Émilie, her visits to the Gradot halted abruptly, if temporarily. *"Why did you never tell me that M. de Voltaire is the paragon of men?"* she asked the Duc de Richelieu in a scolding letter. She had found the grand passion of her life, and their association would help her achieve her ambitions.

VI

The date that Émilie du Châtelet and Voltaire
first slept together was not recorded and is an irrelevant detail.
By mid-summer of 1733 their affair was in full blossom,
blighted only by the severe illness of her third child, soon to
die in infancy. Voltaire was almost forty, a busy, cynical man,
worried by the official reaction to his two recently published
treatises, preoccupied by several other major writing projects
in which he was immersed. In addition he was suffering from
the worst series of stomach disorders he had experienced in
years, and, as he well knew, he needed rest, relaxation, and
a carefully supervised diet.

Émilie, on the other hand, was in superb health, could eat
or drink anything she pleased—provided she dieted periodically
—and was endowed with so much energy that she exhausted
anyone who spent considerable time with her. She was in a
manic state, and supposedly, at least according to her own
dubious word, required even less sleep than the two to four
hours she considered normal. She could memorize long passages of either prose or poetry at will, and she confided to
Voltaire that, one night when she could not sleep, she not only
read but mastered one volume, or approximately one-third, of
Sir Isaac Newton's *Principia*. In spite of her intellectual
prowess and her romantic experiences, she fell in love with the

overwhelming enthusiasm of a teenage girl. A lesser man than Voltaire would have been suffocated by her affection, and even he had to struggle in order to survive.

French aristocratic society was proud of its sophistication, its ability to take any romance in its stride, but the combination of the great author and the brilliant but absurdly girlish Émilie was almost too much. Paris was incredulous, and young Louis XV, when he was told of the affair, refused to believe the story.

Until now Émilie had not realized that she was an iconoclast, but she quickly realized she shared Voltaire's contempt for society's opinions. Both thought themselves indifferent to the views of others, but they recognized only a portion of the truth. In reality both wanted to shock the world, and both went out of their way to create scandal.

From the beginning they broke all the rules ladies and gentlemen were required to observe. A man was allowed to take his mistress to cafés that served women, but not to the older, infinitely more respectable inns. They could appear together at the theater, but not at the opera. They could go to Versailles together, and, if they wished, spend all of their time there together, but they were expected to go separately into the audience chamber when they made their obeisances to King Louis. And, even if they were living together, tradition insisted they maintain the fiction that they were living apart.

When Voltaire spent the night at the Hôtel du Châtelet or Émilie went to his apartment on the Rue de Long-Pont, all of their friends knew it the next day. They dined together openly at the most fashionable inn before going on together to the opera, and they delighted in making a joint appearance before King Louis. Rarely had any couple found such pleasure in flouting custom.

Their conduct was so flagrant that, under the best of circumstances, they would have caused the nobility to wonder whether Émilie's husband would be forced to intervene. But the actual situation in which they found themselves was one that called for the exercise of great discretion. Voltaire's *Temple du goût* had just created an uproar, and although the authorities could find nothing in it that would cause them to take disciplinary action against the author, they once again were looking at him askance. Of far greater significance was the interest his *Lettres philosophiques* was generating. Written for an intellectual readership, it was slow to catch the attention of the court, but was causing increasing excitement in the summer of 1733. Late in August it was read by Cardinal Fleury, who ruled in the name of the King, and His Eminence quietly sent word to the author that he was no longer welcome at Versailles.

The handwriting was written in large letters on the wall, but Voltaire and Émilie ignored it. Not only were they immersed in their own love affair, but were busily and enthusiastically trying to promote a marriage between the Duc de Richelieu and Mary-Elizabeth-Sophie, the very young and beautiful Princess de Guise of the semi-royal family from Lorraine that had played such an important role in the development and history of France. The wedding was arranged, with Voltaire acting as the principal intermediary, and the ceremony was held at Montjeu, in Lorraine, where the bride's father owned a large palace.

For complicated reasons of state France maintained the semi-fiction that Lorraine, lying on her eastern border, was an autonomous, completely independent nation, ruled by her own monarch, Stanislaus Leczinski, the former king of Poland, whose title was Grand Duke of Lorraine. Stanislaus kept his own court, and although his realm followed France in peace and war, contributed taxes to the French treasury, and otherwise was administered as a major province, Lorraine was considered a "foreign" land, and French citizens who went there were required to carry their passports.

Émilie and Voltaire packed their passports in their luggage before setting out for Montjeu early in September. It was the wedding that brought Voltaire and Émilie's husband together for the first time. The General was with his troops in the German states, a new war having broken out, but he took a leave of absence for several days, and appeared for the festivities in the company of his new mistress. The girl was called Mlle. d'Anjou, and although her Christian name is lost to posterity, it is known that she was blonde, young, and very attractive.

For the sake of appearances the Marquise and her lover shared a suite with the Marquis and his mistress, but Émilie went everywhere with Voltaire, and Mlle. d'Anjou never left Florent-Claude's side. Voltaire and the Marquis established cordial relations at once, laying the groundwork for a friendship that would last for many years. Voltaire dedicated a short verse to Mlle. d'Anjou, paying tribute to her large breasts and tiny waist, and the General, who appreciated the compliment, reciprocated by telling the author the prescription for an elixir that would soothe the autumn cough Émilie soon would catch.

Everyone at the wedding, including the bridegroom, was fascinated by the budding friendship of Voltaire and the Marquis du Châtelet, and Émilie enjoyed every moment she spent in the spotlight. Voltaire, of course, knew precisely what he was doing, and not only understood the military mind but wanted no trouble with a professional soldier who was reputedly one of Europe's best swordsmen. What the Marquis may or may not have understood is difficult to determine. He was first and foremost a pragmatist, and, as his wife made no objection to his affairs, he saw no reason to interfere in hers. In addition, he probably knew that Voltaire was very wealthy, and had just loaned a considerable sum to Richelieu, among others. The author not only earned substantial royalties on virtually everything he wrote, but had a remarkable business sense as well, and would have prospered as a financier and investor had he never put a single word on paper. He was not averse to making loans to responsible aristocrats who happened to own valuable

73

property, and his terms were somewhat more attractive than those offered by Paris bankers. Florent-Claude was in no position to forget that his own circumstances were reduced, that his wife was one of the most extravagant women in France, and that his pretty mistress had developed a fondness for jewelry.

The wedding was held as scheduled, and the whole company followed the custom of escorting the bride and groom to their fourposter, prompting Voltaire to observe, *"I have traveled eighty leagues in a carriage without springs for the purpose of seeing a man and a woman in bed together."*

The festivities lasted for seventy-two hours, at the end of which time the military men, including the bridegroom as well as the Marquis du Châtelet, went off to rejoin the army, which was besieging Philippsburg. Everyone else stayed on at Montjeu, prolonging the celebration, and no one relished the respite more than Voltaire and Émilie. Less than twenty-four hours after the wedding Voltaire had received a letter, delivered from Paris by special courier, telling him that he was in even greater difficulty than he had anticipated. The secret police were confiscating every copy of the *Lettres philosophiques* they could find, and the author would be sent off to the Bastille for a long term the moment he returned to France.

Voltaire sensibly decided the climate of France would not be beneficial to his health. Instead he made extensive plans to visit the army in Germany, then travel to Switzerland, Holland, and, if necessary, other countries. Émilie, torn from his side by the fate that mocks lovers, accompanied the new Duchesse de Richelieu back to Paris.

There, to an extent, she resumed the life she had known before meeting Voltaire, and held her daily meetings with Maupertuis and other scientists. But there was a difference: she wrote long daily letters to Voltaire, giving them to friends and acquaintances who were going abroad for mailing beyond the borders of France, where the secret police could not intercept them. Voltaire also wrote her daily, other friends bringing his communications to Paris from distant points outside the country. It sometimes seemed as though the entire French aristocracy was engaged in a conspiracy to thwart the crown's secret police.

Unfortunately, this correspondence was either lost or may have been destroyed, perhaps by Voltaire himself after Émilie's death. It is known that they wrote many hundreds—perhaps thousands—of letters to each other over the period of more than a decade and a half, yet all but a handful have vanished. Voltaire engaged in such voluminous correspondence with so many people that large and important discoveries have been made, down to the present day, but there has been no sign anywhere of his letters to Émilie or of those she wrote to him. Although no one knows what may have happened, literary detectives are inclined to suspect that Voltaire, perhaps acting in concert with the Marquis du Châtelet, burned them.

Because of this missing information, nothing is known regarding the most important decision ever made by Émilie and Voltaire, or which of them conceived the original idea. Only one fact stands out: Early in October Voltaire arrived at the ancient country house that had belonged to the Châtelet family for the better part of nine hundred years. There he lived, alone, except for workmen, until Christmas. No one in Paris except Émilie and a few trusted friends knew his whereabouts, and he could not have found a better hideout if he had invented the place himself.

The Château de Cirey was a huge, rambling structure, which, rebuilt by Émilie and Voltaire, still stands today. It is located in deep woodlands at the eastern edge of Champagne, a short ride from the Lorraine border and also close to the area's best road, which, in the eighteenth century, led directly to Holland. A man living there could, with only short notice, make good his escape out of France in either of two directions.

The forest was literally impenetrable in places, and only a

single, rutted dirt road led to the old manor house. Travel through the woods could be dangerous, because old iron mines used by the ancient Romans were covered with a thin layer of underbrush, and the unwary could fall twenty feet or more into a pit. The cellars dated back to the tenth century, but the building itself was relatively modern, having been erected in the sixteenth century by the Marquis's wealthy great-grandfather after the previous structure had been burned to the ground by partisans of Voltaire's idol, Henry IV, during the religious civil wars.

Émilie, who had paid a single visit of less than twenty-four hours to the place, knew what Voltaire faced when he arrived at the bleak, isolated château. A portion of the building was sound, although its roof leaked here and there, but approximately forty percent had never been completed, and a skeletal superstructure was exposed to the elements. The primitive kitchen, a separate outbuilding connected to the main house by a covered passage, could be used, but that was all that could be said for it. Two large stone hearths were in working condition, and so was a wood and charcoal burning stove.

The house itself was dismal. In the lord-of-the-manor's suite stood an ancient bed with a rotting mattress, and Voltaire was forced to purchase a new bed on the day of his arrival, traveling eleven miles to the nearest village for the purpose. There was not one stick of furniture in the place, so he also had to buy a few simple tables and chairs he could use until he could acquire divans and other pieces that better suited his tastes.

The building was damp and, even in October, bitterly cold. Luckily there were fireplaces that still worked in most of the rooms, and firewood was in ample supply in the nearby forests. On the day Voltaire arrived, he hired several workmen to chop fallen trees into logs.

Working with the intense fury of the compulsive, Voltaire managed to accomplish near-miracles in the three months before Émilie joined him. Hoping to keep his purpose from the ears of French police, he sent an agent to Lorraine to buy furniture, linens, tablewear, and other household goods. Friends in The Hague, Geneva, and Basel bought paintings, rugs, and tapestries for him and shipped them to Cirey. Meanwhile a small army of laborers was at work finishing the château, painting it and putting glass in the newly completed windows. Voltaire literally started his task with a hollow shell, and it is a tribute to his great powers of concentration that, during this same period, he wrote his play *Alzire,* soon thereafter a tremendous success, and continued work on the *Pucelle.*

Like Émilie, Voltaire needed an audience, and the company of no one but illiterate workmen drove him to distraction. He amused himself in his free time by drawing extensive plans for the addition of new rooms, and he also made detailed sketches for the formal and kitchen gardens. Most of his ideas were utilized by the architects and landscapers. In addition, predictably, he called on the two ladies of noble birth who lived in the neighborhood and soon was happily accepting dinner invitations from them.

But he missed the mistress whose home he was rehabilitating and furnishing, and very much wanted her at his side. Although his letters to her during this period have disappeared, his correspondence with several of his close friends in Paris indicates that his patience was strained to the breaking point.

Why Émilie elected to remain in Paris for eleven or twelve weeks is something of a mystery. She followed her usual routines there, studying and translating, working with her tutors and absorbing the wisdom of Maupertuis and other scientists at the Gradot. She also paid calls on friends, played cards with them, and, when she had nothing better to do, allowed her small, neglected children to be brought to her. Her treatment of her son and daughter, it might be noted, was no worse and no better than the attitude displayed by her aristocratic contemporaries. Children of the nobility were reared, in the main, by governesses and tutors, and the Marquise du Châtelet, herself trained in the system, was unfamiliar with any other.

Émilie was in such an emotional state during these months that each day she spent apart from Voltaire were a torture. Her new, dear friend, the young Duchesse de Richelieu, was forced to listen to her talk interminably about him, and Richelieu received a number of communications in which his bride hinted rather delicately that she was growing weary of Émilie's sighs and postures.

A dutiful wife according to the standards of the age, Émilie did not neglect to inform her husband of the transformation in progress at his ancestral home. She relayed to him the information she received from Voltaire on the reconstruction work and was delighted to tell him of the furniture her lover was buying for the house.

At the same time, however, she was afraid that his taste might not meet her standards, and considered it dangerous to allow a man to furnish a house himself, without close feminine supervision. *"His rooms in the city were dreary,"* she said in a worried letter to the Marquis, *"and I can but hope that Cirey offers him its own inspiration before I journey there."*

Florent-Claude did not share her concern, nor did it bother him that a stranger had taken possession of the château. The place had been worthless, uninhabitable, and of no use to him. Now, without reaching into his own purse, he would be the beneficiary of a complete restoration. Legally, if not in fact, he was the master of the estate, and he pursued his campaign against the Germans with a light heart, knowing he would have a home other than the Paris town house that he could visit when the war ended. He was not fond of metropolitan living, and in one letter to his wife he reminded her of a promise she had made him in a previous communication. She intended to urge Voltaire to erect a fence around a portion of the forest that lay directly east of the manor house, where game abounded. There were few pastimes that Florent-Claude enjoyed more than a day of hunting, and he was making certain that his wife's lover did not neglect the preserve he wanted.

It may be that Émilie tarried in Paris because the secret police appeared to be earnest in their resolve to apprehend Voltaire, and were watching the mail of the friends with whom he ordinarily corresponded. Émilie and Voltaire were maintaining elaborate precautions to keep their own letters to each other out of the hands of the authorities, so it is logical to assume they were afraid Émilie might be followed if she left the city. She had no intention of leading the hunters to their quarry, if hints in the letters of Mme. de Richelieu are interpreted correctly.

Cardinal Fleury was in an embarrassing position, to be sure. His own stature and dignity were at stake, as he had not been spared in the *Lettres philosophiques,* but at the same time he did not want to subject himself to undue criticism abroad. Certainly he would have been ridiculed if he jailed the man universally regarded as the genius who exemplified the best of French culture. The Cardinal was wise enough to realize that Voltaire's attacks on him were lampoons that caused people to laugh, but did not in any way denigrate or harm his real authority. So he presumably ordered the secret police to show less zeal in the search for the missing author.

Bureaucracy has moved at a snail's pace in any era, and weeks passed before the secret police displayed sufficient signs of decreasing vigilance to convince Émilie that it was safe for her to leave Paris and make the long journey to Cirey. Certainly her mode of travel was so extravagant that any novice secret policeman would have had no difficulty in trailing her. The caravan of the Marquise du Châtelet consisted of five large carriages, and her party included her children, her personal maids, her principal cook, and several other servants.

One carriage was filled with her clothes, and before leaving Paris she made arrangements for other coaches to leave the following week with still more of her wardrobe. She also stuffed still another carriage with books. Apparently it did not cross her mind to bother with pots and pans or other household goods, much less favorite paintings or bric-a-brac.

Voltaire best describes Émilie's arrival, in a letter sent to Mme. de Champbonin in December, and his humor did not desert him:

"Mme. du Châtelet is here, having arrived from Paris yesterday evening. She came just at the moment when I received a letter from her, by which she informed me that she would not be coming soon, expressing her deepest regrets and asking me to show patience until I might see her again. Her journey was neither planned nor executed on the notice or whim of a moment. She is surrounded by two hundred packages which arrived here the same day as she, but which she sent separately, thus ensuring madness. She left Paris without the many items she wishes, and sent messengers back to the city for them, also to make purchases. What a mad place this quiet island has become! There are beds without curtains, apartments without windows; china cabinets, but no armchairs, charming phaetons and no appropriate horses to draw them.

"Amidst all this disorder, Mme. du Châtelet laughs and is charming. She arrived in a kind of tumbril, bruised and shaken, without having slept, but she is well. I have not yet learned what happened to the coach in which she left Paris, and she is so filled with so many things to say that I doubt I shall ever learn. She asks me to send you a thousand compliments for her. We are going to patch the old tapestries. We shall search for curtains 'in the shops,' but I know of no shops in the area. We shall make doors ourselves, the workmen being too slow for the taste of Mme. du Châtelet, and it does not deter her that neither of us has ever used a chisel or a saw. So, as you see, we are doing everything to receive you. But I swear, joking apart, all will be done if you will visit us soon, and you will be very comfortable here."

Two strong-willed people, each sure that what he or she

wanted was right, were setting up housekeeping together for the first time, and the basic situation, combined with the chaotic conditions and the long separation that had created tensions, brought on a minor crisis. In a letter to Mme. de la Neuville, Voltaire declared, *"Mme. du Châtelet is going to put windows where I have put doors. She is changing staircases into chimneys and chimneys into staircases. Where I have instructed the workmen to construct a library, she tells them to place a salon. My salon she will make into a bath closet. She is going to plant lime trees where I have proposed to place elms, and where I have planted herbs and vegetables (at last, my own kitchen gardens, and I was already taking great pride in them!), nothing will make her happy but a flowerbed."*

But he was a man deeply in love for the first time in his adult life, and a feeling of tenderness inspired unaccustomed patience, and tempered his annoyance. *"I beg to assure you, however,"* he continued, *"that she is a sorceress who is doing magical work in this horribly incompleted house. She is changing rags into Gobelin tapestries and rude logs into chairs that even a man with aching legs, such as Cardinal F., would find comfortable and pleasing to the eye of those who abhor all but the fashions of the moment. In short, she has found the secret of furnishing Cirey out of nothing."*

Émilie threw herself into the task of finishing the reconstruction work and furnishing the château, and her energy was inexhaustible, her dedication unflagging. A shipping venture in which Voltaire had invested brought him a far larger profit than he had anticipated, and a quantity of furs he had purchased in the New World sold in Paris for the highest price that merchants had paid in many years. The author suddenly found himself in possession of the present-day equivalent of twenty-five thousand dollars. Ordinarily he would have reinvested the money in other enterprises, but he made the mistake of telling Émilie what he had just earned, and she had ideas of her own.

Never again would he write to Mme. de la Neuville or anyone else that his clever, frugal mistress was furnishing Cirey out of nothing. Émilie had found a man able and willing enough to indulge her exceptionally expensive tastes, and she went on a wild buying spree, requesting various friends in Paris to make purchases for her from cabinetmakers, art sellers, and linen merchants, among many others. Her lists were endless, and she seemed determined to empty Voltaire's bulging purse.

The more he indulged her insatiable appetite, the more she demanded, but both of them were very happy. Voltaire was tired of living in rented lodgings and other people's homes, while Émilie was enjoying her first opportunity to decorate a house precisely as she wished. They were thinking, quite literally, of settling down together for a long time, and neither was willing to accept less than perfection.

Apparently it did not cross their minds that they were restoring and furnishing someone else's château. Voltaire, always careful in handling funds that were his own, opened his pursestrings and poured money into his mistress's hands. He was not in the least bothered by the knowledge that, once a chair or rug or tapestry was installed at Cirey, it became the legal property of the Marquis du Châtelet.

Émilie recognized her debt to Voltaire, but did not bother with ethical questions. Her lover was wealthy as well as brilliant, generous as well as famous, and the upholsterers and masons were creating a dream house, her dream house, tailor-made for her. For the moment she was so busy she put aside her reading, which was unprecedented, but she did not lose sight of her long-range goals. Daily orders were sent to booksellers in Paris and London, The Hague and Geneva. Voltaire wanted a great many books, too, some for reference purposes, some because of his intellectual curiosity, and a very few because he wanted to read them for pleasure.

They were so thorough, continuing to buy books at a rapid rate, that by the late spring of the following year the main library at Cirey boasted more than ten thousand volumes, making it one of the largest collections of its time in France. Voltaire kept another five thousand in his work quarters, and Émilie, who used two workrooms, eventually accumulated another three to four thousand for each of them. Cirey, located in the most remote wilderness in France, housed more books than most European universities.

Before Émilie permitted herself to read, however, she was determined to put every last finishing touch on the château. Never had she been more indefatigable, never more energetic. She was awake at dawn, and, according to Voltaire's correspondence, she made her initial inspection of the day before the workmen reported for duty. At this juncture food meant little or nothing to her, and she ate her meals hurriedly, scarcely noticing what was on her plate. Then, long after the laborers' twelve-hour day came to end, she was still measuring windows for new drapes, deciding which samples of upholstery she preferred in what rooms, and trying to decide what sort of rugs would look best on the parquet floors being installed everywhere. She was a woman obsessed, but she thrived on very little sleep.

Voltaire was physically unable to maintain the same pace, and his interest in architecture and home decorating waned. The place was becoming increasingly comfortable, Émilie's taste in furnishings won his complete approval, and he was satisfied. Other matters claimed his attention, and he returned to his writing, retiring to the temporary work quarters set up for him in the manor house. The first real friction grew out of his resumption of his profession.

At the end of a long day of labor on a manuscript, the ever-sociable, audience-demanding Voltaire was ready for a relaxed evening, and craved good food and wine, interesting companions, and stimulating conversation. But Émilie was unable to concentrate on anything but color schemes and wallpaper, fabrics and her latest project, the building of a small theater in the château so her lover could test his new plays there. Her own narcissistic demand for an audience was laid aside until Cirey became an accurate reflection of her personality, and she refused to consider the entertainment of guests. In fact, she vetoed Voltaire's request that, at the very least, they return the dinner invitations of the good ladies who had been so kind to him during the months he had spent at the estate alone.

But Émilie would not listen, and, according to his correspondence with friends in Paris, announced without equivocation that she would make no guests welcome until Cirey was ready for company.

Voltaire made the surprised discovery that he was not quite the master in a vast dwelling that was not quite his house. He stormed, became sarcastic, and threatened, but to no avail.

Émilie was so preoccupied that she failed to appreciate his sardonic wit, his anger left her unmoved, and she paid no attention to his threats. She told him, he wrote to Richelieu, that she insisted she was transforming Cirey into a heaven on earth exclusively for his sake, and she claimed that his lack of appreciation crushed her.

Like so many husbands of other periods, the great author was trapped. He had not married Émilie, it was true, but by openly setting up housekeeping together they had forged bonds more difficult to weaken or elude than marriage ties. While Émilie continued to whirl madly, Voltaire had no choice, and returned once again to his writing table. He was surprised to discover that his hostility was short-lived. True love, which he had mocked in prose and poetry, was proving stronger than his hostility, and he was content to wait a trifle longer for a life in paradise.

VII

Voltaire's *Mémoirs,* written and frequently revised in his later years, long after the death of Émilie du Châtelet, offer a calm, remarkably objective description of the "ideal life," as both called it, that they lived together for a decade and a half. He told only a portion of the story, to be sure, but that was his privilege, and what he did reveal was accurate, even though he omitted any mention of turbulence, eccentricities, or dissension. He said:

"I was tired of the lazy, quarrelsome life led at Paris, and of the multitude of 'little geniuses,' of bad books printed with the approbation of censors and the privilege of the King, of the parties and cabals among the learned; and of the mean arts, plagiarism and book-making which dishonor literature.

"In the year 1733 I met a young lady who happened to think nearly as I did, and who took a resolution to go with me and spend several years in the country, there to cultivate her understanding far from the bustle and tumult of the world . . . and those amusements which were adapted to her sex and age; she, however, determined to quit them all, and go, and bury herself in an old, ruinous château upon the borders of Champagne and Lorraine, and situated in a barren and unhealthy soil. This old château she ornamented and embellished with tolerably pretty gardens; I built a gallery and formed a very good collection of natural history; in addition to which we had a library not badly furnished.

"We were visited by many of the learned, who came to philosophize in our retreat: among others we had the celebrated Koenig for two entire years, who has since died professor at The Hague, and librarian to the Princess of Orange. Maupertuis came also, with Jean Bernoulli, and there it was that Maupertuis, who was born the most jealous of all human beings, made me the object of a friendship-of-the-mind which has ever been to him exceedingly dear.

"I taught English to Mme. du Châtelet, who, in about three months, understood it as well as I did, and read Newton, Locke and Pope with equal ease. She learned Italian, too, as readily and with equal facility. We read all the works of Tasso and Ariosto together, so that when Algarotti came to Cirey, where he finished his Newtonianismo per le Dame, *he found her sufficiently skilled in his own language as well as familiar with the works of Newton to give him some very excellent information from which he profited.*

"In this, our delightful retreat, we sought only instruction, and did not trouble ourselves with matters that concerned the rest of the world. We long employed all our attention and powers upon Leibnitz and Newton. Mme. du Châtelet attached herself first to Leibnitz, and explained a portion of his scientific philosophical system in a marvelous book, exceedingly well written, entitled Institutions de Physique. *It is this same book that continues down to this day to be the best exposition of Leibnitz in our language. Mme. du Châtelet did not seek to decorate philosophy with ornaments to which philosophy is a stranger; such affectation never was part of her character, which was masculine and just. The qualities of her style were clarity, precision and elegance. If it be ever possible to give the semblance of truth to the ideas of Leibnitz, it will be found in that book. I deplore that, at present, few people trouble themselves to know how or what Leibnitz thought.*

"Born with a love of truth, Mme. du Châtelet soon abandoned the rigid philosophy of system, and applied herself to

the discoveries of the great Newton. It was she who translated his whole book on the principles of mathematics into French, a feat so sweeping that there are not two persons alive today capable of duplicating it, nor are there likely to be others.

"Afterwards, when she had enlarged her knowledge, she added to this book (which so few people have the education and wit to comprehend) an Algebraical Commentary, *which likewise is not to be understood by the general reader. Alexis Claude Clairault, who may be the greatest geometrician of our century, has carefully reviewed this* Commentary, *and has found it not only sound in every respect, but so advanced is the thinking of the author that she opens new philosophical and experimental paths to the student of mathematics.*

"At Cirey we cultivated all the arts. It was there I composed Alzire, Mérope, l'Enfant Prodigue, *and* Mahomet. *For the edification and instruction of Mme. du Châtelet I wrote my* Essay on Universal History, *from the age of Charlemagne to the present. It is this work, slightly enlarged, that later was printed upon my orders and offered to the general reader; although it was not composed for this purpose, I would have grieved had a word of this magnitude not been made into an edition."*

With reticence that is unique in Voltaire, he fails to mention in his *Mémoirs* that he and Émilie also collaborated on a major project, a long and intricately detailed treatise on the works of Sir Isaac Newton, which covered the whole spectrum of Newton's philosophical, scientific, and mathematical studies. It was called, simply, *Newton.*

When word of the project first leaked out, in 1736, the newspapers of Paris, promptly supported by every self-styled wit in the city, ridiculed the idea. It seemed absurd that the great Voltaire would collaborate with anyone, much less a woman, much less his own mistress, on a subject as difficult for the layman to understand as the thinking of Sir Isaac Newton. That the beautiful, eccentric, and extravagant Marquise du Châtelet happened to be the lady in the case made the jest all the more amusing. She put on airs, to be sure, and pretended she was the equal of such ornaments to France as Voltaire, Maupertuis, and Clairault, but Paris refused to believe that any one woman who bared as much of her bosom as Émilie did, who gambled as recklessly or made it her business to be seen at every important ball, fête, or party when she was in the city, could be a real intellectual.

Voltaire, immersed in the writing of his great history of the reign of Louis XIV, did not reply to the jibes. This, too, was not like him, but Émilie was responsible for his discretion, begging him to say nothing and let *Newton* speak for itself. Her judgment was vindicated, and she enjoyed the long, last laugh. The study was hailed as a masterpiece by every scientist of consequence in France and abroad, and the style of Voltaire being eminently distinctive, it was easy to identify Émilie's contributions to the project. Philosophers, academicians, and members of the scientific community throughout Western Europe, and particularly in England, recognized the Marquise du Châtelet as an independent thinker, a woman of powerful intellect, and treated her with the respect that was her due.

The next year Émilie followed the achievement with another, which was equally impressive. Her translation of the *Aeneid* of Virgil was published in Paris, the result of many years' intermittent but hard labor. It, too, was hailed in the circles that rcognized its worth, and the translator was called the feminine genius of the age. The translation had a long life, and was used almost universally in French schools down to the present century. This accomplishment alone would have established Émilie du Châtelet as a woman of stature.

Her aristocratic contemporaries refused to give her credit of any kind, even though few of them were familiar with the classics, and still fewer were capable of reading the *Aeneid* in the original Latin, much less judging the translation. It was enough, for their purposes, that the flighty, notorious, jewel-loving Mme. du Châtelet had been responsible for the effort.

She was just showing off again, they said, and, aside from ridiculing her, they dismissed her *Aeneid* as a silly trifle.

Strangely, Émilie was indifferent to high society's opinion of her work. Personally sensitive to every facial expression and conversational nuance, she knew her own worth as a scientist and mathematician, classicist and translator, and was deeply gratified by the respect she won from those who understood what she was doing. One of her problems was her need to compete on every level, to be accepted by the intellectuals as one of their breed, and by the aristocrats as a member of their company.

But she had the good sense not to confuse the two worlds. She no more expected a philosopher or a physicist to admire a new gown than she looked for the applause of the salon habitués when she published a new book. There was a time to drink champagne and a time to eat bread, and she did not make the error of trying to do both simultaneously.

What did bother her was the predictable reaction of every literate man and woman in France to the ménage that had been established at Cirey. The eighteenth century was morally permissive; the cardinals and bishops of the period may have been hypocritical, and certainly they were practiced in closing their eyes to the romantic attachments of their more prominent parishioners, but they could not ignore the challenge posed by Émilie and Voltaire. Not until the couple brazenly persisted in their mode of living over a period of years did high-ranking members of the clergy finally consent to visit Cirey.

In 1734 Émilie made several trips to Paris, each of a few weeks' duration, and she was not too surprised to find that a number of prominent ladies made a point of snubbing her in public. With one or two exceptions these women were themselves engaging in adulterous relations with gentlemen of standing, but they were conducting their affairs with discretion. The code, that of pretending to live according to one standard while actually abiding by another, may have been absurd and outrageous, but those who ignored it did so at their peril.

Voltaire, to be sure, delighted in flouting convention, and Émilie was willing to be a leader in breaking down taboos. What caused her deep concern was the possibility that social pressure would force the Marquis du Châtelet to react unfavorably. Florent-Claude was an unthinking traditionalist, and she was afraid he might become upset when he realized that everyone was not only talking about him but laughing at him.

A cause for even greater apprehension was the possibility that he might feel his honor was at stake. The code of honor was still considered sacred. Every gentleman observed it, and a soldier whose imagination was limited might be particularly sensitive.

Florent-Claude had already indicated by his conduct at the Richelieu wedding that he did not object to his wife's affair with Voltaire, so there was virtually no chance he would challenge the author to a duel, which only the professional swordsman could win. Therefore Voltaire was safe. But Émilie herself was in great physical jeopardy. A husband who had been publicly humiliated and disgraced by his wife had the right to order her put away, a move that would win him the complete and unquestioning support of upper-class society in general and the justices of the law courts in particular. A wife subjected to such treatment by her husband was sent to a convent, usually one located in a remote rural district far from Paris. There she would languish until such time as her husband elected to set her free again, and if he did not relent, she would be forced to remain there until he died. There was no appeal from his ruling, and no escape. Émilie had no desire whatever to spend the rest of her busy, enjoyable life behind the walls of a convent.

She had known she was taking the risk when she had conceived of the idea of living at Cirey with Voltaire, of course, and she still thought the risk worth taking. Obviously she believed she could handle the Marquis, but Voltaire was far less amenable to manipulation. Not only was he a social lion in demand everywhere, but he quickly became bored with people and his surroundings. So Émilie was convinced their romance might best be prolonged if she could isolate him at Cirey and keep him there for the better part of the time, cut off from the hectic life at Paris where he would be more susceptible to the charms of other attractive women.

She explained herself in blunt terms in a letter she sent to the Duc de Richelieu late in 1734, saying:

"I wish to confide in you a matter of discretion. On this matter there are things which I have never said, either to you or to anyone, least of all Voltaire. I feel there is heroism, and perhaps folly, in my shutting myself up with him in circumstances of frank intimacy. Nevertheless the decision has been made. I still believe that I shall be able to master and destroy any ugliness my husband may feel more easily than to curb the imagination of Voltaire. In Paris I should lose him beyond return and without a remedy. At Cirey I can at least hope that love will render still more opaque the veil which ought, for his own happiness and ours, to shield my husband from the malice of those who have nothing better to do than to create suspicion in the hearts of those who are themselves too kind and pure to harbor mean thoughts of their own volition.

"I pray of you to have the kindness to say nothing of all this to Voltaire. He would be overcome by anxiety, and I fear nothing more than to afflict him, especially if it be uselessly. Keep your eloquence for my husband, and prepare to love me when I am unhappy, should I ever become so. To prevent my being entirely miserable, I am returning to Cirey for three uninterrupted months, the happiest of my life. I leave in four days, and I am daring to write to you in the midst of the confusion of departure. My mind is weighed down with the thought of it, but my heart is full of joy.

"The hope that this step will persuade Voltaire that I love him above all else hides all other ideas from me, and I see

nothing but the extreme happiness of curing all his fears and spending my whole life with him. You see you were wrong, for assuredly my head has been turned; but I confess that, in spite of this, his anxiety and distrust sensibly affect me. I know that this jealousy, which he cannot curb himself, is the torment of his life. It may well be that on this very account it will poison mine.

"But perhaps you and I may both be right. There is a great deal of difference between jealousy and the fear of not being loved enough. One can brave the one if one feels that one does not merit it, but one cannot refrain from being touched and afflicted by the other. One is a troublesome feeling, and the other a gentle sense of uneasiness against which there are fewer weapons and fewer remedies, except that of living together at Cirey, where we are happy. There, in truth, is the metaphysics of love, and that is where the excess of this passion brings one. All this appears to me to be the clearest thing in the world, and the most natural."

Toward the end of the year Émilie was still concerned about Voltaire's feelings, and referred to the subject in another letter to Richelieu:

"The more I reflect on Voltaire's situation and on mine, the more I think the steps I have taken to preserve that situation are necessary. Firstly, I believe that all those who love passionately should live in the country together if that is possible for them, but I think still more that I cannot keep my hold on his imagination elsewhere. I should lose him sooner or later in Paris, or at least I should pass my days fearing to lose him and in having cause to lament over him.

"I love him enough, I confess it to you, to sacrifice all the pleasure and delight I might enjoy in Paris for the sake of the happiness of living with him without fears, and of the pleasure of wresting him, in spite of himself, from the effects of his own imprudence and fate. The only thing which causes me anxiety, and which I shall have to manage carefully about, is the pres-

ence of M. du Châtelet. I count greatly on your conversations with him. A permanent peace would destroy all our hopes, although I cannot keep myself from longing for it on your account.

"My position is indeed embarrassing, although I take pains to conceal that embarrassment from all, particularly from Voltaire, whose discomfort in all matters is always greater than mine. But love changes all the thorns into flowers, as it always does among our mountains of Cirey, our terrestrial paradise. I cannot believe that I am born to be unhappy; I see only the delight of spending all the moments of my life in the company of the one I love."

Émilie's tension eased somewhat when Maupertuis and Clairault arrived for a short visit. They were the first important guests to come to the idyllic hideaway, and both she and Voltaire were delighted. All four chatted and argued day and night, and everyone got along on far too little sleep. Émilie was setting the pace, and, needing little sleep, she apparently did not think that others sometimes preferred rest to conversation.

Meanwhile the Duc de Richelieu obeyed her bidding and had a number of heart-to-heart talks with the Marquis du Châtelet. The Duke's letters to Émilie were as vague as they were brief, but he emphasized the theme of his talks very strongly: he was trying to convince Florent-Claude that a wise man would ignore the whispers and titters of gossips and would follow his own practical inclinations.

The Marquis was expected to arrive at Cirey in time for Christmas, and by then the two scientists had departed. Husband, wife, and Voltaire would be alone, unless Florent-Claude brought a mistress with him. Émilie, increasingly apprehensive, brought her daughter home from a nearby convent school where she was a boarder, in time for the paternal visit.

One member of the household caused Émilie particular concern. Michel Linant, her son's tutor, was a former abbé who had left the Church and subsisted on the kindness of Voltaire, who had befriended him for years. The author saw, or professed to see, literary talents in the man, who had sponged on him for years while allegedly writing a tragedy based on the Pharoah Rameses II. Better educated than most, Linant should have been a first-rate tutor, but he had other interests that kept him preoccupied. In all fairness to him, he probably was no worse than most members of his calling.

Food was the great passion of his life, and, no matter how much he ate, he was still hungry. Émilie, who had known him only slightly before Voltaire brought him to Cirey, was astonished when she saw the quantity of food he consumed at a meal. Inclined toward overweight from childhood, Linant grew enormous while at the château. His second interest was gossip, and he found himself living under the roof of the couple whose names were on every fashionable tongue in France, a situation he relished.

Unfortunately, the former abbé was a malicious troublemaker, and could not refrain from stirring up his brew. He was curious, and when he failed to learn enough about Émilie and Voltaire to satisfy his appetite for tidbits, he read their mail. Unfortunately for him, Émilie was a reader of other people's mail, too, particularly Voltaire's. She made it her business to take the mail sack when it arrived, and to read communications to her lover before passing them along to him. On several occasions she found that Linant had reached the mailbag first, and became furiously angry.

Occasionally there were references in her own incoming mail that she didn't understand, sly or subtle remarks about incidents that had not taken place, expressions of concern over rifts in her relations with Voltaire that hadn't occurred. When a number had accumulated she bluntly asked her friends the source of their misinformation, and in every instance Linant proved to be the culprit.

Émilie's first real disputes with Voltaire took place when

she demanded that the tutor be discharged. In each instance Voltaire defended the man with such vigor that she backed down, even though Cirey was her house and the education of her son was at stake. Knowing her lover as she did, she realized he was slowly changing his opinions of Linant, and she was content to play a waiting game rather than risk a major quarrel with him.

The approaching visit from the Marquis posed a new, grave problem, however. With her own security at stake, she wanted no complications created by a talkative gossip-monger who loved to stir up tempests. She had succeeded in isolating Linant, to an extent; his gourmand appetite was so disgusting to her that he now ate his meals with the children. But there was no telling what he might say or do when the proprietor of Cirey arrived on the scene. In spite of her desire to keep Voltaire isolated and cause him no unnecessary anxiety, she knew the situation forced her to speak candidly.

She confessed her fears to him, and Voltaire promptly took charge. He held a long, private talk with Linant and then told Émilie to relax. Without saying what he had done to extract a promise of circumspect behavior from the tutor, he said that he felt certain Linant would cause no trouble.

A few days before Christmas the Marquis arrived, and his wife was dismayed when she learned he was alone. Mlle. d'Anjou, who had not seen her own relatives for a long time, had gone off to visit them, he said. Whether the girl really had relatives was beside the point. Knowing what high society would and would not condone, Châtelet was not forcing his wife and mistress to sleep under the same roof.

Ordinarily Émilie would have appreciated his tact, but this was no ordinary situation. With nothing else to distract him, the Marquis was now in a position to concentrate most of his attention on his wife and her lover.

Voltaire, who loved his comfort, made the supreme sacrifice, offering to go off to Holland until Châtelet departed. It would be easy enough for him to say he had been called away on literary business, and no one would ever know he had invented the excuse.

But Émilie refused to allow him to make the journey. An unusually heavy snowstorm had made travel difficult, and what was more important, she had no intention of being separated from her lover over Christmas. She showed common sense, too, in a letter to Richelieu, explaining to the Duke that tongues would wag even harder if she gave her consent. Voltaire would be accused of cowardice, and it would be difficult for him to deny the charge, as he couldn't explain he was motivated by a desire to protect his mistress from embarrassment.

It would be far better, Émilie declared, to live a normal life, changing no day-to-day routines. If they did no boat-tipping, Florent-Claude well might accept the situation.

In his first days at Cirey the Marquis spent an hour each morning becoming acquainted with his daughter, and another trying to hold man-to-man conversations with his son. Then, his duty as a parent done for twenty-four hours, he had nothing to keep him busy. So, while the weather remained inclement, he spent long hours making a detailed inspection of the château.

Even though he had been aware of the rehabilitation, its scope impressed and delighted him. Cirey was completely restored, and was as sumptuously furnished as the palace of a royal prince. No man could have asked his wife and her wealthy lover to do more, and Florent-Claude was grateful.

Meanwhile, at Émilie's instigation, the household routines remained unchanged. Voltaire slept fairly late, but she was awake at dawn, and went to her private sitting room for a light breakfast of grilled fish, a small veal stew, and a roll or two soaked in honey, washed down with a small bottle of wine. Then she retired to her library to attend her correspondence, look after her accounts, and receive the reports of the housekeeper and chef. Usually she crowded in a brief visit with the children, and then went off to her workroom on an upper floor, where she worked on her writing projects and scientific experiments until dinnertime.

There was no regular dinner hour at Cirey. The principal meal of the day was served whenever Émilie and Voltaire remembered they were hungry, and if one was not yet ready to eat, the other was accommodating and waited. Thereafter they returned to their separate work quarters, where they stayed until hunger brought them together again for a supper that, depending on their mood and appetite, ranged from light to sumptuous.

Florent-Claude gallantly tried to acclimate himself to their erratic way of life. He wasn't certain whether it was worse to be forced to wait for a meal until he was ravenous, or to subject himself to the company of his wife and her lover. They discussed Leibnitz, Descartes, and Newton at length, argued interminably over mathematical equations and natural science formulas, and read aloud from their current writing projects. As Voltaire wrote to friends in Paris, the poor man didn't understand a word they were saying.

Both exerted themselves to be pleasant to the nominal master of Cirey, to be sure. Émilie, who had less in common with him each time she saw him, tried to regale him with the latest Paris gossip. Florent-Claude replied politely, but the affairs and feuds of the aristocracy bored him, and he lacked the grace to dissemble.

Voltaire did far better in attracting and holding his attention. It is possible that the author had an understanding of theoretical military strategy and tactics superior to that of the General, and certainly he could converse cogently on the subject. He coaxed Florent-Claude into discussions of the current campaign in Germany, and his own interest as a historian was aroused. Both men enjoyed these conversations.

But Émilie vehemently disliked being ignored, and when the two men became so engrossed they forgot her presence, she was quick to let them know she was not pleased. Voltaire always became apologetic, and the Marquis, who hated to be rebuked, sulked in silence.

A day or two after Christmas Florent-Claude solved the problem in his own forthright way. He was a man who had always lived a carefully regulated life, and he could see no reason to change now, under what was supposedly his own roof. The children ate their main meal of the day promptly at two o'clock in the afternoon, the hour when the Marquis liked his dinner. So, saying nothing to Émilie and Voltaire, who were locked away in their workrooms, he joined his son and daughter.

When Émilie discovered what had happened, she was horrified. Michel Linant, the tutor, also ate with the children, and if the gossip-monger discussed at length what Paris thought of the Marquis du Châtelet, there could be trouble. She wanted to insist that Florent-Claude continue to eat his meals with her.

But Voltaire, assuring her Linant would behave, urged her not to make a scene.

She agreed, but her misgivings were so great she wrote the Duc de Richelieu a nine-page letter.

Voltaire was right, as things turned out, but not for the reason he thought. Linant, who subsequently acquired an almost universal reputation for biting the hands that fed him, might have stirred up trouble had he been given the chance. Florent-Claude gave him no chance. The blunt soldier had no use for the simpering gossip who, when he paused in his overeating, made only viciously snide remarks about everyone he knew. Addressing himself exclusively to the children, the Marquis resolutely ignored the man, and his attitude was so consistent that Linant believed he was deaf, commenting to that effect in his correspondence.

So the visit passed pleasantly, without incident, and Émilie was saved the fate of being locked away in a convent. By the time Florent-Claude returned to his division in the field, he had developed an abiding respect and admiration for Voltaire, and their friendship, although never close, continued long after

Émilie's death. Voltaire, who took excellent care of his health, made it his practice to take a long walk late every afternoon. Émilie, who under the best of circumstances disliked aimless walks, was not enamored of hikes through the muddy forest and rarely accompanied him. But Florent-Claude, who missed his own exercise, became his daily companion.

The character of virtually no man was safe from attack when Voltaire dipped his quill pen into a jar of ink, but neither then nor in later years did he write a single sarcastic or uncomplimentary word about the Marquis du Châtelet. His friends marveled at his discretion when he mentioned Florent-Claude's name in his letters, but the truth of the matter is that the cynical author developed a feeling of genuine admiration for his mistress's husband. The Marquis's mind was limited, and his lack of imagination was appalling, but he was the rarest of humans, a truly honest man who hated sham, cant, and hypocrisy. Voltaire could not fail to appreciate someone endowed with these virtues and to appreciate him for them.

Émilie breathed a sigh of relief after her husband's departure, and knew that thereafter the machinations of the gossips could not touch her. By condoning her relationship with Voltaire at Cirey on this visit, Florent-Claude had established a precedent, and no justice in any French court of law would support an attempt to punish her for her boldness.

The household immediately settled back into its routines, or the lack of them, but the quiet soon was shattered. Voltaire discovered that Linant had been gossiping about his writing, and had made a number of offensive remarks about his work in recent correspondence. This was a situation far worse than that which Émilie had just managed to circumvent, so he discharged the tutor immediately and sent him away.

VIII

By the early spring of 1735 Voltaire had spent the better part of eighteen months at Cirey, never traveling farther than the immediate neighborhood. At no time in his adult life had he remained in any one place for more than a small fraction of that time, and his friends, knowing his need for the stimulating company of people from all walks of life with conflicting opinions, wondered if Émilie du Châtelet might be a sorceress or a witch. The educated were inclined to regard witchcraft as a mere superstition, but even in the Age of Reason men sometimes entertained doubts.

So it is small wonder that Émilie was called a witch, a charge she thoroughly enjoyed when friends wrote to her about it. She felt far less equanimity when she assessed the real situation in which she found herself. She could sympathize with Voltaire's growing restlessness, and she realized that for vocational as well as personal reasons he needed a respite from the isolation of his life at Cirey. His *Alzire* was scheduled for April production in Paris, but the playwright had never heard the play read aloud or performed in rehearsal by professional actors. He was dissatisfied with portions of it, but was uncertain how to cure its faults, and would not know what to do unless he saw the company that would present it running through rehearsals.

He had been making strenuous efforts to arrange a visit to Paris, he confessed to Émilie, and he believed he had reason to hope his request would be granted. As a matter of fact, the secret police had grown weary of playing a farce, of pretending not to know where to find him, and when Voltaire's friends besieged Cardinal Fleury with requests to rescind the order that would place him under arrest, the secret police indicated they would be happy to cooperate.

The Cardinal, relieved to extricate himself from an embarrassing situation, signed the necessary order. That same day the commandant of the secret police, who had been a classmate of Voltaire's, wrote him he was free to come and go as he pleased, and, in a postscript, begged him not to offend the authorities again.

Forty-eight hours after Voltaire received the letter, in mid-March, he and Émilie left Cirey for Paris. He was excited, full of plans, and she was suffering from the greatest fear she had ever known. The worst had materialized at last; she was convinced she would lose him.

They could not live together openly at the Hôtel du Châtelet, so they parted when they reached the city, Émilie going to the town house while Voltaire, reverting to his old ways, rented inexpensive quarters in a lodging house. Thereafter they saw relatively little of each other, and made a point of traveling separately to Versailles for the purpose of paying their obligatory respects to the court. Obviously they were sensitive to criticism, and saw no reason to encourage additional gossip when Voltaire was just being readmitted to the good graces of the authorities.

Émilie plunged into her usual heavy social life in the capital, visiting the salons of friends, receiving academicians for long discussions of scientific subjects, and, on occasion, continuing these talks at the Gradot. She made fewer appearances at the café than she had done in the past, perhaps out of deference to the situation in which she and Voltaire found themselves, but she did not halt them completely. That would have been a sign of surrender to public opinion, and Émilie had no intention of admitting defeat to anyone.

She continued to spend money at her usual, reckless pace. Her dressmaker made daily visits to the Hôtel du Châtelet, and so did booksellers, whose wares she sent to Cirey in a convoy of carts. A jeweler was a frequent caller, too, and in addition to such baubles as gold earrings and bracelets, she purchased a magnificent emerald ring and matching pendant. Certainly the Marquis could not afford to buy such gems, so it was assumed by Paris society that they had been a gift from Voltaire. For the first time since they had started living together, however, the couple behaved discreetly, and neither mentioned the source of the emeralds. If Voltaire paid for them, he kept the fact to himself, and Émilie, too, maintained a consistent silence. It might be added that the emeralds were her favorites for the rest of her life, and, no matter how many other jewels might be sparkling on her fingers or at her throat, she usually wore the matched gems, too.

Her friends and enemies noted that she indulged in very little card playing during her sojourn in the city, and on the few occasions she did engage in a game of *vingt-et-un,* she played for modest stakes. No one thought she had reformed, however, and her caution indeed proved transitory. On subsequent visits to the city she returned to her old ways, and her recklessness again became the talk of the town.

Voltaire, after his protracted absence from Paris, was busier than he had ever been. He attended rehearsals of *Alzire,* was dissatisfied with the play, and made extensive revisions in it before it opened later in the spring. He conferred with his printers, saw scores of old friends and acquaintances, and made the rounds of the cafés to catch up on the literary, academic, and social feuds of the city.

He also proved that he had learned nothing from his banishment, and that he was still indifferent to the good will of those who might be in a position to help him. He resumed his own feud with the Academy, somehow finding time to lampoon most of the members, by name, in a satiric verse. The poem was not published, but copies made the rounds of the cafés, and he did not endear himself to the Academy membership, from which he was still excluded. In addition, he made no secret of his continuing contempt for Roman Catholic theology, and it was rumored that he had written a new version of the story of Adam and Eve. He blandly denied the allegation, a denial that subsequently proved to be a lie, for within a few months his observations on the origins of man would outrage the French clerical hierarchy and cause him fresh trouble.

Émilie must have been nervous and afraid she would lose Voltaire, as she had indicated so strongly in her correspondence with the Duc de Richelieu, but she was wise enough not to hold him on too tight a rein during their visit to Paris. Presumably they saw each other on occasion, but they made no public appearances together. In fact, Émilie did not attend any performance of *Alzire,* and her absence caused considerable speculation. High society wondered whether the affair had come to an end, and a number of ladies made themselves available to the author. The correspondence of the inveterate gossips indicates that he was charming and gallant, but personally disinterested.

A group of Émilie- and Voltaire-watchers also wrote to friends who happened to be away from Paris that Voltaire made no appearances at any of the dinner parties Émilie gave in town during the spring season. Whether he went to the Hôtel du Châtelet on the evenings she spent alone there was their own business, and they kept their own counsel on the subject. It is unlikely that Émilie paid any private visits to Voltaire's lodgings during this time. His friends drifted in and out at any time of the day and night, and someone would have been sure to see her. Inasmuch as everyone in town was wondering and keeping the couple under close observation, the fact would have been reported in a dozen letters the next day.

La Pucelle, Voltaire's long poem that ridiculed virtually everyone in high places, proved to be the author's undoing again. He could not stop adding new verses to the satire, and he found it impossible to refrain from reading them aloud to friends. Although he always swore his listeners to secrecy, they could not refrain from repeating lines of his wit to others, and it wasn't long before tidbits of *La Pucelle* were being repeated all over town. Government ministers and bishops smarted under the lash of his pen, and soon the secret police became active again. Voltaire's apartment was visited and searched, but no copy of the poem was found there. Even though he could not keep silent about his work, he had the good sense to hide his manuscript.

It was rumored that the original of the poem was in Émilie's possession, but this was unlikely. She was a natural object of suspicion, and if the secret police had chosen to call at the Hôtel du Châtelet and had found the manuscript there, her reputation would have been damaged so badly that her husband would have been compelled to send her off to a convent, no matter what his own inclinations in the matter might have been.

The authorities had no concrete evidence that would have enabled them to place Voltaire under arrest, but they proceeded on the theory that a fire was burning somewhere beneath the clouds of smoke. Someone, an official whose name has not been recorded for posterity, paid the author a private visit and warned him that trouble was brewing for him. The warning must have been severe, for Voltaire vanished from the city overnight, to the astonishment and dismay of his friends, who had no notice that he intended to leave.

Émilie was besieged by eager and anxious questioners, but she took refuge in pretended innocence, and denied any knowledge of her lover's whereabouts. It was learned at a much later date that she was literally the only person in Paris who knew where he had gone. But she was proving adept at keeping her mouth shut, and no one learned anything from her.

The usual rash of rumors proliferated, and within a few days stories reached Paris, each of them supposedly authentic, to the effect that Voltaire had been seen in such far-flung places as Brussels, The Hague, Berlin, and Geneva. Almost a fortnight passed before the truth was ascertained and verified: he had gone to visit the court of Lorraine, arriving there without advance notice, so hasty had been his departure from Paris.

When the flurry of gossip had subsided somewhat, Émilie paid a quiet, private visit to Cardinal Fleury at Versailles. Neither was willing to discuss the subject, but no genius was required for members of the court to know that Voltaire's name must have come up. Émilie and the Cardinal refused to confirm or deny the obvious.

What happened at the meeting was revealed, much later, in Voltaire's own correspondence. Émilie sought the assurances of the Cardinal that her lover would not be followed and persecuted if he returned to Cirey. Cardinal Fleury, himself the object of ridicule in a section of *La Pucelle* devoted exclusively to him, could not prove that he was being mocked, and, in any event, he could take no legal action against the author until the poem was published. He was still reluctant to place Voltaire under arrest. It was enough, for his purposes, if the volatile author was removed from the mainstream of French life. So he was relieved to inform Émilie that no action would be taken against "any person who might happen to be visiting Cirey in the near future." Voltaire was safe and could return with impunity to the retreat near the Lorraine border.

Émilie saw the Cardinal one day in early July, 1735, and within forty-eight hours she had closed her Paris house again and was traveling with her entourage to Cirey. Obviously she wrote to Voltaire as soon as she received the good news because he reached Cirey within twenty-four hours of her arrival. The bucolic privacy of the place had a greater appeal than ever to them, and they settled down once again in domestic bliss.

According to no criterion had the Paris visit been a failure, and Émilie was delighted with all that had happened. As she wrote to Richelieu, she had taken a risk and had allowed Voltaire to be exposed to the temptations and joys of Paris. He had been faithful to her, showing no interest in any other woman, and love had triumphed. The bonds that held them together had grown tighter.

The renovation and repair work on the château was virtually finished, and Voltaire felt a need for a separate wing that guests would use, a section removed from the mainstream of "family" activity. He felt inspired to play the role of architect, and Émilie, who considered herself a supervising architect, made extensive revisions in the plans and added ten or fifteen rooms. Never one to think in niggardly terms, she wanted a home that would rival the great palaces of France in grandeur, and, thanks to Voltaire's generosity, she got it.

It is little short of miraculous that the workmen accomplished their goals. When Voltaire wanted a respite from his writing, he wandered over to the construction area and gave the men the benefit of his latest thinking regarding the location of an arch, a window, or a door. If the men were annoyed by his interference, they were still relatively pleased to see him, principally because Émilie drove them wild. She paid several visits each day to the construction project, and at no time did it cross her mind that her genius did not extend to architecture. She changed her ideas several times each week, issued new streams of instructions and drew new blueprints, confusing the workmen so thoroughly they scarcely knew what they were doing.

Eighteenth-century laborers would not have gone on strike in protest, of course, but the situation became so muddled that the men appealed to Voltaire for help. None of the details of his intervention are known, so he may have told Émilie to stop interfering, he may have attracted her interest and enthusiasm into other channels, or he may have used reason to ensure a greater consistency on her part. Whatever his technique, it was effective, and by mid-autumn there was visible progress on the construction of the new wing.

Émilie was now able to concentrate on her work, and threw herself into her scientific studies with an enthusiasm that even Voltaire could not match. She had acquired a number of books in English and Dutch on the theories of Newton, and, after reading them, she devised a number of tests to try them out on what she thought was a practical basis. Needing space that was unavailable in most of the château's cramped rooms, she utilized the great hall for the purpose.

In time the chamber resembled a mammoth physics laboratory. Metal pipes and rods were everywhere, attached to each other in geometric shapes. There were wooden balls hanging from the rafters, some of them swinging in the breeze and making life hazardous for anyone walking beneath them. The ancient Roman iron mines of the neighborhood provided her with almost unlimited raw material for her paraphernalia, and she devised so many experiments to prove the accuracy of Newton's concepts of the inter-reacting physical forces of the universe that the cluttered great hall soon became a virtually impenetrable maze.

Voltaire was fascinated and sometimes invented a test of his own, but he took little active part in conducting the experiments. Émilie invited him to observe what she was doing, and he undoubtedly saw all of her experiments, but he wisely made no attempt to interfere in the work she considered her own. His contribution was the preparation of several essays that explained her tests, their purpose, and the way they functioned, and his descriptions were crisp and lucid. Physicists of later periods, down to the present day, have agreed that Émilie's experiments were soundly conceived and executed. No matter how foolish or extravagant her behavior in some realms, her scientific thinking was sound.

It is surprising that Voltaire could afford to devote any time to Émilie's work, and only a man of his prodigious talents was able to manage it. He was concentrating on his *Siècle de Louis XIV*, in which he successfully portrayed the whole spectrum of the civilization of an age. As a relief from this labor he also wrote a play, *La Mort de César*, which he called a part-translation, part-adaptation of Shakespeare's *Julius Caesar*. His creative talent made the work his own, to be sure.

Experience having taught him that a play was worthless until it had been tested by actors performing for an audience, he made arrangements with a nearby boys' school, the Collège d'Harcourt, for a production. Not trusting the interpretive powers of the clergymen on the school's faculty, he directed the players himself.

Émilie, who was fascinated by the theater, wanted to watch the rehearsals, and insisted they be held in the newly completed playhouse in the château. Voltaire agreed, and she had the pleasure of watching him direct the amateurs every afternoon. The play was so successful that an unauthorized, somewhat inaccurate version was published in Amsterdam without the author's permission, so the angry Voltaire published his own edition in Paris.

There were no women's parts in the play, so Voltaire had not thought in terms of a professional production, but Émilie told him that Paris would succumb to *La Mort de César*, and he agreed to a showing in the city. The play was produced there, its author remaining at Cirey, and, like all Voltaire's plays, was a huge success. The newspapers were critical, but audiences paid no attention to the derogatory comments. The public wanted to see any play that Voltaire wrote and didn't care what the experts thought.

By accident Émilie saw the opening night of *César* in Paris. She hurried back to the city when she received word that her mother was critically ill, but the report was exaggerated, and she arrived to find Mme. de Breteuil in the best of health. So, unable to resist the opportunity, she spent an evening at the theater before rushing back to Cirey. In all, she was gone only a week.

By 1736 word of the unusual living arrangement at the château had spread throughout Europe, and the attention of the Continent, as well as that of Great Britain, was focused on the unorthodox establishment. Thousands of people who had never read a word of Émilie's scientific treatises or her translations of Latin classics knew of her. This notoriety in no way diminished the regard in which she was held by the distinguished intellectuals of the age. Maupertuis publicly declared that she was endowed with "sublime knowledge," and called her learning "marvelous." He also praised her for her beauty, wit, and, undeservedly, for her alleged refusal to say an unkind or nasty word about anyone.

It was inevitable, perhaps, that wild stories about life at Cirey began to circulate everywhere in Europe. According to the most persistent of them, Voltaire made a business trip to Brussels, and during his short sojourn there he had an affair with an attractive young noblewoman of Spanish descent. When he returned to Cirey he found an angry Marquis du Châtelet waiting for him, and Émilie's husband upbraided him for his infidelity to her.

The story was widely believed, and was generally accepted down to the present century. No verification can be found for it, however, and there is no reference to it in the correspondence of any of the principals. Even though it appears to have been invented out of whole cloth, the basic point it emphasizes contains a grain of truth. The Marquis, having accepted his wife's mode of living, could not repudiate her affair without making himself appear doubly ridiculous.

Regardless of whether the story and others like it are true or false, French and foreign society was hungry for details of the affair between the great author and his lovely scientist-classicist paramour. This appetite was satisfied, early in 1736, by one M. de Villefort, who served as a gentleman-in-waiting to the Comte de Clermont. Villefort, himself something of a physicist and poet, received an invitation to spend a few days at Cirey, and his subsequent description was copied in literally scores of letters written by others.

When the young man arrived in mid-afternoon, laborers were hard at work on the new wing, but the main section of the château appeared to be deserted. The shutters were closed, drapes were drawn, and when he knocked at the door, no one answered his summons. He would have departed had the work-men not assured him that the household was in residence. So he continued to pound at the door, and at last a servant admitted him.

It was broad daylight outdoors, but the interior of the château was so dark that the servant was forced to carry a candle. Villefort was led through the great hall, which was filled with so many strange contraptions of metal and wood that it resembled a medieval torture chamber, and the visitor had to proceed cautiously so he wouldn't trip over devices that jutted into the narrow aisle that traversed the hall.

Most of the rooms through which Villefort walked appeared unused. There was furniture in them, but these pieces were covered with linen dust-cloths on which thick layers of dirt had gathered. Another servant appeared with a lantern and led him up a narrow, winding flight of stairs to the top floor, where he was admitted to Émilie du Châtelet's work suite.

His hostess was seated at a large work table in a tightly shuttered room, the illumination provided by a score of the expensive smokeless tapers that no one but the wealthiest of French aristocrats could afford. The table was strewn with books, scientific calculations, and papers on which mathematical formulas were scribbled. Émilie, at first glance, looked as though she were dressed for a court ball. Diamonds gleamed in the candlelight on her fingers and wrists, and others, at her throat, emphasized the low cut of her extravagantly brocaded gown. In fact, her dress was cut so low that only the nipples were covered. Her fingers were ink-stained, and her hair, which she had neglected to brush, streamed down her back in a tangled mass.

Émilie greeted the guest graciously, poured him a glass of rare wine from a carafe in the workroom, and pressed him with questions about the latest news in Paris society, frequently interrupting to tell him about some of her latest experiments. He thought of himself as a student of science, but she was doing such advanced work that he found himself incapable of understanding her explanations.

Eventually she suggested they visit Voltaire, and herself led him through a winding, secret passage to another part of the château, where she tapped at a door. Voltaire called out, asking her to leave, but she persisted, and eventually he opened the door. He was working in his shirtsleeves, although the room was bitterly cold, and his wig was hanging on a wall peg. He was furious because Émilie had interrupted him at his work, and in no time they were engaging in a violent argument, both shouting, both using the colorful epithets of the Paris gutters.

But the argument ended as abruptly as it began, Villefort was invited to sit, and for a half-hour Voltaire, exerting his charm, discussed poetry. Émilie contributed her share to the conversation, and Voltaire listened to her opinions with respect. Then a clock chimed, Voltaire returned to his writing, and Émilie took the visitor down a staircase to a reception hall, where she turned him over to one of the servants he had seen since his arrival. Émilie immediately vanished down a dark corridor, and the visitor, by now carrying his own lantern, was conducted to his bedchamber.

Everything imaginable had been done to ensure his comfort, even though the drapes and shutters were closed here, too, making it impossible for him to determine whether it was day or night outdoors. A fragrant fire was burning in the hearth, a servant appeared with hot water for his bath, and took away his soiled linen for laundering. Still another servant, the fifth, brought him a huge cup of hot, spiced wine, which he found delicious, and he was left with a stack of books on a variety of subjects.

Two or three hours later a gong sounded, and one of the servants reappeared, conducting Villefort through the paraphernalia-cluttered great hall to a dining room located on an upper floor. Here he found Émilie and Voltaire awaiting him, both immaculately dressed in elegant attire, she with her hair piled high on her head, diamond pins holding it in place.

It was considered a serious breach of etiquette for members of the French aristocracy to wait on themselves at table, but there were no servants in sight. A trap door opened, and the first course appeared on a serving table, the trio carrying their food to the places already set for them. Thereafter each course appeared through the trap door, the dirty dishes vanishing through another trap door on the opposite side of the room. Émilie and Voltaire explained to the guest that they had invented the system themselves in order to ensure their privacy and the opportunity to talk without interruption.

The food and wine were superb. Every dish had been prepared by the master chef, and Villefort, who apparently considered himself something of a gourmet, said he had never tasted better. Émilie, who was ravenous, consumed large quantities of everything in sight, but Voltaire ate sparingly, taking care to avoid the rich sauces, which, he said, disagreed with him. The meal lasted for hours, but time did not drag. Villefort reported that Émilie and Voltaire conversed brilliantly on many subjects, and that both were animated, remarkably well informed, and witty.

At last the meal came to an end, and they adjourned to a sumptuously furnished sitting room. When they had made themselves comfortable, a gong sounded, and Émilie announced the time had come for moral and philosophical readings. She politely asked the guest's permission, which he granted, and the readings took place, Émilie and Voltaire alternating. The readings, Villefort discovered, complemented each other; Émilie and Voltaire seemed to be playing an intellectual game, in which one would try to match the last reading of the other.

One hour after the readings started, another gong sounded, and the session came to an end. It was time for bed, Voltaire said, so Villefort went off to his own chamber.

At four o'clock in the morning the guest was awakened by the sounding of yet another gong, and a servant appeared at his door to tell him that Mme. du Châtelet hadn't felt sleepy, and wondered if M. de Villefort would like to attend a poetry reading. His curiosity made it impossible for him to refuse.

Émilie, wearing a fur-embroidered dressing gown, was waiting in the handsomely furnished sitting room of her private suite. Voltaire, who apparently slept elsewhere, appeared in a shabby robe, his eyes puffy. In spite of his sleepiness, however, he read a number of poems with animation, and Émilie applauded him. The readings ended abruptly after an hour had passed, Voltaire stamped off to his own suite and Villefort returned to his chamber.

The days began early at Cirey. Promptly at 8 A.M. a servant appeared at M. de Villefort's door with a tray containing a large, succulent breakfast, which included broiled meats and fish, an omelet, and a variety of cheeses. The guest was astonished when his drapes and shutters were opened to admit bright morning sunlight. He was informed the weather was so pleasant that Émilie and Voltaire had decided to take a partial holiday, hence the admission of daylight was permitted. Ordinarily, Villefort gleaned, even a glimpse of the outdoors was prohibited because the conscientious Émilie and compulsively driven Voltaire wanted to allow nothing to distract them from their work.

As the guest was finishing his breakfast the major domo came to his door to inquire whether he would like to join Madame and Monsieur on a picnic outing. Since there was snow on the ground this was not the season for picnics, but the curious Villefort agreed. An hour or so later he went to the main courtyard, where he found a caravan of carriages lined up. Émilie and Voltaire rode in the first, with the guest on horseback beside them. The second carriage was filled with books, and in the third rode several servants who were bringing the food and various items of equipment.

The party rode slowly down a rutted, narrow dirt road deep into the forest. When the road ended they proceeded on foot up a narrow trail that led to a sheltered clearing beside a half-frozen brook. The servants spread layers of blankets on the ground, there were satin cushions for comfort and fur lap robes for warmth, and huge hampers of food were placed close at hand. The servants withdrew, and the trio ate cold chicken cutlets, fish cutlets, and veal cutlets, Émilie believing that a cutlet of any sort was appropriate picnic fare. There were cold vegetables that had been soaked in wine, delicious bread, and at least a dozen different kinds of cheese, each of them perfect.

The conversation was stimulating almost beyond Villefort's belief. Émilie and Voltaire had talked incessantly whenever he had seen them, but they appeared to be inexhaustible. They debated such topics as British drama, Dutch financial policy, and the Swedish "military temperament" that had produced such geniuses as Gustavus II Adolphus and Charles XII. According to the ground rules of the discussion, the guest gleaned, every assertion had to be verified before it was accepted. So good use was made of the books the couple had brought with them, and a servant shuttled back and forth between the carriage and the picnic site, fetching books that would prove or disprove a point.

In spite of the endless flow of warm talk, however, the day was cold, and Villefort, sitting on the blanket-covered ground, huddled beneath his fur robe. When the effect of the wine he had consumed wore off, he became even chillier, and later wrote that his hands and feet felt colder than the chunks of ice he saw floating in the brook.

But Émilie and Voltaire were impervious to the weather. Seemingly unaware of their surroundings, they argued amiably, incessantly, and with unflagging spirit. When the guest could tolerate the cold no longer he interrupted their debate to beg a favor: if they did not object too strenuously, he would retire to their carriage and wait there for them until they were ready to return to the château.

Both immediately became solicitous and told him there was no reason to suffer any inconvenience. They were intending to go back to the manor house themselves in a few more minutes. So Villefort, trying to be accommodating, decided to wait for them, which proved to be a mistake. They lost themselves in talk again, and another hour passed before they were finally ready to call an end to the picnic.

Villefort spent the better part of the afternoon sitting before a roaring fire in his bedchamber, drinking a mulled wine laced with rum imported from the West Indian Islands. The drink made him sleepy, and, already tired because of his lack of rest the preceding night, he crawled into bed for a long nap. It was night when he finally sat up, and he was afraid he had missed dinner, but a hastily summoned servant assured him the meal would not be served for some time. He would be notified by the ringing of the now-familiar gong. The wait proved almost interminable; several more hours passed, and the guest felt famished before the gong at last sounded.

A liveried servant appeared and conducted him to a different chamber than the one that had been used the preceding night. This was a state dining room, with scores of tapers burning in crystal chandeliers, a table already set with gold plate for a party of twenty. There was no sign of either Émilie or Voltaire, but several other guests were present, and Villefort joined them, listening with amusement as those who were new to Cirey found it strange that there should be no servants on duty in the dining room.

One of the most outspoken was Germain-Louis de Chauveron,

later to become a minister in the government of Louis XV, a man of early middle age who was accompanied by his young, exceptionally pretty wife. M. de Chauveron's cousin, Bishop de Chauveron, was also present, and he appears to have been one of the first clergymen of high rank to pay a visit to the estate. A general and a colonel were among the other guests, the former escorting his wife, the latter accompanied by his mistress, a Mlle. de Chantilly, who was very talkative and told everyone she was a poet.

Villefort felt sudden, excruciating embarrassment when the Marquis du Châtelet came into the dining room, the blonde Mlle. d'Anjou on his arm. But the proprietor of the estate appeared completely at home, and his conversation made it clear that he and his companion had arrived earlier in the day. No one else seemed in the least upset by his appearance, and, as nearly as Villefort could judge, he was relaxed and in a talkative mood.

At this juncture Émilie made her grand entrance in a low-cut, fur-trimmed gown better suited to Versailles than a house in the far reaches of rural France. Diamonds and emeralds blazed on her fingers and at her throat, and she wore a large number of diamonds in her elaborate hairdo. She immediately took charge of the conversation, delivering a monologue for the better part of a half-hour. Few of the others tried to interrupt, and those who did were simply ignored.

She appeared to be on very amicable terms with her husband and with Mlle. A'Anjou, whom she called, "My dear." Everyone drank wine, the guests helping themselves from several bottles placed on a convenient sideboard. Then a gong sounded somewhere outside the dining room, which meant it was time to eat, though Voltaire had not yet arrived. Émilie, who appeared annoyed, summoned a servant and sent the man to fetch him.

The company waited, Émilie's growing anger creating tensions, and eventually she sent a second servant for the missing author. There was another, equally long wait, and by the time

Voltaire finally appeared, resplendent in a velvet coat and silk breeches, she was furious. But he neither apologized nor offered any explanation for his tardiness; not until an hour or two later did he reveal, in the course of casual conversation, that he had been writing and had refused to interrupt his labors until he reached a place in his manuscript that he considered a natural spot for a pause.

Pouring himself a little wine, to which he carefully added water, he made the rounds, greeting each of the others in turn. He and the Marquis du Châtelet treated each other with great cordiality that Villefort found unfeigned, and the author complimented Mlle. d'Anjou at length on her radiant appearance.

Most of the company seemed somewhat embarrassed when, in greeting Bishop de Chauveron, Voltaire tenderly inquired after the health of the Almighty.

Mlle. de Chantilly provided something of a diversion when she recited excerpts from her poetry for Voltaire's edification. He politely tried to avoid making a comment of any sort, but the young woman was so insistent he told her his frank opinion of her creative efforts, thereby reducing her to tears.

Émilie took command of the situation by pounding a gong, and the dining room doors were closed from the outside. Food appeared through a trap door similar to that built into the smaller dining room, and the astonished guests were required to help themselves to each course, depositing their dirty dishes on the second trap door on the opposite side of the room. In response to M. de Chauveron's questions, Émilie explained that the absence of servants made conversation livelier and less inhibited.

The meal, Villefort later reported, was as delicious as that served the previous night, but was even more elaborate. There were nine separate courses, he wrote, and the company sat at the table for more than four and a half hours. The wines were good, too, and everyone enjoyed the meal.

For the first hour Émilie and Voltaire did not address each

other, and for a time Voltaire conducted a private conversation with the Marquis du Châtelet, who sat two seats to his right, at the head of the table. Émilie, who was dominating the talk at the other end of the table, made repeated efforts to interrupt, but her lover and her husband paid no attention to her.

Eventually Voltaire grew tired of her efforts, and tried to take charge of the general conversation by telling one of his amusing stories.

Émilie gave him no chance, however, and interrupted him repeatedly.

Thereafter, for at least an hour, they engaged in a spirited competition, each attempting to capture the attention of the audience. Neither won, but neither lost, and the atmosphere, Villefort later said, resembled that found on a battlefield. At last Voltaire brought his heavy cannon into play, and captured the others by reciting to them from the *Pucelle*. The presence of the Bishop de Chauveron and the two visiting army officers made the gesture a foolhardy one, as they could testify against him and would be considered extremely reliable witnesses. But Voltaire was willing to gamble, and they laughed as heartily at his thrusts as did the rest of the company.

Émilie had lost the battle, and Villefort thought she might sulk, but he was surprised when she accepted her defeat with good grace. Her anger at Voltaire disappeared, and she treated him with all the loving charm she was capable of manifesting. He grinned at her down the length of the table, indicating that he had no desire to continue the fight, either.

Thereafter they dominated the conversation together, and Villefort described their joint effort as breathtaking. Witty, urbane, and learned, they leaped from one subject to another, dazzling the company with their knowledge, exploring a topic in depth before going on to the next. They gave a virtuoso performance that was unique in Villefort's experience, and what made it doubly impressive was the ease with which they spoke. Both were relaxed, and Émilie ate her usual hearty meal; Voltaire, although he consumed less than anyone else present, nevertheless did not allow the conversation to interfere with his appreciation of the meal.

The most bizarre touch of Villefort's stay was yet to come. When the party finally left the dining room, Émilie led the way to the great hall, where conversation was resumed. Chunks of wood and metal balanced overhead appeared to be in danger of toppling over and falling as far as ten or fifteen feet onto the heads of the company below, and the guests had to make themselves as comfortable as they could by hauling their chairs away from the cumbersome machinery of Émilie's various scientific experiments. Only Émilie and Voltaire found it easy to converse in this atmosphere, and they regaled the company until the small hours of the morning.

The next day Villefort took his leave without seeing Émilie, Voltaire, or the Marquis du Châtelet again. He encountered two of the other guests walking on the grounds as he rode away, but otherwise, except for the workmen building the new wing, the tightly shuttered château appeared to be deserted.

IX

Crown Prince Frederick of Prussia, who was twenty-four years of age in 1736, was universally regarded, by everyone except his father, Frederick I, as a remarkable young man. The Crown Prince of Prussia had spent a year in prison because he had failed to live up to his father's harsh standards. The young man's character was undergoing changes in some respects, however, and in time, when he would be known as Frederick the Great, his tyranny would be greater than that of the father he despised, his military exploits would outshine those of the older Frederick, and he would prove himself a far more able administrator and innovator of far-seeing reforms.

It was an open secret that young Frederick was a homosexual who avoided his wife, Princess Elisabeth Christine, but he managed to conceal some of his other likes and dislikes from his father, and they did not become public knowledge until he succeeded to the throne in 1740. A passionate lover of literature and music, he was himself the author of several exceptionally well-written books on politics and philosophy. He despised every facet of German civilization, and, an ardent Francophile, spoke and wrote only in French. A rebel who decried the status quo until the time came for him to preserve it, he turned against all organized religion and made no secret of his contempt for Christianity.

While still in his teens Frederick discovered the writing of Voltaire and became his devoted pupil, and the first duty of his representative in Paris was that of buying every work of the author's that was published. Early in 1733, soon after his release from prison, Frederick initiated a correspondence with Voltaire that grew in the following years.

Like all authors of the era, Voltaire was sensitive to the patronage of royalty, ever conscious of the comforts that a king's pension or subsidy could buy. He knew Frederick only through letters, but soon realized that the Prince had qualities that set him apart from the dull, unimaginative men who sat on most of Europe's thrones. It was in their correspondence that Frederick first developed his concepts of justice, administration, and international relations that subsequently appeared in his book, *Anti-Macchiavel*, and the Prince gave Voltaire full credit for helping him.

The rumor that King Frederick I was illiterate was a canard, although it was true that he never read either for pleasure or the increase of knowledge. When he heard of his son's admiration for Voltaire he forced himself to look through some of the Frenchman's work, and was deeply impressed by his study of Charles XII. So, in 1735, he approved of the correspondence.

This gave Prince Frederick the opportunity to invite Voltaire to pay him a visit at the estate he maintained in the forest near Berlin. But Voltaire, who had many other matters keeping him occupied, managed to side-step without causing offense. He received the invitation while attending the rehearsals of *Alzire* in Paris, and thereafter he returned to Cirey to resume his exceptionally pleasant life there with Émilie du Châtelet. Besides, Berlin was far from France, and he disliked making long, uncomfortable journeys.

From the moment Émilie first heard of the proposed visit, she vehemently disliked the idea. She and Voltaire were in love and sharing a home under circumstances that innumerable other couples who were similarly enamored had good cause to envy, and she had no desire to see life in paradise disrupted. Furthermore, even though Voltaire had not turned away from her after his visit to Paris, she thought it unwise to take unnecessary chances. A visit to Prussia would be unlike his short journeys to Holland and Belgium, where she sometimes followed him for a stay of a day or two that broke up the tedium of their separation. If he traveled to Berlin, she believed, he would stay there for many months, and she didn't want him to become accustomed to living without her. If the independence that characterized his previous existence reasserted itself, he might never come back to her.

Émilie had heard enough gossip about Frederick's estate to realize there was no possibility that Voltaire might develop an interest in another woman there. Literally no women except middle-aged and elderly servants ever set foot on the property. The danger was that he might become intrigued by one of the highly intelligent, talented, and ravishingly beautiful creatures who lived on the estate. There were few women anywhere, according to rumor, whose beauty and wit equaled that of Frederick's private stable of transvestites.

How much Émilie actually knew of Voltaire's past is debatable, since portions of that past have remained concealed down to the present day, but many scholars have suspected that. prior to falling in love with Émilie, Voltaire indulged in several brief homosexual affairs. Émilie may have known of these affairs, or have heard gossip about them, which could account for the almost hysterical vehemence of her opposition to the proposed visit. If her lover had homosexual tendencies, she would go to almost any length to prevent him from visiting Frederick. Perhaps she could cope with another woman who tried to take her lover from her, but she would find it very difficult to compete with charming, wily transvestites.

Prince Frederick, who made it his business to keep informed, knew a great deal about Voltaire's relationship with Émilie, and the brilliant young Prussian realized she was an extraordinary woman. Therefore he conceived a new plan: He would use Émilie to win Voltaire's favor. He had no sexual interest in the great Frenchman, to be sure, but wanted the glory of becoming the literary patron of this author he admired above all other living men. Headstrong and in his own way supremely selfish, Frederick not only sought Voltaire's intellectual companionship, but knew his own reputation would be enhanced if he could persuade the author to visit him.

By 1736 Émilie's name appeared with increasing frequency in Frederick's correspondence with Voltaire. He praised her beauty and scholarship, declared that he stood in awe of her charm, and called Voltaire the luckiest of men.

Émilie was not fooled, of course. Fully aware of Frederick's loathing for women, she knew that every word he wrote about her was totally lacking in sincerity.

Voltaire, however, was flattered. Not even the most brilliant of men is flawless, and Voltaire, although he claimed he felt little respect for the institution of royalty, nevertheless was gratified by the attentions of kings and princes. He was a welcome guest at the palaces of the reigning monarchs of England and Holland, and he would add Prussia to his list of conquests.

Émilie's feminine intuition made her aware of nuances that escaped Voltaire, and she realized that, in spite of the torrents of praise Frederick heaped on her, she had never once been included in his invitation to visit Berlin. When she taxed Voltaire with the fact, he told her she was imagining things; she had received no separate invitation to be sure, but Frederick was including her. She knew better, and challenged her lover to prove her wrong by raising the question openly with Frederick.

Voltaire carefully composed a letter to the Prince, explaining that he found it difficult to tear himself from the side of Mme. du Châtelet for more than very brief periods.

Frederick's reply was succinct. *"If my destiny does not favor me to the extent of possessing you altogether, at least I hope to*

see, one day, the one whom I have long admired from afar."
His letter made no specific mention of Émilie.

Voltaire was forced to agree that Frederick was not inundating her with hospitality, but argued that the Prince was not the complete master in his own house. Perhaps his straight-laced father objected to a visit from a man accompanied by a woman married to someone else.

Émilie regarded the excuse as absurd. If King Frederick I allowed his son's hunting lodge to be filled with homosexuals, he would not object to a visit by a man and woman who didn't happen to be married to each other. But she guarded her tongue with great care in her direct approach to Voltaire. If she opposed his trip to Berlin too strongly, she might goad him into making the visit.

She made no attempt to conceal her true feelings, however, in her correspondence with Charles Augustin de Ferriol, Comte d'Argental, Voltaire's close friend and literary adviser, who had also become her friend. In fact, when d'Argental wrote to Voltaire late in the autumn of 1736, urging him to accept Frederick's invitation, Émilie completely lost her poise. Writing privately to d'Argental, she said:

"I positively wish that he should not go to Prussia, and I go down on my knees to you. He will be lost in that country; entire months would pass before I could have news of him. I should die of anxiety before he returned. The climate is dreadfully cold.

"Besides, how can he return at any given moment. In Holland it is almost as though he were in France. One could see him from one week to another, and there would be news. His affairs are not at all desperate, and no one can prove he wrote the verses about Adam and Eve; you flatter me in the hope that all will be settled within a few months and that he will not be forced to take refuge in exile.

"Why, then, should he go so far? If it were necessary for

him to leave France for a time, he could go to the court of Lorraine, where I could follow him with ease.

"A stay in Holland is always useful to him, but only harm could come to him in Prussia. All these reflections are nothing compared to those which the character of the King of Prussia furnishes. The Prince Royal is not yet King. When he is, we will both go to see him; but until that takes place there is no surety about anything. His father sees no merit in men other than being ten feet in height. He is suspicious and cruel; he hates and persecutes his son; he keeps him under an iron yoke; he will believe that M. de Voltaire may give him dangerous counsels.

"The King is capable of having M. de Voltaire arrested at his court, or of giving him up to the Keeper of the Seals. In one word, NO PRUSSIA, I beg you. Do not speak of it again. Recommend to him only that he be wise."

Voltaire's Adam and Eve verses, in which he ridiculed the Church doctrine on the origin of man, complicated an already tangled issue. An unauthorized version of the poem had been published, and at first Voltaire had been angry only because of the errors he found in the text. But the authorities, prodded by angry members of the clerical hierarchy, were at last exasperated, and a number of Voltaire's friends wrote him to the effect that he should leave France until tempers cooled.

If he elected to go to Prussia now, this was the right time, and there was nothing Émilie could do to stop such a visit. Apparently she persuaded him, however, that they could see each other occasionally if he remained closer to home, and early in December, 1736, they parted. It appeared inevitable that they would spend Christmas apart.

It did not occur to Émilie to return to Paris for a pleasant holiday. Instead she remained in isolation at Cirey, ready to join her lover in the Low Countries if he should send for her. She was afraid, too, that if she put too much distance between them he might change his mind and make the long journey to

Berlin, but for the present she carefully refrained from mentioning the possibility to him.

Voltaire had the time of his life. Traveling under an assumed name, he pretended he was a merchant, but it soon became very clear that he made no serious attempt to conceal his true identity. In Antwerp, his first stop, a performance of *Alzire* was given in honor of the merchant who called himself M. Rèvol. Word preceded him to Brussels, where the honor was repeated, and when he crossed into Holland performances of the play were given in Amsterdam and Leyden.

The frantic Émilie did not hear from him until the last day of the year, when she received a short note in which he complained that the translation of *Alzire* into Dutch had been sloppy and unimaginative.

"My heart is breaking with anxiety and grief," Émilie wrote, and begged him to write more frequently.

But Voltaire knew better. Realizing that the authorities would do anything in their power to discredit him if they were serious in their intent to arrest him, he had no intention of being embarrassed by sending love letters to a married woman. He guessed that the secret police were reading letters sent to Cirey, and, regardless of whether he was right, he preferred to take no chances in a delicate situation. He sent Émilie infrequent notes, addressing her formally as Madame and confining himself to a few brief, impersonal remarks.

It did Émilie's peace of mind no good to be informed by friends that newspapers in the Lowlands were reporting with great glee on Voltaire's triumphal tour. At Aix-la-Chapelle a banquet was given in his honor. In Leyden he conferred at length with scholars who were experts on Newtonian philosophy and physics. In Utrecht the university students serenaded him, and he was the principal guest at a great banquet that lasted until the small hours of the morning.

The crowning blow was an article in the Utrecht *Gazette*, dated January 14, 1737, stating that M. de Voltaire was departing in the immediate future for the purpose of paying a visit to the Prince Royal of Prussia.

Émilie had no idea whether the story was true or false, and she did not know where to write Voltaire for his confirmation or denial. In her anguish she turned to d'Argental and wrote him a letter in which she stripped herself of all pride:

"Persuade M. de Voltaire, I beg you, to return to Cirey at all costs. I am ill; I have had fever for two days; the violence of my feelings is capable of killing me in four more.

"Who is there could save him in spite of himself? I, at least, have nothing to reproach myself with, but that is a sad consolation. I am not born to be happy; my brain is mazed with grief."

Voltaire was not entirely to blame for keeping Émilie in the dark. He was enjoying himself, to be sure, but other activities were keeping him busy. He was working on a major project that strained his talents to the utmost and had valid reasons for wanting to keep his efforts a secret.

Nothing was known of Newton's scientific hypotheses in France other than in the very limited circles that understood both Latin and algebra. Voltaire had believed for several years that a comprehensive survey of Newton's thinking should be written and published in French for the edification of the educated classes, and he had conducted a long study, with Émilie, of the great Englishman's work.

Just before fleeing from France Voltaire had completed the manuscript of what he considered the most important book he had written to date, *Les Éléments de la philosophie de Newton*, but he knew that, with the French authorities indicating their disapproval of him, no printer in Paris would dare run the risk of publishing this latest work.

So he made arrangements with an Amsterdam printer to do the job for him, a decision that vastly increased his own responsibility. The printer's unfamiliarity with the French language meant the work would have to be supervised with the greatest care, and Voltaire planned to remain in Holland until April or May, when the task would be completed.

He was still intrigued by the reception he had been promised in Prussia, to be sure, and continued to toy with the idea of going there for the spring months. In cautiously worded letters to d'Argental and one or two others he admitted the possibility, but did not find it necessary to urge his friends to refrain from mentioning the idea to his mistress.

Émilie learned, late in January, that he had settled in Amsterdam on a semi-permanent basis and began to bombard him with letters. Meanwhile friends were finding it difficult to keep the secret that Voltaire had passed on to them, and Émilie began to receive hints from Paris: Voltaire, she was told, was being subjected to increased pressure from Prince Frederick, who was writing to him regularly. She responded promptly by increasing the pace of her own already frenzied correspondence.

Unfortunately, these letters are a portion of the Émilie-Voltaire legacy that has been lost, so they can be judged only by their results. Voltaire stepped up the printer's schedule, and the *Éléments* was ready for the French reading public by the end of February, four to six weeks early. Voltaire sent a letter of cordial but evasive regrets to Berlin and then deliberately passed the word that he was returning to the country he considered an earthly paradise, England.

He was so clever that Émilie heard the story, believed it, and was heartbroken. She recovered swiftly, however, when Voltaire made a totally unexpected and dramatic reappearance at Cirey. He had given out the story about making a journey to England only for the purpose of throwing the secret police off his scent, and was risking arrest by going back to France, but the attraction exerted by his mistress proved too strong to resist.

A few days later the Marquis du Châtelet made one of his brief visits to the château, and, as he was traveling to Paris, he obligingly took with him a letter from Voltaire to d'Argental.

Surely Émilie's husband was the best of all possible couriers to keep mail out of the hands of the secret police. In the communication Voltaire spoke with even greater candor than was his frank custom:

"I confess to you that if I had not been recalled by a friendship stronger than all other sentiments, I would willingly have spent the remainder of my days in a country where at least my enemies could not harm me. I have only to expect persecutions in France; that will be the whole of my reward. I should regard my presence in this country with horror if it were not that the tenderness and all the great qualities of the person who holds me here did not make me forget where I was.

"I have become a willing slave for the sake of living with the individual near whom all disagreeables disappear.

"I have always said that if my father, my brother, or my son were prime minister in a despotic state, I would leave it tomorrow, but Mme. du Châtelet is more to me than father, brother or son. I ask nothing more than to live buried in the mountains of Cirey."

For the moment, at least, love had conquered all, and Prince Frederick of Prussia lost a battle in his campaign to woo Voltaire to his estate outside Berlin. But Frederick, who had underestimated his adversary, immediately shifted ground, and in a letter he sent to Voltaire in the spring he resorted to gross flattery: *"How much I approve of a philosopher who knows how to take his relaxation in the company of the incomparable Émilie! I know very well that I should greatly prefer to make her acquaintance than to understand the center of gravity, the squaring of the circle, potable gold, or the sin against the Holy Ghost."*

Frederick was an accomplished hypocrite and liar. He had no intention of meeting Émilie, and took pains to ensure that he did not set eyes on her. It would have been a very simple matter to win Voltaire's acceptance of his repeated invitation:

All he needed to do was include Émilie, but the studied omission of her name revealed his true desire.

Émilie understood the nature of the tug-of-war and was annoyed by the density that Voltaire displayed. She had to exercise great care in her handling of the matter, however, and could not let him see that she was impatient. He would be certain to lose interest in her if she showed jealousy, a trait he despised.

In July an emissary from Prince Frederick arrived at Cirey. Baron de Keyserling was an accomplished diplomat, one of Prussia's few genuine intellectuals and a member of Frederick's inner circle of homosexuals who not only felt contempt for women but, Émilie feared, could read their minds. The farewell letter that Frederick had given his envoy, which was carefully shown to the hostess, was so flowery it confirmed her fears of Frederick's motives and convinced her, more than ever, that he intended to separate her from Voltaire. The letter said:

"Remember that you are going to a terrestial paradise, to a spot a thousand times more delightful than the Island of Calypso; that the goddess of this place yields in nothing to the beauty of Telemachus; that you will find in her all the charms of the mind, so superior to those of the body, and that this marvel among women occupies her leisure in searching after truth. It is there that you will see the human mind in its highest degree of perfection, wisdom without austerity, surrounded by tender loves and smiles!"

Voltaire was delighted by the letter and took the compliments to Émilie at face value.

She smiled, but knew beyond all doubt that the future monarch of Prussia was her deadly enemy, that his ego demanded her surrender of Voltaire to him. The situation in which she found herself was delicate enough without this added complication, as she lived in daily fear that the secret police might arrive unexpectedly at the château and place her lover under arrest before he could escape into the forest and make his way across the border.

Voltaire's pleasure in the gifts Frederick sent him was so naïve it was almost childlike. He put the portrait of the Prince on the wall of his bedchamber and prominently displayed the books Frederick had sent him, keeping them on his work table even after he had read them, usually aloud.

Émilie made no protest, however. Instead she exerted all of her considerable charm. Dramatic performances and fireworks displays were provided for the evening entertainment of the Prussian envoy. She gave a series of dinner parties in his honor, and such guests as the Richelieus traveled all the way from Paris for the express purpose of attending some of these affairs. Keyserling spent more than a month at Cirey, and in all that time Émilie's poise did not falter. Until the very end.

Then she discovered that the Baron had an immediate as well as a long-range goal. He had been ordered by his master to bring back to Berlin a copy of the much-discussed *Pucelle*. Frederick wanted the glory of being the first man in Europe, other than the author himself, to read the scurrilous work in its entirety.

But Émilie held the whip hand and refused to relinquish it. Not trusting Frederick, she knew that the publication of only a small portion of the *Pucelle* would cause Voltaire's permanent banishment from France, were he fortunate enough to escape. If he fell into the hands of the authorities, he would spend years languishing in the Bastille, and the combined influence of all his friends would be insufficient to win his release.

Before Voltaire had made his last trip out of France she had persuaded him to give her the original manuscript of the *Pucelle* for safekeeping, and she had concealed it, with great care, somewhere in the château, or, for all Voltaire himself knew, on the extensive grounds.

The drama that took place behind the closed doors of Émilie's and Voltaire's private quarters at Cirey during the last week of July, 1737, is revealed, at least in part, in the correspondence of the frustrated, angry author. *"I have begged and threatened in vain,"* he told d'Argental, *"but Mme. du Châtelet is adamant, and will not release into my custody those documents which are mine. In vain have I argued with her that the work which my efforts alone have produced is as much mine as the dairy farm in Normandy that I purchased a few months ago for a bargain sum."*

His friend's reply could not have caused him to rejoice. *"Mme. du Châtelet,"* d'Argental wrote, *"displays wisdom as well as caution, and I applaud her for both."*

"How I wish you would return to this lovely retreat," Voltaire said in a long letter to the Duc de Richelieu. *"When our charming friend is seized by one of her righteous moods, nothing will dissuade her from the course she has chosen. How I long for your calm reason to set her on the course that my best interests demand."*

"I have heard from our friend as well as from you," Richelieu replied bluntly, *"and it appears to me that the force of logic lies completely on her side. Any other approach to the problem you have presented to me would be folly, perhaps madness. You are fortunate that you have a calm and philosophical approach to life to guide you."*

In short, Émilie steadfastly refused to reveal the hiding place or give Voltaire the manuscript.

Making the best of an embarrassingly uncomfortable situation, Voltaire sent an apologetic letter to Prince Frederick, saying, *"Your ambassador will tell you it was impossible to fulfill your request, through no fault of my own. For many months the little work you wish to read has been in the charge of Mme. du Châtelet, who will not allow herself to be deprived of it. The friendship with which she honors me does not permit me to risk a thing which might separate me from her forever. She has renounced everything to live with me in the bosom of this retreat and study; she knows that the least knowledge of*

132

this work would certainly raise a storm. She fears every accident."

It was Frederick's turn to force a smile. He had been defeated by a stubborn woman and felt increased respect for her as an opponent.

Émilie did not bother to rejoice in the victory she had just won, but turned with her characteristic energy to something new. The Academy of Science was sponsoring an essay contest in the general realm of physics, and some of the most prominent men of science in France were submitting articles. Voltaire, undeterred by his status as an amateur scientist, had spent months working on an essay, with which Émilie was thoroughly familiar. Now, with the September 1st deadline for submissions only a month away, she decided to enter the contest, too.

She realized that Voltaire would insist she had too short a time for the preparation of an appropriate essay, so she didn't tell him of her intention. This meant she had to work on her article at odd times, without his knowledge, and in order to accomplish her end she was forced to sacrifice sleep. For two weeks she worked very late, sleeping for no more than an hour or two each night. She utilized her own unique method of staying awake, plunging her hands into a bowl of ice water until they became numb, then pacing up and down and beating her arms until the circulation was restored.

Not until she had sent off her essay did she reveal to Voltaire that she, too, had entered the contest. Their ideas were opposed to one another, with Émilie, of course, enjoying an advantage, since she knew what her lover had written.

Voltaire maintained that light and fire were separate entities. Each, he said, was material, each exerted pressure, each divided, and each propagated. Émilie took the opposite view and attempted to prove that light and heat were the same element, luminous when moving in a direct line, creating heat when the movement of the particles was irregular.

What she failed to see was that the movement was only vibratory, and that different effects were caused by different speeds. What she did claim, however, was that light rays of different colors did not emit equal degrees of heat, a theory that was validated the better part of a century later. In spite of her unorthodoxy, her scientific reasoning was sound.

Characteristically, perhaps, Émilie's essay ran to eighty-four closely written pages. Voltaire, who had worked for months on his paper, had prepared a document of less than half that length. He considered her essay far superior to his, and she returned the compliment, each feeling certain the other would win the prize.

Both were bitterly disappointed when the Academy of Science announced its decision early in 1738. The prize was divided between three professional scientists, one of them a Jesuit, and that which won first prize was a concise sixteen pages in length. *"We are in despair,"* Émilie wrote to Maupertuis. *"It is hard that the prize should be divided and that M. de Voltaire should be given no share of the cake."*

The couple won a consolation, however. The mere fact that the dramatist-poet-historian and the lady of high rank had submitted essays had created extraordinary interest in the contest, and the judges decided that, although their views were radical, they merited publication. The question was submitted to the membership of the Academy of Science, and the learned gentlemen voted unanimously in favor of printing the two essays in the same pamphlet that contained the prize essays. The celebrated pair enjoyed the last word, their efforts being rewarded with far greater publicity than that accorded the actual winners.

Prince Frederick lost no opportunity to soften the foe he had found worthy of his steel, and it is possible that he felt genuine respect and admiration for Émilie's work. *"Without wishing to flatter you,"* he wrote her, *"I can assure you that I should never have believed your sex, usually so delightfully gifted with all the graces, capable also of such deep knowledge, minute research and solid discovery as appears in your fine work. Ladies owe to you what the Italian language owes to Tasso. This language, usually soft and deprived of forcibility, appears in a masculine and energetic form when used by this clever poet. Beauty, which ordinarily is the highest merit ladies possess, could only be reckoned among the least of your advantages."*

He wrote to Voltaire about Émilie's essay in the same vein, saying, *"I was astonished when I read it. One would never imagine that such a treatise could be produced by a woman. Moreover, the style is masculine and in every way suitable to the subject."* He could find nothing to criticize except for a few minor quibbles with her observations on the possible origins of forest fires, and it was obvious to anyone reading his letter that he was straining in an attempt to find something wrong.

Émilie had cause to feel smug, and was relieved when Voltaire stopped reading Frederick's own literary efforts aloud every evening. Whether her own enhanced stature was responsible or whether Voltaire was becoming bored with the writing of the future monarch is impossible to determine.

Frederick, privately more insistent than ever that Voltaire, unaccompanied, pay him a visit, continued to write lavish letters of praise to the author and his paramour.

Voltaire found it easy to return the compliments in kind, and dashed off letters with such flattery as, *"Every time we pass Your Royal Highness' portrait we sing the hymn of old Simeon in the Temple."*

Émilie felt a measure of relief, and although she knew the threat was not yet ended, she believed the immediate danger was diminished. Therefore it was easy for her to lie, and in letters to all of her friends she blandly announced that she and Voltaire would go together to Berlin as soon as Frederick succeeded his father on the throne of Prussia.

X

Voltaire's oldest brother, with whom the author had been on bad terms for almost all his adult life, died early in 1738, and as no one else thought of the future of the two orphaned daughters of the deceased, Voltaire elected to take care of them. The elder of his nieces, Louise Arouet, who was twenty-six years old and unmarried, paid a visit to Cirey, and Voltaire was impressed. A handsome young woman, she was remarkably similar to Émilie in temperament, considered herself an intellectual, and had as passionate an interest in music as Émilie had in science.

Promising her a large dowry, Voltaire wanted to marry her to the son of a neighbor, but Louise, whose independence was responsible for her single state at an age when most women were considered old maids, immediately balked. She was city bred, and the mere idea of spending the rest of her days in rural Champagne was unbearable. She had a suitor in Paris she wanted to marry, a pleasant young man of the middle class named Denis, and Voltaire agreed that she should live her own life in her own way. So Denis was paid the dowry, Louise married him, and Voltaire rubbed his hands in relief from afar, having refused to attend the wedding on the grounds that all such affairs were alike and insufferably boring.

Mme. Denis's description of life at Cirey was one of pity,

awe, and condescension. It was obvious she disliked everything about the place. During her visit several performances of new plays were given, but it was necessary to use puppets, and most of the roles were played by Voltaire and Mme. du Châtelet, neither of whom was expert in the handling of marionettes. Mme. Denis felt the spectacle was demeaning to her uncle's genius.

Voltaire, as usual, was working too hard, and his stomach was causing him trouble again, so he confined himself to a light, bland diet. Mme. du Châtelet, the young woman reported, was growing plump, a claim that was actually untrue. Louise admitted, however, that Émilie was very pretty, very charming, and was devoted to Voltaire, sparing no effort to make certain he was comfortable and happy. Both appeared as much in love as they had ever been, and it was Mme. Denis's opinion that her uncle was bewitched. She indicated in several letters that she did not blame him.

Émilie did not reciprocate the good will of her lover's niece. It did not bother her that Louise was a handsome young woman, her own beauty making her impervious to the threat of any other woman, no matter how physically attractive she might be. What was unbearable, however, was the incisive mind of someone who seemed to have inherited a slice of Voltaire's own genius. When Émilie spoke on intellectual matters, she was accustomed to the awed silence of her feminine listeners, and only rarely did a man, other than Voltaire himself, dare to contradict her.

Louise, however, challenged every assertion, demanded proof of every theory, debated every question. At first Émilie was amused, then annoyed, and finally she felt outraged. But she made certain that neither Voltaire nor his niece knew how she felt, and she confided in no one but a few old friends, to whom she wrote long letters of complaint. She felt great relief when the young woman returned to Paris to be married.

Domestically, at least, 1738 was a quiet year for the couple who had renounced society. Émilie and Voltaire worked, read, and debated, living the isolated life they had chosen for themselves. But the outside world continued to intrude, and the removal of the latest secret police ban on Voltaire's work made it easier for him to take part in the active literary life of France. Apparently he had no desire to visit Paris, and happily remained at Cirey throughout the better part of the year.

Voltaire drew the plans for a new darkroom Émilie wanted to install, a chamber where she could conduct some of her more advanced experiments in physics. She disagreed with his ideas and developed a set of blueprints of her own. They argued amiably for days, but could not come to a meeting of minds, and finally decided on what seemed a sensible solution: they would build two darkrooms, and then would see which was better for the experiments. This project occupied much of their spare time for weeks.

When the workmen were finished the couple conducted identical experiments in the two rooms. The chamber Émilie had designed proved eminently superior, but Voltaire was delighted he had lost, and boasted of her intellectual prowess in letters to his friends. He took positive pride in the knowledge that his mistress could beat him in a contest of this sort.

Émilie was gratified by her victory, but proved that she could think in practical terms from time to time, too. The darkroom built according to Voltaire's specifications was sitting idle, and although there were many other chambers in the huge château that were unoccupied, she hated waste. A huge hearth was located at one end of the room, so she conceived the idea of converting the chamber, at small cost, into an auxiliary kitchen where the light meals they sometimes enjoyed very late at night could be cooked.

This idea was a revolutionary concept in the eighteenth century. For centuries the kitchen of the aristocrats and of the small middle class had been an outbuilding, a separate structure connected with the main building or manor house, but never actually a part of it. Thus the cooking odors never permeated the great houses, and the danger of fire was reduced, since a kitchen fire could be confined to that chamber alone.

But Émilie and Voltaire were indifferent to the smells of cooking food, and their convenience meant more to them than running the risk of starting a fire when such snacks as jugged hare or venison stew were being prepared in the small hours of the morning. Their new kitchen was a delight, and Voltaire boasted in letters to friends that it was a great contribution to their mutual comfort.

So, without knowing what they were doing, Émilie and Voltaire were responsible for a fad that would, in time, lead to the inclusion of kitchens in new homes rather than adjoining them. Émilie's only known comment on the subject is contained in a brief line near the end of a long letter to the Duc de Richelieu. Food, she told him, remained hot when prepared in the same building in which it was eaten. Others, imitating the celebrated recluses of Cirey, made the same discovery, and the beginning of a kitchen revolution was under way.

Occasional visitors to Cirey provided diversions, too, and none was more welcome than Mme. de Graffigny, who arrived there on December 4, 1738. Inadvertently, this woman, who would have lived and died unknown had she not made the journey to Cirey, contributed more facts than any other individual to the history of Émilie du Châtelet and Voltaire. Forty-three years old at the time of her visit, Françoise d'Issembourg-d'Happencourt de Graffigny was a member of a noble but impoverished family who had been married at a very early age to the chamberlain at the court of the Duc de Lorraine. According to all accounts, de Graffigny was one of the most unpleasant men of the era, a brutal, penny-pinching tyrant who made life miserable for almost everyone who had the misfortune to associate with him. His wife found her existence with him intolerable, and, in an attempt to escape, she turned first to literature, then to friendships with authors.

In spite of the hardships she had suffered, Mme. de Graffigny was an incurable romantic, a gushing idealist who thought of her literary heroes as inhabitants of Mt. Olympus. Late in 1736 her marital situation became so desperate that she took the unusual step of applying to the royal and ecclesiastical courts for a separation, which was granted. She was free of her husband, but had no home of her own and was virtually penniless, which made her situation precarious. Friends took pity on her, and she lived by making prolonged visits to those from whom she wheedled invitations.

She had been acquainted with Émilie for a number of years, although the time and place of their first meeting is not recorded, and she first met Voltaire in 1735. Both had felt deeply sorry for her, and had been pleased to ask her to pay a visit to Cirey, but had they been aware of her secret nicknames for them they might have hesitated. She called Voltaire Idol, which would have made him shudder, and she referred to Émilie as Nymph, which was absurd. The uncommonly tall, statuesque Mme. du Châtelet, who had never overcome the awkwardness of her childhood and who still broke bric-a-brac or crashed into furniture on occasion, could by no stretch of even the most fertile imagination be considered a nymph.

Mme. de Graffigny's greatest asset, if it could be called that, was her very limited talent as a letter-writer, which was valuable to posterity because she substituted quantity for quality, and no detail of daily life escaped her attention and pen, regardless of how trivial it might be deemed by others. Unlike Mme. de Sévigné, regarded through the centuries as the finest letter-writer of the age, Mme. de Graffigny did not apologize for the length of her communications by saying, *"If I'd had time, I'd have written a shorter letter."*

Most of her correspondents were eager young authors, some just beginning to make their mark in the world, others as yet completely unsung. All these young men, naturally, were curious about the private life of the century's greatest dramatist-poet-essayist-historian, and if Mme. de Graffigny merely hinted at something, or failed to fill in enough details, they asked for more. The net result of the two-month visit was a vast collection of facts, details, opinions, and unimportant trivia that, nevertheless, helped to round out a picture of life at Cirey.

Unfortunately, Mme. de Graffigny's personality and prejudices were bound to color her reports to her youthful friends, and it was even more unfortunate that the stars in her eyes were shining so brightly when she arrived at the château. No one knows what she might have imagined before she reached the remote estate, and it is probable that she herself was so thrilled she did not pause to remind herself that Idol and Nymph were human, and therefore had feet of the usual mortal clay. Her eventual disillusionment was as intense as her initial enthusiasm, so her reports must be read and weighed carefully, with her own opinions screened out where possible.

Mme. de Graffigny's arrival at Cirey was anything but auspicious. Heavy rains had reduced the rough country lanes to their muddiest condition, and the roads, in her opinion, had been built by "the devil himself." Her carriage had become mired repeatedly, and long delays had ensued; she was cold, wet, and in a state of near-exhaustion when she finally pulled up at the main entrance to the château at two o'clock in the morning.

Émilie was fully dressed, and, having awaited the guest's arrival, came to the door herself. She was her most charming, gracious self, conducted Mme. de Graffigny to the suite she would occupy, and went off to bring her a bowl of hot soup, a loaf of bread, some wine, and a wedge of "the most delicious, aromatic cheese." Émilie returned with the food simultaneously with Voltaire, who was wearing a long robe, carried a candle, and obviously had been sleeping.

Anyone well acquainted with Voltaire knew that he was not at his conversational best when he had just been awakened. But the guest was a complete innocent and failed to realize that his delight at seeing her was feigned, and that he gallantly kissed her hand in lieu of making small talk. Then he inquired, politely, after the health of several of her young author friends, and she replied at great length. He listened for a quarter of an hour and then hauled himself back to bed.

By the next day Mme. de Graffigny felt completely at home, and settled down to her task of writing literally everything she heard, saw, felt, and smelled to her correspondents. The bulk of her letters were sent to François-Antoine Devaux, a handsome young man in his mid-twenties who scorned a career as a professional man, and, for want of anything else, called himself an author. Older women, to whom he dedicated his light poems, were overwhelmed by what they considered his dazzling personality, and the affection-starved Mme. de Graffigny, knowing no better, referred to him as her "beloved son," and addressed him as Pan-pan.

Her letters to her darling Pan-pan constitute one of the most remarkable chapters in the history of the written word. It would have been a considerable feat had she written a daily letter of ten to fifteen pages, but Mme. de Graffigny wrote a number of such letters every day of her visit to Cirey, without fail. No sooner did she hear, see, or become aware of something that interested her than she reduced it to paper. On some of her more verbose days she actually wrote as many as seven or eight letters to Devaux. Her handwriting was small, she filled every inch of the large pages on which she wrote, and it is astonishing that she was able to turn out as much as one hundred pages of trivia in a single day.

No infinitesimal detail at Cirey was beneath her notice. She could devote a paragraph to the way a satin bow was attached to a lace curtain. She counted the number of stone steps that led from the terrace to the kitchen garden, and she discussed in almost fantastic detail every vegetable and herb there, even though this was not the growing season, culminating this minor triumph by listing which plants were Idol's, which were Nymph's, and which had been put into the ground by servants on the household staff. She set the tone on the morning after her arrival, when she wrote to Pan-pan:

"I should like to describe everything that I see and everything that I hear in this fascinating place, dear Pan-pan. In short, I should like to afford you as much pleasure as I am having. I would like you to enjoy this visit as though you, too, were here. But I fear lest the heavy touch of my hand—and I am not an author, so you must forgive my bumbling efforts —should mix up and spoil everything. So I believe it will be far better to tell you everything plainly, not day by day, as I might become confused in recalling details, but hour by hour."

She began her recital with surface descriptions of her hostess and almost-host. Émilie's most obvious trait was her constant stream of conversation, and her chatter, Mme. de Graffigny said, was astonishing. But she hastily amended the comment by saying, *"She speaks like an angel."*

The range of Nymph's conversation was equally impressive. She could chat about personalities at the court of Versailles or in Paris, even though she had not seen some of these people in years, and seemed to be aware of the latest gossip about them. She was familiar with every detail of Voltaire's publishing and theatrical worlds, had read the latest books and plays and could discuss them with critical detachment. When her own fields of endeavor were under discussion, she delivered non-stop monologues, and became so profound that the guest had no idea what she was saying. She could also talk about such feminine matters as clothes and food, and she delighted in concocting the recipes for new dishes, although, being a great lady, she did none of the actual cooking herself.

She wore a gown of East Indian design, with threads of silver and gold cloth making a pattern in the material, and over the dress a fetching, large apron of black taffeta. Her hair, which was growing darker as she matured, was very long, fastened at the back of her head and falling in ringlets "like the hair of little girls." The style suited her well.

Voltaire surprised Mme. de Graffigny by wearing a powdered wig, silk stockings, and a handsome suit, looking as he might if he were spending a busy day in Paris. The guest was uncertain whether the elegance was intended for her benefit, but she later discovered that he always dressed with care, making no concessions to the fact that he was living in the country. *"I think,"* she wrote Pan-pan, *"he enjoys making a display. It is a vanity, I know, but one to which a Genius surely is entitled."*

By chance the Marquis du Châtelet arrived at Cirey on the first day of Mme. de Graffigny's visit, and it happened that, as he was traveling on crown business, with a military matter to attend to in Brussels, he was not accompanied by a mistress. His presence for a few days gave the busybody an unparalleled opportunity to observe the relationship between Émilie, her lover, and her husband, but Mme. de Graffigny either found very little to report or was bored by the soldier who had virtually no interests in common with the other inhabitants of his ancestral home.

The Marquis was a bluff, hearty man who dressed plainly, ate and drank more than anyone else, and spent most of his time outdoors, riding across the small meadows and through the sodden forests. He and his wife were on good terms, and, although they said little to each other, neither appeared under tension. Voltaire and the Marquis seemed very friendly, and went for a stroll together, which was their custom whenever they found themselves under the same roof. In mid-afternoon the visitor happened to come upon them in a sitting room, where they were discussing the details of a campaign waged by the forces of Louis XIV against the English, Austrians, and Dutch in the War of the Spanish Succession. Both men were polite and preoccupied, and although they went through the motions of including her in the conversation, it was obvious that this was a "men's hour." So Mme. de Graffigny, after listening to them for a time and making no sense out of their talk, wandered away again.

144

There were two other guests at the château, both of whom spent the better part of their time alone. One was the elderly Marquis de Trichateau, a semi-invalid related to the Châtelet family, who was helping his cousin settle details of a complicated lawsuit involving some of the extensive property located at the far end of the estate. He knew nothing whatever of literature, so in Mme. de Graffigny's opinion he was a deadly bore, and she spoke to him only when it would have been rude to remain silent.

The other guest was a neighbor, Mme. de Champbonin, who lived about fifteen miles away. She was young, with a pretty face, although considerably overweight, and was one of the gentlewomen of the area who had been kind to Voltaire when he had first arrived at the estate. She was a frequent visitor, staying for a day or two at a time, and Voltaire apparently felt indebted to her. Émilie, on the other hand, made it plain that she merely tolerated the woman for his sake.

A casual conversation made it clear that Mme. de Champbonin was a semi-educated member of the rural nobility. She was unfamiliar with literature, and the little she read was trash, unworthy of the attention of anyone who had literary pretensions. But she considered Voltaire the most wonderful, fascinating man on earth, and her opinion coincided with that of Mme. du Graffigny, who became friendly with her, knowing that anyone who worshipped at the throne of the Idol was necessarily a fine person.

The evening meal was the highlight of the day, and Mme. de Graffigny was transported into ecstacies because it was served in Voltaire's sitting room, as a convenience to him because he was in the climactic throes of a writing project. The guest counted five globes, a number of instruments used in physics experiments, which she described, and vast numbers of books. She memorized as many titles as she could, and listed the volumes for the edification of Pan-pan.

She was given the place of honor between the Marquis du

Châtelet and Voltaire, and the occasion lived up to her fondest dreams of Cirey. *"I found this supper made delightful,"* she wrote, *"by all that I felt within myself as well as by my surroundings. What did not we discuss? Poetry, sciences, the arts, all in a tone of badinage, and good humor. How I wish I could reproduce them for you—these charming discourses, these enchanting discussions—but that is beyond me."*

The meal was *"choice, tasty and dainty,"* and Mme. de Graffigny spent several paragraphs describing each dish served, speculating at length on the ingredients of the sauces. She was impressed by the quantities of heavy silver used at the table, and she found the crystal exquisite. But a faint note of criticism appeared in her writing for the first time. Even though the food was delicious, it was not as plentiful as she might have wished; the plump Mme. de Graffigny liked rich food, in quantity, and it disturbed her to see the Marquis du Châtelet taking the lion's share. As always, Voltaire ate sparingly, and so did Émilie, who told the guest in confidence that she was on a diet, having gained too much weight recently.

The Marquis contributed almost nothing to the occasion. He was silent, taking no part in the conversation, and yawned frequently; in an aside to the guest he remarked that he was accustomed to an earlier supper hour when he lived with his troops in the field. He ate very quickly, consuming large portions while others were busy talking, and then went off to bed, making no apologies for his abrupt departure from the table. He was not sullen or unpleasant, however, and Mme. de Graffigny assumed he was following the routines he usually observed at Cirey.

When the meal ended the guest seized the opportunity to make a tour of Voltaire's private suite, and she described it in full detail, ranging from the furniture upholstered in crimson velvet, with a fringe of gold, to his porcelain ornaments, marble clock, and other bric-a-brac. Everything was so clean, she said, that *"you could kiss the parquet."*

There were vases and other ornaments of heavy silver, and Voltaire kept his rings, more than two dozen of them, some with diamonds and some set with engraved stones, in special cases of gold-tooled leather. Everywhere was the luxury the great author needed, and the guest repeatedly felt overwhelmed. What money had gone into the furnishing of the suite, she exclaimed, and what labor!

The simplicity of Voltaire's workroom stunned her, however. The walls were painted a soft shade of gray, and the only ornament in the chamber was a miniature portrait of Mme. du Châtelet. The drapes that stood at the sides of the windows were made of a drab, gray cloth, and the small rug on the floor was woven of a matching, solid gray. There was no sofa, no chaise in the chamber, and the single chair that sat before a table of unpainted wood was not upholstered. There was no comfort here, much less luxury, and no opportunity to lounge. Well-thumbed books stood in solid rows, as did a number of instruments used in physics experiments, and the guest was shocked by the battered condition of the two globes on a far shelf.

The spartan atmosphere was beyond her comprehension, and did not fit the picture of the Voltaire she thought she knew. He explained to her, gently, that he permitted nothing to distract him when he was working, and he emphasized that he permitted himself no comforts because they, too, might cause him to relax. Had she not seen the workroom with her own eyes she would have thought he was joking, but it was obvious that he meant every word, which did not fit her concept of her literary Idol.

Mme. de Graffigny was somewhat confused when she went to bed that night, but her faith in the luxury of Cirey was revived the next day, when she made a tour of Mme. du Châtelet's suite, conducted by Émilie. The beauty of the furnishings was breathtaking and befitted a Nymph who was unique.

The bedroom was wood paneled, varnished in light yellow with edges of pale blue. Everything in the chamber harmonized, even the dog's basket. The bed was blue, and both canopy and coverlet were of watered silk; there was a glimpse of blue silk bed-curtains as well. The wood of the armchairs, the chest of drawers, the corner cupboards and the writing desk were done in yellow, with blue trim. The mirrors were set in huge, expensive frames of heavy silver, and were brilliantly polished. Another, full-length mirror was set in a door that led to Émilie's private library, a room that was not yet finished.

The boudoir was so lovely that Mme. de Graffigny wanted to drop to her knees so she could worship at the shrine of beauty. The wainscoting was blue, and the ceiling, which featured full-length portraits of Émilie, her mother, and Voltaire's mother, had been painted and varnished by a pupil of the renowned Robert Martin, but the guest could not recall his name at the moment.

In the smaller panels were a number of paintings which the hostess did not identify, but which Mme. de Graffigny thought had been painted by Watteau. Actually, she was less accurate as an observer than she imagined; most had been done by Pater, and were gifts of Voltaire's wealthy English friends. The corner cabinets and chimney piece were crammed with treasures that made the visitor's eyes gleam, and the most impressive object in the room was a writing desk made of pure amber that had been a gift of Prince Frederick of Prussia. There was an armchair upholstered in white taffeta, and two stools covered with the same material.

A pair of French windows led to a small, private terrace, from which the view was charming. Mme. de Graffigny was guessing, in all probability, because the fog was so thick the morning she was taken on the tour that she could not have seen the view clearly.

On one side of the boudoir was a huge clothes closet, as large as most women's bedchambers. It was lined with marble, hung with gray linen and decorated with lovely prints. Even the muslin curtains that covered the small windows of the closet

148

were embroidered, and Mme. de Graffigny was convinced she had never seen anything so lovely. She could not satisfy her curiosity completely, however, because her hostess did not offer to show her the clothes hanging in long, neat rows beneath linen dust covers, and Mme. de Graffigny lacked the courage to ask for the privilege of seeing them.

She was shown some of Mme. du Châtelet's jewels, however, and was overwhelmed. The contents of the jewel closet, a small, separate chamber that was secured with three separate locks, were even richer and more ornate than those belonging to the Duchesse de Richelieu. Mme. de Graffigny could remember when she had owned only one modest snuffbox, made of tortoise shell. Now she had fifteen or twenty of gold, of precious stones, of beautiful lacquer, and of enameled gold, which was a new, exorbitantly expensive fashion. She had a dozen or more incense boxes, some of which matched the snuff containers; she had watches set with diamonds, enameled watches, and watches of new types that were not yet popular at Versailles. Her rings, set with precious stones, were almost without number, her diamonds filled several boxes, and her famous emeralds were breathtaking.

"Indeed," Mme. de Gaffigny wrote, *"I cannot stop telling you about her jewels, and will have to describe her trinkets and charms on another occasion, for my writing hand grows weary. What I find intriguing is that the Châtelet family has never been wealthy, and Mme. du Châtelet's family could afford to give her only the most modest dowry."*

The guest, who would become less circumspect later in the visit, was hinting, of course, that Émilie's jewel collection was the result of Voltaire's generosity. Her guess was right. Voltaire was earning vast sums of money, and his investments were making him one of the wealthiest men in Europe. He still believed that Émilie was isolating herself at Cirey exclusively for his sake, and he felt indebted to her because of the "sacrifice" she was making for him. He knew she loved finery, particularly jewelry, so he showered her with a queen's ransom in gems.

It is small wonder that the pangs of jealousy began to stir in the impoverished bosom of Mme. de Graffigny. Paradise was not what it had seemed at first glance, and, as her attitude changed, so did her opinions of the Idol and the Nymph.

XI

In Mme. de Graffigny's first letters to her beloved Pan-pan, she described her living quarters as snug and cozy, but she regarded them in a far different light after seeing the personal suites of Voltaire and Mme. du Châtelet. Her main chamber was a room into which the wind crept through a thousand chinks and crannies, and the fireplace was so absurdly small it could not provide enough heat, even on a mild day. The windows were small, and the walls, painted a dull white, did little to relieve the dullness. An arid mountain stood outside the windows, *"so close I can almost touch it,"* and provided an uninspiring view. A huge tapestry stood near the window, but its subject was unfamiliar, and the guest thought it ugly.

In fact, most of the furniture was not only ugly, but was surprisingly shoddy, and she found cause to complain about even the expensive furnishings: *"There is a nook, hung with very rich hangings, which are disagreeable to the sight, because they do not match."*

The quarters provided for her servingmaid were so small they were shocking. In fact, the only daylight that filtered into the room came from the corridor outside and entered through a glass transom. There was a magnificent old staircase outside her room, Mme. de Graffigny said, and ordinarily she would have admired it, but it was so steep that her heart pounded every time she climbed it.

What disturbed her more than anything else was the disgusting state of filthiness everywhere in the château except the private suites of Idol and Nymph, which the servants were kept busy cleaning and polishing. A few of the general rooms, she conceded, were fairly clean, but her own chamber was a veritable pigsty. It was impossible for any staff to maintain a semblance of order in an ancient castle, portions of which were still being rebuilt, and she suspected the servants were lazy. It was also her opinion that Nymph was not the best housekeeper in France, and was happy as long as her own rooms were kept immaculate, but cared nothing about the comfort of her guests.

The awakening of Mme. de Graffigny's critical faculties undoubtedly was due, in part, to the peculiar nature of the routines at Cirey. Her hostess and near-host did not spend all of their time entertaining guests and looking after their comforts. Far from it. There were books in every bedchamber, books in the library, books in the great hall, and books in the bathroom, a handsomely furnished chamber the size of a large drawing room, in which Voltaire sometimes read poetry aloud. So guests were actively encouraged to spend a great deal of time in their own chambers, reading.

In fact, there were a number of unwritten laws that governed the conduct of visitors. Mme. de Graffigny, bored because Idol and Nymph were locked away in their respective workrooms, went to the chamber of Mme. de Champbonin for a chat. The younger woman showed signs of increasing nervousness, and finally confessed that Mme. du Châtelet and M. de Voltaire discouraged social gatherings under their roof when they themselves were at work. So the duly chastised Mme. de Graffigny went back to her own quarters, found a book she might enjoy, and settled down to read it.

She had always claimed she had too little time to read all the books that interested her, but now time dragged. Her breakfast was served in her room, and she was expected to spend the entire morning there, cut off from human companionship. She could go for a walk or a drive, of course, but had no desire to venture out of doors in such cold, wet, raw weather. Around noon, when the mail was delivered, she sometimes caught a brief glimpse of Émilie, who, dressed in her regal finery, made a point of accepting the mail bag in person from the postman.

When Émilie was busy, as she was most days, Mme. de Graffigny was served a light meal in her room in the early afternoon. Otherwise she and a few others were invited to join the hostess for a very brief meal; conversation was held to a minimum, and the preoccupied Émilie not only gulped her food but expected everyone else to do the same. When she was finished, the dishes of others were cleared away, too, even though they might still be eating.

One of the worst frustrations of daily life at Cirey was the complete absence of Idol, who remained in isolation until he elected to appear in the evening. Mme. de Graffigny understood that genius had to be protected from distractions, of course; after all, she was a worldly woman with a literary bent who understood these things. But, in her considered opinion, at Cirey they went too far.

One of her goals in coming to this remote place was that of watching Voltaire at work, of actually standing at his side as a fascinated observer while he penned his glowing poetry or immortal prose. Her eyes would be the first to see the words, the sentences, the paragraphs as they took shape on paper. *That* would be a memorable occasion she could report in thrilling detail to her darling Pan-pan!

She had said nothing at the château of her ambition, realizing she would be discouraged. She had no doubt that Mme. du Châtelet, who hovered over the author and insisted on placing a screen between him and the world, would be quick to block such a move. But she convinced herself that the gallant and charming Voltaire, who invariably treated her with every warm courtesy, would be delighted to receive her whenever she paid him such a visit.

Assuring herself and her correspondent that she would not be denied this rare treat, she made her way to Idol's workroom one afternoon when her patience gave out after she had spent the entire day alone, seeing and speaking to no one except her maid and the servant who had brought her meals to her room. What she did not know, but soon discovered, was that a servant was stationed at the head of the stairs that led to Voltaire's suite. There the man stood vigil, polishing silver and performing other tasks as he passed the dreary hours.

With great politeness the servant announced that M. de Voltaire was at work on a manuscript, and consequently could not be disturbed, even if an emergency should arise.

Mme. de Graffigny refused to listen to such arrant nonsense. Unnamed persons might try to hold M. de Voltaire prisoner behind the closed doors of the suite, but she would foil them, permitting no one to stand in her way.

The servant did not argue or protest, but hurried off down the stairs.

Mme. de Graffigny believed she had cowed him, and, congratulating herself on her courageous stand, she boldly knocked at the door.

There was no reply.

She thought it inconceivable that Idol could have failed to hear her, so she knocked again, pounding on the door at length.

He remained silent, and although she strained to hear what might be happening on the far side of the door, she heard nothing.

Quickly convincing herself that he was ill or in trouble of some sort, Mme. de Graffigny called out her name to him and rattled the latch, feeling deep disappointment when she discovered that the door was locked.

At that moment Mme. du Châtelet raced up the stairs, and never had she looked less like Nymph. Coldly furious, she demanded to know what the guest was doing there.

Resenting her tone, Mme. de Graffigny replied that she had come to see M. de Voltaire on a private matter.

Mme. du Châtelet became still angrier, and replied that she could imagine no matter, private or otherwise, of sufficient urgency to disturb him when he was working.

Mme. de Graffigny began to feel annoyed and revealed her real purpose in trying to gain admittance to his suite.

At this Mme. du Châtelet completely lost her poise, and with it her self-control. Shouting, cursing, and screaming, she made a dreadful scene. It was an inviolable rule that no one could interrupt M. de Voltaire when he was writing. This was the first law of Cirey.

It was the private opinion of Mme. de Graffigny that her hostess was jealous, but she kept the opinion to herself, which was fortunate, as Émilie might have ordered her to leave the house at once.

As it was, Mme. du Châtelet made her attitude unmistakably clear. Guests were expected to fulfill their obligations to their hosts and were required to obey the rules of the household. She could not emphasize too strongly the gravity of the attempted infraction. Had M. de Voltaire been interrupted, the rhythm of his thoughts might have been disturbed, causing him to lose a whole day's work.

Again Mme. de Graffigny entertained private thoughts. The woman was exaggerating, so determined was she to keep Genius to herself. She might fool someone who was unfamiliar with artists and the arts, but Mme. de Graffigny was a close friend of many authors, among them her dearest Pan-pan. On any number of occasions she had interrupted him—had she not?—when he had been busy in the throes of composition, and he had not minded in the least, but had returned to his labors without difficulty after chatting with her.

Mme. du Châtelet was not to be denied, however, and making it plain that Cirey was her domain, she glowered at the guest.

Mme. de Graffigny was forced to beat the most undignified of retreats, and retired to her own room. The worst of the experience was the knowledge that Mme. du Châtelet continued to stand at the head of the stairs, watching her ignominious withdrawal.

The guest wondered whether she should pack her belongings and leave Cirey forthwith, but decided that her departure would be an admission of guilt, and she considered herself guilty of no wrong-doing. In addition, she admitted, her curiosity about the celebrated inhabitants of this strange place had not yet been satisfied, and she didn't want to be cheated of her opportunity to observe them at close range. She made no mention of still another factor that must have been important: She had made no arrangements to visit other friends, and if she left Cirey she had no place to go.

That evening Mme. de Graffigny felt apprehensive as the time approached to meet her hostess and near-host for dinner, but her fears proved groundless. Émilie was charming and vivacious, the personification of Nymph, and made no mention of the afternoon's unfortunate incident. Voltaire seemed somewhat withdrawn, however, and Mme. de Graffigny couldn't decide whether he had been influenced against her.

She decided to find out, and at her first opportunity she remarked to him, privately, that she hoped she had not caused him inconvenience.

His attitude quickly revealed that he had literally no idea what she meant.

Mme. de Graffigny gave him a "candid and honest" report, telling him what had transpired.

Voltaire seemed slightly amused.

His lack of anger caused her to believe she would be welcome in his workroom, and she pressed him for an invitation to visit him there the following day.

His attitude changed instantly, and he informed her, with unaccustomed brusqueness, that he would and could consent to no such arrangement. He permitted no one to visit him when he was writing, and even Mme. du Châtelet was not allowed to set foot in his workroom at such times.

Mme. de Graffigny could draw only one conclusion. He had fallen so completely under the spell of a woman who was obviously a sorceress rather than a nymph that he merely echoed her thinking and her desires. If left to his own devices, the guest was convinced, he would be delighted to receive her, but he was helpless, unable to do as he pleased in this isolated place, where he was being held captive without his knowledge.

Thereafter Mme. de Graffigny's attitude changed sharply, and the rose-colored lorgnette through which she had been peering was smashed. She now began to find fault with everything that Émilie said and did, and Voltaire came in for his share of criticism, too. Although it must be granted that she saw the couple from the viewpoint of a new, unfavorable bias, some of her observations became far more realistic. She was prejudiced, to be sure, and she exaggerated. Also, it must be remembered that she had known no normal married life of her own, and therefore had no understanding of the ordinary annoyances, tensions, and disturbances that strain even the most blissful of domestic ties. At the same time, however, she was able to give Pan-pan a new perspective on daily life at Cirey.

Émilie, she discovered, had an exceptionally volatile temperament. When Voltaire spoke to her caustically, she sulked, making what Mme. de Graffigny thought was a flimsy excuse when the hostess explained that, rather than reply in kind and cause an upheaval that might disrupt his work schedule, she preferred to take refuge in silence. When others defied, disobeyed, or otherwise displeased her, however, the mistress of Cirey was not reluctant to unleash her frightful temper, and she stormed, raved, and ranted until the guest grew weary of hearing her voice.

Another of Émilie's annoying traits was that of catering to M. de Voltaire at the expense of common courtesy to others.

157

When he felt hungry, the supper hour was moved forward, and when he was otherwise occupied the evening meal was delayed, sometimes interminably. The entire château was searched for a book he had misplaced, and never had Mme. de Graffigny seen such a commotion, such an uproar.

What really disgusted Mme. de Graffigny was Mme. du Châtelet's habit of making a fuss over M. de Voltaire. She catered to him as though he were an idiot or an invalid, and when he suffered from an upset stomach, she behaved as though nothing else on earth was important. One day, for example, he received some letters in the mail from Paris that annoyed him. Soon thereafter he began to suffer "stomach convulsions," and Mme. du Châtelet sent the entire household staff flying for hot poultices, medicines, blankets, and pillows. Finally she herself brewed him a mug of a herb tea that supposedly contained healing properties, and she held the hot mug herself while he sipped from it. Such fatuousness was unbearable.

M. de Voltaire was so bemused by this fawning attitude that he replied to it in kind. Although it was obvious that he resented the constant interference of his mistress, he pretended to be grateful for her interest in his affairs. He even returned the compliment when it was obvious that her business privately bored him. For example, Mme. du Châtelet insisted on reading aloud to him, in the presence of supper guests, an essay she had just composed on a scientific subject. Mme. de Graffigny could not understand a word, and she felt certain M. de Voltaire thought it was gibberish, too. In fact, she saw him yawning several times during the reading.

But he pretended to overcome his fatigue, and launched into a long discussion of the piece with her. The haughty baggage was incapable of accepting the advice of this great man, however, and had the temerity to dispute several points at length with him. Naturally the discussion became heated, and the guest could not blame Genius for his anger. What made the scene revolting was that, at the end, he conceded—or, in Mme.

de Graffigny's opinion, pretended to concede—that Mme. du Châtelet was right, and he even humbled himself by congratulating her on the astuteness of her intellect.

Most of the quarrels recorded by Mme. de Graffigny, and she recorded many, were trivial domestic arguments, no worse and no more significant than countless similar disturbances of the peace that have taken place in homes without number since man and woman started living under the same roof. The dispute over Voltaire's coat, which only Mme. de Graffigny regarded as meaningful, was typical.

Voltaire appeared in one of the sitting rooms for afternoon tea, an English custom he sometimes enjoyed, and Mme. du Châtelet told him his coat didn't match the rest of his attire. She requested him to change it, but he refused; she pressed, and he made excuses. He was already suffering from a head cold, he said, and didn't want to make it worse.

Émilie was not impressed and replied that she didn't see how the changing of his coat would affect his cold.

Voltaire sighed and announced that, for the sake of restoring domestic tranquility, he would send his valet for another coat. Then, rather abruptly, he left the room.

The tea arrived, but Voltaire did not return, and Émilie sent a servant to fetch him.

He replied with a message to the effect that he was not feeling well and preferred to remain in his room.

Émilie drank her tea alone and retired to her own quarters. Shortly thereafter she was notified that a visitor had arrived, so she spent a few minutes primping and then went downstairs.

There she found Voltaire, miraculously recovered from his "illness," gaily chatting with the visitor. His manner changed the moment Émilie entered the room, however, and he glowered at her, fell silent, and refused to take further part in the conversation.

Émilie paid no attention to his sulkiness, and complimented

him extravagantly on the appearance of his handsome new coat.

Voltaire appeared lost in thought and pretended he didn't hear her.

But she persisted, and before long he began to weaken. He made an occasional, grudging remark as he rejoined the conversation, and eventually he made a brief, cryptic remark that only Émilie understood. Both laughed merrily, the quarrel was forgotten, and soon the visitor was being entertained with a reading of Voltaire's play, *Mérope*.

On another occasion, when a number of guests were present at a dinner, a sudden argument caused embarrassment for the whole company. Voltaire accepted a glass of Rhone wine, and Émilie reminded him that he always found that type of wine indigestible.

He shrugged, remarking that he had lived for a great many years and had consumed considerable quantities of wine. Therefore he knew what he could tolerate and what might upset his delicate stomach.

Émilie retorted that whenever he took that attitude he caused trouble for himself.

Voltaire informed her, with icy disdain, that he was under no obligation to obey her commands and would do whatever he wished. Then, deliberately defying her, he took a swallow of the wine.

Émilie informed him that his behavior was childish, and, before anyone could stop her, she leaped from her chair, hurried to his place, and snatched his glass from him.

He tried in vain to regain possession of it.

She emptied the glass into a bowl of Italian greens, the flavor of which, according to Mme. de Graffigny, was improved.

Voltaire forgot himself and began to abuse her, attacking her with the sardonic wit that had won him renown.

Émilie retaliated in kind, and even Mme. de Graffigny was impressed, admitting she held her own.

Voltaire became exasperated and shouted, "Stop staring at me with those haggard, squinting eyes."

Several of the ladies gasped, the gentlemen squirmed in their seats, and Voltaire realized he had gone too far. No sooner had he uttered the words, Mme. de Graffigny reported, than he regretted them.

Émilie seemingly refused to allow herself to be dragged down to his level. She looked through him without seeing him, smiled sweetly at the company, and began to praise something written in the recent past by Rousseau.

The first house rule at Cirey was very strict: it was best not to mention the name of Rousseau, whose work Voltaire already loathed, although they did not feud until many years later. If a reference to him proved unavoidable, it was essential that he and all his literary efforts be damned. His laws of nature and the "natural order" were anathema to the cynical Voltaire. Everyone at the table knew of the rule, and the guests froze, undoubtedly wishing themselves elsewhere.

Voltaire said nothing, but he grew very pale, indicating that the thrust had been felt.

Émilie apparently believed anything she might add would be superfluous, so she, too, fell silent.

There was no sound in the dining room but the clinking of silverware. Some of the guests, desperately aware of the need to fill the void, made sporadic attempts to chat about inconsequentials, but all these efforts failed. The hostess ate mechanically, gazing into space, and Voltaire, although he consumed very little, seemed to be concentrating on his food.

Suddenly the warring couple appeared to communicate without utilizing speech or gestures. Even Mme. de Graffigny, who did not believe in the occult and took pride in her reliance on reason, claimed she felt strange "waves" traveling back and forth from the opposite ends of the table.

Whatever may have been happening, Émilie and Voltaire found some way to declare a truce, decide the fight had been absurd, and agree to drop the matter. They began to speak more or less simultaneously, both of them in the best of good humor, and exchanged several light remarks, with neither mentioning the dispute. Then Voltaire told a very amusing story, and Émilie launched into a brilliant discourse on new styles in architecture. She had never mentioned the subject in Mme. de Graffigny's presence, but she soon proved to be an expert, and made many learned references to the principles of architecture and the fads in building that had predominated in Europe, the Orient, and the civilized portions of the New World for centuries.

The unsettled guests were still trying to regain their equilibrium, but Émilie and Voltaire acted as though nothing untoward had happened, discussing many subjects, engaging in priceless repartee, yet taking care not to hurt each other's feelings.

Mme. de Graffigny had to admit, in spite of her prejudices, that she had never known a more talented couple. Voltaire could play on an audience as a musician played on a violin, and he could make an audience laugh or weep at his pleasure. Émilie, the guest conceded, was even more versatile. One night she sang the entire score of an opera, accompanying herself on the harpsichord, and what made the performance impressive was the professional, lyric quality of her voice. Had she been born into another class she would have become one of the leading personalities of the Paris theatrical world. She could read any role with great conviction, and her own character became submerged in the part she was playing. She, too, could tell stories effectively and could evoke responses of gaiety.

One of Émilie's brothers, the Abbé de Breteuil, the Grand Vicar of Sens, arrived at Cirey for a visit over the Christmas holidays, and the atmosphere became livelier. The Abbé shared his sister's love of luxury, her high spirits, and her appreciation of good food and wine, as well as her dedication to intellectual pursuits. Although he and Voltaire had not been well acquainted, they quickly discovered they were kindred spirits, and the author honored the new guest by reading portions of his excruciatingly cruel, amusing, and dangerous *Pucelle* after dinner one evening.

Émilie rearranged her schedule for the first time in years, and actually gave up some of her work time in order to spend more of each day in his company. Then Voltaire unbent, too, cutting his own work time in half each day. He and Émilie dressed in their finest clothes, dazzling the entire company, and never had the mistress of Cirey been more beautiful. *"When she wishes,"* Mme. de Graffigny wrote Pan-pan, *"she can be lovelier than any other woman in France."*

A performance of one or another of Voltaire's plays was given nightly in the little theater, and everyone in the neighborhood who was literate was directed to participate. No excuses were tolerated, and none were offered. Even Mme. du Châtelet's twelve-year-old daughter, Gabrielle-Pauline, came home from school, ostensibly to see her uncle, but actually, according to Mme. de Graffigny, to act in the plays. The girl was almost as talented as her mother and could recite with ease in English, Latin, or Greek, but she lacked Mme. du Châtelet's wild abandon on the stage.

When the Abbé left at the end of a week's visit, Émilie and Voltaire returned to work with a vengeance, determined to make up for lost time. Her energy and zeal were awe-inspiring; she slept little, ate breakfast and dinner at her desk, and, except for the supper hour and a brief respite for coffee and conversation late in the morning, took no relaxation. Voltaire, who required more sleep, drove himself just as hard, and did not arrive at the table for supper until the meal was half-finished. Displaying little appetite, he hurried back to his workroom as soon as he was done, and was so preoccupied that he made few attempts to take part in general conversation.

Mme. de Graffigny was left largely to her own devices, and utilized her time in her own way. She had been so busy during the Abbé's visit that she had been unable to write Pan-pan more than two or three letters each day, but now she had her chance to fill in all the details of that crowded week.

The foolish woman was intrigued by the notorious *La Pucelle*, potentially the most explosive manuscript of the century, a document whose publication could send the author to prison for life, a poem the secret police had been trying in vain, for years, to pin down. Mme. de Graffigny's memory was very sharp, and she spent the better part of a day committing to paper all the verses of the *Pucelle* she could recall. Happy in her ignorance, she sent the material to Devaux, delighted because she could contribute to his enjoyment of the scandalous, forbidden rhymes.

It occurred to her, vaguely, that something might be amiss when Devaux's daily letter to her failed to arrive on time. Sometimes several days passed before she received a packet of letters from him. Studying them, she thought the seals had been broken and felt disturbed. But the significance of the mystery did not dawn on her.

One night, when Mme. de Graffigny was sitting in her room, Voltaire burst in without ceremony, crying, "I am lost! My life is in your hands!"

The bewildered woman gaped at him and muttered something.

"What do I mean?" he shouted. "Why, that one hundred copies of some verses of the *Pucelle* have been circulated. I must leave at once, and I am off. I shall flee to Holland—to the end of the world—I hardly know where."

Mme. de Graffigny began to realize the enormity of what she had done.

The excited Voltaire begged her to write Devaux and ask him to use his influence in withdrawing the verses from circulation. Suddenly he lost his temper and accused her outright of copying verses and sending them to her dear friend.

In vain the poor woman tried to tell him that she had remembered some lines of the poem and had written them to Devaux.

Then Émilie burst into the room, and launched into an even more violent tirade. Mme. de Graffigny, she insisted, had sneaked into her suite stolen the original of *La Pucelle* and copied long sections of it for the benefit of the young poet.

Again and again the guest, now reduced to tears, tried to explain what had really happened.

But Émilie produced "proof," a brief letter from Devaux to Mme. de Graffigny in which he said he found a canto of the *Pucelle* charming. So furious she scarcely made sense, Émilie revealed that the letter had arrived with the seal broken, and that her own curiosity had impelled her to read it.

Voltaire was forced to intervene and restrain his mistress before she physically assaulted the weeping, frightened guest.

The emotionally charged scene did not end until five o'clock in the morning. By that time Voltaire understood the truth, and although it was disconcerting to realize that Devaux had been the recipient of even a few fragments of *La Pucelle*, he knew it was his own fault for giving in to the temptation to read portions of the poem aloud.

The unyielding, still furious Émilie remained convinced that the guest had stolen and copied the poem for the financial benefit of her young friend.

Had it been possible for Mme. de Graffigny to go elsewhere, she would have left Cirey immediately. But a small sum she was expecting would not arrive for several weeks, and until then she was penniless. She did not dare impose on other friends whose homes she hoped to visit in the future, so she was compelled to remain at Cirey, no matter how humiliating and miserable the circumstances.

The situation was even worse than she had realized, as she knew when she grew calmer. From the time of her arrival at the château she had seen Émilie personally accept the mail from the postman each day, and herself had seen the hostess open much of Voltaire's correspondence. If she chose to read his incoming letters and he did not protest, that was their business. But it occurred to the badly upset guest that Devaux's letters to her had not been opened by the secret police; she felt certain that Émilie had been breaking the seals and reading them before passing them on to her. It became evident to her that Émilie had read Pan-pan's comment about the canto of *Pucelle*, and had leaped to her own false conclusions.

This belief hardened into a conviction when Voltaire quietly stayed on at the estate, making no attempt to flee to Holland or anywhere else. He was very quiet in the days that followed, exerting little of his celebrated charm, but he made no attempt to leave or, for that matter, change any of his routines.

Meantime Émilie made no secret of her intense dislike for Mme. de Graffigny. Regardless of whether she had opened Devaux's letter herself or had merely read it after it had arrived unsealed, she considered the guest guilty of perfidious disloyalty to Voltaire. So intense was her own love that she demanded the same unswerving devotion to him from others, and anyone who failed to live up to her standards was unworthy of her friendship or his. She glared at Mme. de Graffigny whenever they met, did not acknowledge her presence at the supper table, and in scores of little, feminine ways made the guest feel she was no longer welcome.

Voltaire found the atmosphere uncomfortable, and his common sense impelled him to clarify the situation if he could. He persuaded Émilie that they had been mistaken in their hasty assumption of the guest's guilt, and repeatedly urged her to apologize. Émilie finally complied with his request, but her apology was flat, almost curt, and totally lacking in sincerity. Thereafter she made vague references to the possibility of inviting Devaux to Cirey, an idea seconded by Voltaire with equal vagueness, but neither actually wrote to him.

Meanwhile other guests were coming and going. Among them was Maupertuis, who stayed for five days, and Mme. de Graffigny, who no longer had her heart in the affairs of Cirey, was unable to understand a word of the high-flown scientific discussions and esoteric philosophical debates she heard on the night of his arrival. Thereafter, for the rest of the scientist-explorer's stay, she had her supper served to her in her own room.

Mme. de Graffigny could scarcely wait until she was able to leave the estate, and rejoiced when she received a letter from the Duchesse de Richelieu, asking her to come to Paris. The dreadful exile was at an end. Émilie expressed few regrets when she left, and Voltaire was polite but restrained.

The former guest enjoyed the last word, and no sooner had she departed from Cirey than she wrote letters to everyone she knew. M. de Voltaire, she declared, was insanely jealous of every other French author who had attained even a limited success. And Mme. du Châtelet was even more insanely jealous of M. de Voltaire. Their household was an unsavory, unpleasant, corrupt place, where licentiousness was demanded of everyone, and a virtuous woman could feel only joy and relief once she was free of the horrid atmosphere.

XII

The hysteria shown by Émilie and Voltaire when they accused Mme. de Graffigny of treacherous disloyalty can be understood only when seen in relation to a far more important matter that caused a real crisis in the lives of the couple. The Abbé Pierre-François Desfontaines, whom Voltaire had befriended some years earlier, had turned against the author, and late in 1738, soon after Mme. de Graffigny arrived at Cirey, he published a book, the *Voltairomanie*, that listed and ridiculed every error, typographical and otherwise, that had ever appeared in any work by Voltaire.

Émilie and her lover had received separate copies of the little book, and, like characters in a French farce, each had spent a week concealing any knowledge of the volume's existence from the other, meanwhile writing furious letters of denunciation to friends in Paris. Desfontaines's assault was so scurrilous that he could not be ignored, and the problem was uppermost in the minds of Voltaire and Émilie during the latter part of Mme. de Graffigny's visit. It is small wonder, then, that they magnified her indiscreet but basically innocent blunder out of all proportion to its significance.

Voltaire instinctively wanted to retaliate in kind against the Abbé, but Émilie believed that a mere duel of words would not suffice. Anyone in France familiar with the written word knew that Desfontaines's wit and acidity were no match for the penetrating barbs that Voltaire was capable of hurling. It was her opinion that a clean-cut legal victory was necessary to restore her lover's damaged dignity, and she urged him to bring suit against the Abbé.

She was supported by d'Argental and other friends, and Voltaire, after mulling the question, agreed. He sued Desfontaines for criminal libel, and the issue was joined. Émilie threw herself into the battle with all of the tremendous energy and enthusiasm at her command, and, like Voltaire, she put aside all her other activities. Never had she worked as hard as she did during the winter and early spring of 1739. While Voltaire devoted himself to extensive correspondence with his attorneys, with friends, and with anyone he thought might be able to influence the court, Émilie did the essential spadework in preparing his case. She made a word-by-word, line-by-line study of the Abbé's book, and, citing precise references from Voltaire's works, she refuted every hint, every innuendo, every cutting remark that Desfontaines had made.

The case came to trial in mid-April, and Voltaire remained at Cirey to await the verdict, it having been deemed unnecessary for him to appear in court. The wait was agonizing, and Émilie and Voltaire could neither eat or sleep. Seeing the problem from the vantage point of the centuries, it is easy to say that they exaggerated the gravity of their situation. As they viewed it, however, the author's entire future was at stake, and even Prince Frederick of Prussia was asked by Émilie to contribute a deposition that could be submitted to the court by the prosecution. That the reluctant Frederick complied, breaking the precedent that prevented royalty from participating in the legal disputes of those beneath them, was a tribute, at least in part, to Émilie's persuasiveness.

The verdict was a total victory for Voltaire. Abbé Desfontaines was found guilty and was given the choice of making a detailed, complete public retraction, or, if he preferred to stand by his guns, go to prison. He did not hesitate, and immediately issued a preliminary statement, which he followed with a pamphlet that made a series of point by point retractions.

Émilie and Voltaire were too tired to rejoice. The battle had exhausted them emotionally, and the author, whose nervous tensions were far greater than those of most people, was suffering from the worst health he had known for years. His stomach was causing him problems, severe cramps in his legs and hands crippled him, and he found it difficult to sleep.

A change of scenery was essential, Émilie decided. They had spent four years at Cirey, and for two years had rarely left the grounds, so the time had come to put aside daily work routines and reenter—at least for a time—the busy world they had both forsaken but still loved.

Her thoughts first turned to Paris, as did Voltaire's, and they agreed it would be pleasant to own a home of their own there. They could not live together at the Hôtel du Châtelet, so the property they purchased would necessarily be Voltaire's. It would be difficult for Émilie to dwell there openly, to be sure, but they could circumvent conventions to an extent. On a strictly unofficial basis she would act as his hostess, in effect supervising the household, precisely as she did at Cirey, and although she would ostensibly make the Hôtel du Châtelet her home, it would be no one's business but their own if she elected to eat her meals and spend her nights at the new dwelling.

The idea of buying a house for Voltaire had occurred to her long before the case against Abbé Desfontaines had been settled, and she had let it be known through friends that they were in the market for a place. A superb mansion on the Île Saint-Louis, known as the Palais Lambert, was available, and Émilie immediately opened negotiations for it. She and Voltaire knew the place well, both of them having been guests there on a number of occasions, and they were delighted they had the chance to purchase it.

The house—calling it a palace was giving it a grandeur it

didn't quite possess—had cost one million livres to build and was in excellent condition. It was for sale at the ridiculously low price of two hundred thousand livres, which, although a large sum in itself, still represented a bargain. The value had declined because the neighborhood had lost its appeal to the aristocracy, and prices in the entire district had dropped appreciably.

But the couple did not care. As Voltaire was quick to point out, their only guests would be philosophers, scientists, classical scholars, and authors, "the scum of the Paris gutters." They bought the house, which was already furnished, and needed only to move in. Their letters to friends spoke in glowing terms of the pleasure they felt at the prospect of returning to Paris.

Instead, leaving Cirey in May, 1739, they went to Brussels on what proved to be a journey through the Low Countries. The reason for the abrupt change in plains was simple: a family lawsuit over an estate in the Netherlands, which would go to the Marquis if they won it, had been dragging for a long time. The Marquis had been supervising the case, but he had no head for the law or matters of finance, and Émilie decided to take the helm herself. Voltaire, who had enjoyed the benefits of her assistance in his case against Desfontaines, felt it was only right that he return the gesture. Certainly his prestige was so great in the Low Countries that his mere presence would be of great benefit to Émilie.

It may be that another factor influenced the couple, too. They had been living together openly for so long that the prospect of being forced to resort to certain measures of subterfuge may not have appealed to them. By going together to Brussels they could, for all practical purposes, travel as husband and wife. In any event, that is what they did.

What's more, they traveled in great style, showing the flair that was supposed to be the exclusive prerogative of royalty. They made the journey in two of the Châtelet coaches, each pulled by a matched team. Émilie and Voltaire went in the first carriage, and with them traveled a young mathematician named Koenig. A protégé of Maupertuis, Koenig had been hired to give Émilie instruction in some of the more advanced, complex phases of algebra that were beyond her present understanding.

It was inconceivable to her, as it was to Voltaire, that they would make any journey for the sake of pleasure alone, and a change of scenery did not mean that either would stop working. Émilie planned to take three hours of instruction from Koenig each day, then spend another three hours working on algebraic equations by herself, and no matter how frantically busy she and Voltaire became at various times during the sojourn, she never fell behind in the schedule.

Riding in the second carriage were the servants. Among them were Émilie's two maids and her seamstress; she did not take her hairdresser, having decided that her simple hair styles did not warrant the expense of paying for a servant who would perform no other function. Instead she would use the services of hairdressers on the household staffs of friends they would see and visit. Voltaire's needs were less complicated; he required only his valet and the young secretary who would take care of the tiresome details of travel. The coachmen, to be sure, were members of the permanent staff and would be on duty every day in Brussels and elsewhere. All, with the exception of the secretary, wore uniforms that Émilie and Voltaire had designed together.

The journey was leisurely, and for a few days the couple enjoyed a real holiday. Often they took their ease at noon and enjoyed a long picnic on the grounds of an estate belonging to a friend. And at every town they received the welcome that was their due as celebrities. In the garrison town of Valenciennes there was so much planned in their honor they were forced to linger for several days. The local theatrical company performed a comedy by Voltaire one evening, and another by Molière on the last night of their stay. A ball was given for them, and on another evening they were the principal guests at a banquet, which was followed by a ballet performance.

The officers of the garrison, including the commandant and his senior colonels, danced attendance on them, too, but for an entirely different reason. Émilie, after all, was the wife of one of the most prominent and powerful generals in the French army, and no officer of high rank at the garrison would have dared to risk offending the Marquis by snubbing her. Nothing in the attitude of either Émilie or Voltaire, whose correspondence indicates they were delighted by the attention they received, indicates they were in the least embarrassed by the homage paid to them solely because they were the wife and good friend, respectively, of the Marquis du Châtelet.

On the last day of May they arrived at the disputed estate in Belgium, at that time known as the Austrian Netherlands, which was the core of the lawsuit. It was a property belonging to the Marquis du Châtelet's ancestors, and he was trying to retain possession of it by fending off the claims of distant relatives. Known as Beringhen, it was located near Liège, on the road to Juliers, and although the family had no use for it, Voltaire was trying to persuade Prince Frederick to buy it, suggesting it might make a convenient and useful place for them to meet.

The luxury-loving couple loathed the estate, and found both of the manor houses located on it lacking every convenience. The bathrooms were primitive, the buildings ugly, the furniture uncomfortable, the view drab. The countryside was desolate, and Émilie complained in a letter to the Duchesse de Richelieu that even the trees were warped and twisted. A description Voltaire sent to d'Argental was even less inviting:

"The people who reside in this unholy land have seen their country ravaged by so many wars that they have forgotten the refinements of civilization. Mme. du Châtelet believes they never became acquainted with civilizing influences, and her theory may be right.

173

*"It is difficult in the extreme not to lower one's own stand-
ards of refinement to those that surround one, and therein lies
the danger. If Mme. du Châtelet stays long in this dismal country she will be in danger of being called the Queen of the
Savages.*

*"Tomorrow we are going to her house at the other end of the
estate, the superb château of Ham, where we are not at all sure
to find beds, windows, or doors. They say that thieves abound
here, but in that case they must be thieves who are doing
penance. No one is worth robbing except ourselves.*

*"We have seen nothing to commend this place other than the
fine avenue of trees that extends from the entrance to the property to the front of the château of Beringhen. Alas! so bleak
is the country and so dismal the spirit hereabouts that Mme.
du Châtelet's dogs refused to accept the convenience of these
trees for the purpose that nature intended them."*

They stayed at the ancestral estate no longer than was necessary to make a rough inventory of the property, and then went
on to Brussels, where they rented a large and comfortable house
on the Rue de la Gross-Tour. Voltaire was cheered by the
receipt of some gifts from Prince Frederick, including an amber
inkstand for Émilie, another for him, and a box of games, including some playing cards, for both of them. Émilie immediately wrote the donor a proper but unenthusiastic letter of
thanks.

As soon as the couple settled into the place, the old, familiar
work routines were restored. Voltaire was finishing his monu-
mental history of the reign of Louis XIV and had started work
on a new play, *Mahomet*. He also found time to ask Frederick
to intervene on behalf of Émilie at the Imperial Austrian court,
a favor that was granted, which meant that the lawsuit was
virtually won.

Émilie was equally busy. She was studying algebra, and, in
order to understand the intricate details of the suit, took a
crash course in law from two university professors. In her

"spare" time she began a translation of Sophocles's great play, *Oedipus Rex*, a translation that would become a classic in the French theater for more than a century. It has been suggested that Voltaire helped her with the translation, but the contention cannot be proved, and is dubious. Not only was he immersed in his own work, but he and Émilie invariably made it their business never to interfere in each other's work. This was one of the secrets of their continuing close relationship. Although it would have been natural enough for Émilie to request the advice of the great playwright while working on the French version of the tragedy that other classicists had been reluctant to translate, it would not have been in keeping with her character. Her pride was too great, her sense of intellectual independence too strong.

Life in Brussels was grim for literate cosmopolitans. Belgium had been a political and military football for centuries, and currently was a province of Austria, which had wrested it from Spain. The natives of the battered country had grown cynical, and no longer dreamed of political or cultural freedom, preferring instead to concentrate on international trade, which would make them wealthy.

Voltaire, who knew the city well, suffered no false illusions, and evaluated the atmosphere accordingly. *"There is not one man of letters in this benighted place,"* he wrote to a friend in Paris. *"There is no painter, no printer, no musician who can play an instrument without striking a sour note. Brussels is the home of ignorance and stupidity, of indifference and obedience without question to laws that undermine liberty. He who lives here too long will find his imagination stifled."*

There was small danger that he and Émilie would suffer from a curtailment of the imagination. When they decided to give a party to repay those who had entertained them, Voltaire insisted on giving the party in Émilie's honor and sent invitations asking people to come to the house on the Rue de la Gross-Tour to meet "the envoy from Utopia." But the compli-

175

ment fell flat because none of the guests had ever heard of Utopia, much less of Sir Thomas More, the English philosopher-statesman who had created the perfect land in one of the most justly famous books written since the beginning of the Renaissance.

The Duc d'Aremberg, one of the highest-ranking nobles in Belgium, played host to the celebrated couple at his vast estate at Enghien for several days, and the visit was a mixed success. The Austrian and Hungarian wines were splendid, and the gardens, which were in full bloom, were spectacularly beautiful. But Voltaire, who considered the sport of hunting a cruel offense against nature, refused to accompany the Duke on a shoot. And he summed up the atmosphere when he wrote, *"There are no books in this place except those that Mme. du Châtelet and I brought here ourselves."*

Émilie preferred no social life whatever to association with dolts, so she insisted they refuse most of the invitations they received. Time began to hang on her hands, so she found a new relaxation by hiring a tutor who would teach her Flemish. Her grasp of languages was so good that, by the end of a month, she could read the language fluently and understand virtually anything that was said to her. It annoyed her, however, that she could not rid herself of a distinctive French accent when speaking Flemish, a liability that did not appear when she spoke English, German, or one of the classical tongues.

Late in August the couple paid a brief visit to The Hague, where Voltaire had business with his Dutch printers, and then returned to Brussels in time for Émilie to win the Châtelet lawsuit. Letters from Paris indicated that the coming social season there would be the most active in many years; the eldest daughter of Louis XV was being married to a scion of Spanish royalty, and the King had finally lived up to the traditions of his predecessors on the throne by taking an official mistress, Mme. de Mailly. The travelers found the lure irresistible, and early September found them in Paris.

Voltaire had rented his new house for an exorbitant sum, so he took his usual, inexpensive lodgings for himself, and Émilie, rather than open the Hôtel du Châtelet for a few weeks, stayed at the palace of her friends, the Duc and Duchesse de Richelieu, who raised no eyebrows if she spent a night elsewhere than under their roof.

Rarely in the history of Paris had so many balls and fêtes, galas and routes, banquets and dinners, supper parties and theater parties and opera parties been crowded into a short span of time. Never had competition for prominent guests been so keen, and every celebrity-conscious host or hostess who wanted his party assured of immediate success sought the company of the renowned and dazzling, notorious and controversial couple who were visiting the city. Émilie and Voltaire plunged into the most hectic life they had ever known.

Émilie loved every moment of the visit. She found Versailles gayer and less inhibited than ever before, and she relished the frivolous life she lived in the city. She ate too much rich food and drank too many fine wines, she danced until dawn one night and played cards until sunrise the next. Her clothes were so daring that other beauties hurried back to their dressmakers for near-copies of her gowns, and she flirted, harmlessly but with amusement, with every interesting man in town.

Only a woman endowed with her unique energies could have maintained the dizzy pace, which would have been exhausting had she done nothing but live the life of a social butterfly. Parties, however, comprised only a minor part of her daily routine. After sleeping for two or three hours at sunrise she cleared her head by working out complicated mathematical problems before breakfast. She spent hours with Maupertuis and her other friends in the world of science, and she began the serious study of the philosophy and scientific theories of Leibnitz, which would lead, less than a year later, to the publication of one of her most profound books.

Voltaire, who had recovered his health, found it impossible

to keep pace with her. He was gallant and made the effort, but soon he began to complain that Émilie was driving him to his grave. At the end of a month he realized he would never again be able to spend more than very limited periods in the city, and wrote a letter to his Cirey friends and neighbors, M. and Mme. de Champbonin, that was destined to become one of the most famous documents he ever penned:

"Paris is an abyss where one loses repose and the contemplation of one's soul, without which life is only a troublesome tumult. I no longer live. I am dragged in spite of myself into the stream. I go, I come. I sup at the end of the town, to sup the next night at the other end.

"From the society of three or four intimate friends it is necessary to fly to the opera, to the comedy, to see curiosities, to be a stranger, to embrace a hundred people a day, to make and receive a hundred protestations, not one instant to oneself, no time to write, to think, or to sleep.

"I am like the ancient who died, crushed by the flowers they threw at him."

Voltaire was as relieved, secretly, as Émilie was dismayed when they received word that the Châtelet relatives who had lost the lawsuit in the Austrian Netherlands had successfully won a petition reopening the case. It was necessary to return to Brussels at once, and the couple set out early in November, after spending two months in Paris. They paused for a week at Cirey, and both found it difficult to tear themselves away from the place they loved. As Voltaire said after their return to Brussels, they had *"abandoned the most agreeable retirement in Europe to bawl in the labyrinth of Flemish chicanery."*

In spite of his protests, the daily life he and Émilie led in Brussels was remarkably similar to their existence at Cirey. They worked all day with furious diligence, then relaxed at elegant suppers, either alone or in the company of a few carefully chosen guests. They argued frequently that winter because of Émilie's preoccupation with Leibnitz, and neither could understand the principle on which the other based a stand.

Émilie did not necessarily agree with the scientific theories or the philosophy of Leibnitz, but felt that her own opinions were unimportant in a book that would try to crystallize his views for a French reading public. Leibnitz was a major contributor to the scientific and philosophical currents of Western thought, exerting a particularly strong influence in the German states, and therefore deserved as wide an understanding audience in France as could be achieved. No new law of physics, no new philosophical concept ever sprang into being by itself out of barren soil; there was no such thing as intellectual parthenogenesis. Therefore every important and influential idea, regardless of one's personal opinion of it, deserved to be studied.

Voltaire, on the other hand, believed Émilie was guilty of muddled thinking. It was self-evident that the world of physics was grounded on the concepts initiated and advanced by Newton, whose cause she, too, had espoused, and it was a waste of time to study anything that contradicted or disagreed with Newton. It was particularly stupid to fritter away one's substance on what he called speculative metaphysics. One might wish to find amusement in reading the works of some philosophers, no matter how inaccurate they might be, but there was no excuse for reading Leibnitz. He was a German, and therefore was guilty of being heavy-handed, humorless, and didactic.

To others, if not to Émilie herself, Voltaire praised her new *Institutions de Physique.* She not only had mastered the most intricate of the propositions that Leibnitz propounded, but explained them with greater clarity, brilliance, and precision than Leibnitz himself had ever shown.

In April, 1740, the book was completed, and Émilie sent a copy of the manuscript to Frederick, whose father was dying and who would, within a month, become the ruler of Prussia. Whether she made the gesture as a diplomatic offering to placate him because of Voltaire's continuing refusal to visit

Prussia, or whether she was believing her own propaganda that she would be included in the invitation once Frederick ascended the throne, is unknown.

Replying in a scholarly vein, Frederick said he thought the book was delightful, which was saying much for a work on metaphysics; Émilie's wit gave new meaning to much that Leibnitz had propounded. Her interpretation was superb, and he admired her French style, wishing that he, too, could achieve her level of fluidity and grace in the book he was currently writing. He expressed only one critical thought: Leibnitz, like so many Germans, methodically repeated himself, sometimes approaching the same idea from several different angles, perhaps, but making the same essential points, and he believed Émilie had been trapped into following the philosopher's example. So, it seemed to Frederick, the book might benefit if some portions of it were compressed.

The book was published in the summer of 1740, and created tremendous excitement in French intellectual circles. Even Émilie's enemies in the aristocracy, who were incapable of understanding a word she had written, were deeply impressed. These noble ladies and gentlemen had been consistent in decrying and denigrating her talents for years, claiming she was incapable of doing any substantial work herself, and that she was totally dependent on Voltaire. Now, however, she had written a book on a subject which her lover openly disavowed, and it was apparent to even the most stubborn of her foes that she, alone and unaided, was responsible for the *Institutions de Physique*. Unwilling and unable to admit that she was superior to them, they were inclined to regard her as something of a freak.

Voltaire replied succinctly to their criticisms, silencing them. *"Only fools and poltroons,"* he said, *"ridicule that which they cannot understand."*

Scientists and academicians were critical, too, but dealt with the three-volume work on its own high level, and they found fault with the attitude of the author rather than the content of her study. "Lady Newton," as she had been dubbed, was regarded as a traitor to the disciples of Isaac Newton, and only a handful of intellectuals realized that Émilie was not necessarily expressing her own views or predilictions, but felt that the Leibnitz school should have an exhaustive hearing in France.

The official hierarchy of the Academy of Science entered into a long correspondence with her, challenging the basis of various theories advanced by Leibnitz. Émilie replied at length, with spirit, and the letters that flew back and forth became so technical that only a few people in all Europe had the educational background to understand them.

Voltaire entered the fray on the side of his mistress. Even though he had disapproved of the project, he refused to let her stand on the ramparts alone, and he defended her ably, adding the weight of his wit as well as his technical knowledge to the ammunition hurled at the membership of the Academy of Science.

The dispute was legitimate, of course, and, in spite of the disagreement, enhanced Émilie's reputation. She may have been the only woman in France who knew or cared what such giants as Newton and Leibnitz were saying. Regardless of the specific opinion of her work formed by scientists in France and elsewhere, physicists and philosophers recognized her effort as a major achievement, worthy of their respect and admiration.

The *Institutions* solidified Émilie's growing reputation, and she won a permanent place in the upper ranks of the intellectuals of the era, a remarkable achievement for someone who belonged to the top crust of the aristocracy. It was even more astonishing that a woman should accomplish so much. She was the only member of her sex anywhere in Europe who was regarded as the equal of men who were advancing the frontiers of human thought.

In the largest sense, Émilie came of age with the publication of the *Institutions*. Until then, although there were many who admired her attainments, she was generally regarded as something of a poseur. Now there could be no doubt regarding her achievements.

Émilie's success was not financial. The publication of the *Institutions* had cost more than two thousand gold louis, a huge sum, and in all probability the project had been financed by Voltaire. Over a period of several years the book earned back its expenses, so nothing was lost, but the enterprise did not show a profit. Émilie was not disappointed, however; she had written the *Institutions* to win prestige, and she succeeded beyond her expectations.

Her new standing caused no changes in her attitudes or way of life. She remained ultra-feminine, violently jealous of Voltaire, emotional in every facet of her personal life. She still loved extravagance, wore daring gowns, decorated herself with far more jewelry than was considered appropriate, and gambled again after a hiatus of some years, yet usually won.

She had matured intellectually, but she was still adolescent in many of her attitudes. That, however, was her charm. Now in her thirty-fifth year, she had reached an age at which most eighteenth-century women had passed their physical prime. Certainly they were regarded as middle-aged, but Émilie refused to acknowledge the passing of the years.

Several portraits of her that were painted during this time indicate that she had lost none of her beauty. And her contemporaries frequently commented on her fresh, clear skin, her sparkling eyes, and her truly inexhaustible energy. She had gained a little weight, it is true, but her figure had not become matronly, and her breasts, her waist, and the long line of her torso were still the envy of other women. She was enjoying life to the full, and her newly acquired stature spurred her toward the winning of more laurels.

XIII

On the last day of May, 1740, Frederick of Prussia acceded to the throne when his father, mourned by none, died after a long illness. Within a week King Frederick wrote to Voltaire. His *Anti-Macchiavel* was completed, and he wanted it published in Holland, anonymously, as a reigning monarch could not retain his dignity if it should be revealed that he was an author. The King also indicated, more strongly than ever, his desire to meet Voltaire.

It was possible to temporize when dealing with the Crown Prince of Prussia, but far more difficult to evade the ruler. Émilie and Voltaire had just returned to Cirey from Belgium, but the author departed again, hastily, and in spite of Émilie's protests. He went straight to The Hague, and there made the necessary arrangements for the publication of the *Anti-Macchiavel*.

Émilie should have been enjoying the fruits of her own labors. The *Institutions* had just been published, and she was engaging in stimulating correspondence with some of the finest minds in Europe. But she had no opportunity to relax, to relish her triumph. Frederick, she felt sure, was stepping up the pace of his correspondence with the absent Voltaire, urging the author to come to him alone, and she felt compelled to guard her own interests.

This she did, assiduously. Since she, too, was corresponding with the King, she could make it very plain to him that she intended to accompany her lover on a journey to Berlin or any other place that the meeting might take place. One letter in particular came very close to ripping away the polite façade of convention that was considered imperative in dealing with royalty. She wrote:

"At last the time is close at hand when we shall meet Your Majesty. M. de Voltaire and I have been anticipating this occasion for so many years that we cannot recall when we felt anything but the joint pleasure in store for us. That feeling is heightened now, and we are prepared to travel, together, to any place that Your Majesty deems convenient for our rendezvous with you."

Frederick knew she was important to Voltaire, but he deeply resented her persisting interference with his own plans. His father had denied him many things, but now that he sat on his throne in his own right, he was determined to do only what he wanted, when he wanted to, and in the way that best suited his own convenience. He respected Émilie's stubborn attitude, but quickly revealed that he, too, could be stubborn. In a private letter to Voltaire, sent to The Hague, he declared:

"To speak to you frankly about Mme. du Châtelet's journey, it is Voltaire, it is you, it is my friend that I desire to see, and the Divine Émilie with all her divinity is only the accessory of the Newtonian Apollo. If it must be that Émilie accompany Apollo, I consent; but if I could see you alone, I should prefer it. I should be too much dazzled, I could not bear so much splendor all at once; it would overpower me. I should need the veil of Moses to temper the united radiance of you two divinities."

Voltaire was caught in the middle, and his dilemma was embarrassing. A stubborn reigning monarch was being insistent in a demand to see him, which was flattering, but the conditions could ruin the author's private life. He had no doubt that his mistress would make his existence miserable for him if he accepted Frederick's strongly worded desires and left Émilie behind. Even a master wordsmith could not solve the problem, so Voltaire temporized.

Émilie, meanwhile, continued to exert pressure on Frederick, bombarding him with letters indicating her eagerness—and Voltaire's—to pay the King a visit.

Frederick capitulated, or seemed to give in, which was not the same thing. In the years that followed he used similar tactics in the establishment and development of his foreign, domestic, and military policies, allowing his foes to think they had won a victory and then snatching it from them. He sent a letter to Émilie and Voltaire, telling both of them he had rented a mansion in Antwerp, would go there incognito in order to dispense with the formalities that a visit to a foreign land otherwise would cause, and would greet them there together.

Émilie was elated; she had won a victory in a long-standing clash of wills with a king. But her joy was short-lived. Frederick left Berlin, and on September 5th he wrote to Voltaire from his country house at Wesel that he had halted there because of a violent attack of fever. He added, *"If the fever does not return I shall be at Antwerp on Tuesday (tomorrow week), where I flatter myself I shall have the pleasure of seeing you with the Marquise. It will be the most charming day of my life. I fear I may die of it, but at least one could not choose a more delightful kind of death."*

The chief seamstress at Cirey and her assistants worked overtime on several new gowns Émilie intended to take with her to Antwerp. The largest and most impressive of the Châtelet carriages was given a fresh coat of varnish, and the principal groom scoured the neighborhood for a larger and more handsome team of geldings than any in the stables.

Then, suddenly, the preparations were halted. Frederick wrote that his fever had indeed worsened, and it would be necessary for him to delay his departure for Antwerp.

185

Émilie, suspecting no trick, waited impatiently, assuming that the young monarch, who had never in his life known a serious illness, soon would be recovered.

Frederick wrote again, this time from a rented estate at Moyland, near Cleves. His case of the ague, he said, was proving to be *"more tenacious than a Jansenist."* The best of all possible cures, he said, would be a visit from Voltaire—alone. He could not permit himself to meet Émilie when his broken health would not tolerate such a meeting, and he was devastated because that meeting would have to be postponed until a later, unspecified occasion.

Now Émilie saw through the scheme, but it was too late. She and Voltaire had already committed themselves to the Antwerp meeting, and therefore could not claim that they were too busy or otherwise occupied. Frederick knew they had set aside the time. A refusal on Voltaire's part to make the journey alone would, under the circumstances, be the ultimate in poor taste. Such a display of ungracious behavior well might win the enmity of Frederick.

There was another factor that Émilie was forced to take into consideration, too. For a long time the flattered Voltaire had been eager to meet the intellectual young monarch who showered him with praises and openly regarded him as the most important living European. Not only would he be bitterly disappointed if he had to cancel his journey, but he would, in time, resent the mistress who had stood between him and Frederick. It wasn't every author whose friendship was so persistently sought by one of the most powerful men on earth.

Summoning whatever good grace she could muster, she wrote Frederick a charming note that undoubtedly hurt her pride. *"I do not know which afflicts me most,"* she said, *"to know that Your Majesty is ill, or to be disappointed in the hope I had of paying court to you."*

Still smiling, she released Voltaire and sent him on his way. Certainly he knew the anguish she was suffering, even

186

though she kept her jealousy under control, and promised her the visit would be a short one.

Émilie made her real feelings clear in a letter to Maupertuis, who had already arrived at Moyland for a visit with Frederick: *"I feel great regret in seeing M. de Voltaire leave, and the King ought to give me credit for this sacrifice. I hope he will soon send back to me the one with whom I intend to spend the rest of my life, and whom I have lent to him for a very few days only."*

She had assumed, as had Voltaire, that Frederick's illness was strictly imaginary, and the author was surprised to find, on his arrival at Moyland, that Frederick was actually in bed, suffering from a slight fever. Remarkably at ease, Voltaire took his pulse and prescribed the cure for fever that his Jesuit teachers had used, quinine.

The royal physicians had never used the exotic West Indian tree-bark product for fevers and objected, but the patient showed sublime faith in the amateur diagnostician and demanded quinine. By evening he was well enough to leave his bed for a gala supper, and thereafter he showed no signs of his ailment.

The visit was a roaring success. Voltaire read his new play, *Mahomet*, and Frederick led the loud applause. The monarch asked questions, the author answered them, frequently delivering long monologues that captured the undivided attention of his audience. Not even in England had Voltaire been treated with such respect, and rarely, if ever, had a reigning king deferred so completely to the opinions of a wordsmith, the son of a mere notary. The incurably vain Voltaire was in his glory, loving every minute of the experience.

Meanwhile Émilie brooded, fidgeted, and wrote him several admonitory letters each day. Thomas Carlyle, in his *Frederick the Great*, summed up her reaction: *"Madame watches over all his interests and liabilities and casualties great and small; leaping with her whole force into M. de Voltaire's scale of the*

balance, careless of antecedences and consequences alike; fly-
ing, with the spirit of an angry brood-hen, at the face of
mastiffs, in defence of any feather that is M. de Voltaire's."

Voltaire kept his promise to Émilie, and remained with Frederick for only a few days before returning to The Hague. But
there he stayed, notifying Émilie it was necessary for him to
supervise the publication of the *Anti-Macchiavel*. His friendship with the monarch made it essential that he remain there
until the book left the hands of the printer.

Émilie learned all she cared about the true situation from
Maupertuis and others. Voltaire had delivered a long lecture
on the principal themes of the works of Plato, and Frederick
had been his pupil. Voltaire had made a speech on personal
liberties and a more impassioned address on censorship. Frederick had taken notes, asked questions, and, in general, behaved
like an undergraduate being subjected to the influence of a
revered professor. Voltaire saw himself as a power behind a
major throne, as a man who would directly and significantly
influence the relations between nations, and was enchanted by
the view he took of his role.

Émilie suspected he would join King Frederick in Prussia
when he left The Hague. Knowing him, she realized the lure
of acting as the ambitious young ruler's mentor would prove
irresistible to him. So she had two choices: she could wait for
him at Cirey or Brussels, meekly accepting his decision to see
more of Frederick, or she could force the issue by insisting
that she join him when he went to Prussia. But she would be
supine if she did nothing and too aggressive if she pursued her
lover. So she followed an unexpected third course.

What had been done at one court could be accomplished at
another, and a court far more powerful and prestigious than
that of Frederick was much closer to home. King Louis XV,
although guided by his ever-present ministers, was taking control of France in his own right, and was the wealthiest, most
powerful ruler in the Western world. It was true, of course,

that he was capricious, undisciplined, and loved luxury too much, but, no matter how great his faults, he still ruled the most civilized, advanced, and sophisticated of nations.

Voltaire, Émilie reasoned, would forget Frederick if his own king made as big a fuss over him, so she decided to win the interest and support of Louis. Besides, it would give her something constructive to do rather than sit at Cirey or in the rented Brussels house, waiting for her lover to reappear.

The French court was in residence at Fontainebleau, so she went there, determined to wring a commitment of some kind from Louis and repair Voltaire's relations with Cardinal Fleury, who was still a power at the age of eighty-seven. The scientist-intellectual-playgirl demonstrated her remarkable versatility: Her finesse and cunning were those of the experienced diplomat.

Quietly dressed, she sought a meeting with the Cardinal and did not have long to wait. The meeting, according to the correspondence of gossips who had nothing better to do, lasted more than three hours, and no one knew what was discussed. But the results of the conference soon manifested themselves.

Cardinal Fleury sent an urgent letter to the author, who had not yet left The Hague. In the past, His Eminence said, the most talented of Frenchman had distressed the crown by flouting its authority, but now he had a chance to rehabilitate himself. The French envoy to Berlin was incompetent, and little was known of the policies Frederick was formulating. What were his domestic plans? What foreign alliances was he thinking of making? Since he was already building up the powerful army of his father, he must have military ventures in mind. Where did he plan to strike, and why? Any information Voltaire could glean in the capacity of undercover ambassador would be greatly appreciated by the French administration, which, if he succeeded, would be willing to forgive and forget his past transgressions.

Precisely as Émilie anticipated, Voltaire happily accepted the assignment. He loved playing the role of a secret agent, and the operation was on such a high level, with so much at stake, that he was flattered by the Cardinal's confidence in him. His hearty, unequivocal acceptance, which arrived while Émilie was still at Fontainebleau, reassured her that he would not become a semi-permanent member of Frederick's court.

Wanting more than one string to her bow, Émilie sought an audience with King Louis, too. Under ordinary circumstances she might have had to wait several months, but she was aided by the Duc de Richelieu, who was at loose ends since the death of his wife earlier in the summer. Émilie had written to him in Paris prior to her departure from Cirey, and he met her at Fontainebleau. Regarding Frederick as too ambitious for the good of France, Émilie's dear friend and one-time lover became her willing ally.

At his suggestion she applied for an audience with King Louis, writing an unusual note. Departing radically from protocol, she requested that the King's current mistress, a particularly feather-brained Comtesse, be present at the audience. Her reason was obvious: She didn't want either Louis or his mistress to think she had any personal designs on the monarch, and the presence of the Comtesse would guarantee that the inevitable court whispers would be held to a minimum.

Émilie presented Louis with a warmly-inscribed copy of *Mahomet*, and after telling him in detail how Frederick had wooed Voltaire for years, she described the author's reception when he and Frederick had met. Louis was a vain, jealous man, and she knew he would react strongly, so she exaggerated with delicate care, her feminine intuition telling her how far she could go without arousing the wrath of His Christian Majesty. Richelieu, who was also present at the interview, later described her efforts as a "clever masterpiece."

King Louis promptly made it clear that he would not permit the most renowned of his subjects to be stolen from him by a Prussian upstart. He was unfamiliar with Voltaire's work, having no interest in science, philosophy, or poetry, and finding the author's plays and works of history too heavy for his frivolous tastes, so he could not match Frederick's intellectual interest. But he knew how to deal with people, and sent the author a friendly letter, enclosing a gold medallion of himself.

Voltaire, whose greatest weakness was his susceptibility to the attentions and blandishments of royalty, replied at once with a long, flowery letter, in which he suggested that, when he finished his book on the reign of the King's grandfather, he would be pleased to do another on the reign of Louis XV.

So Émilie succeeded, brilliantly, in attaining her objectives. She not only made peace between Voltaire and the royal court with which he had been at odds for years, but she had created a powerful magnet, other than her own love, that would draw him back to France from Berlin.

Her conduct at Fontainebleau astonished the court. Her clothes were expensive, as always, but she wore none of the very low-cut gowns that, on previous occasions, had shocked the supposedly shock-proof court. Her gems were dazzling, but she wore only a few of her diamonds at any single time, and no one caught as much as a glimpse of her famous emeralds. She behaved discreetly, refused to become embroiled in arguments, and took part only in token dancing at the two balls held at Fontainebleau during her stay there. If it was her intention to prove to King Louis and Cardinal Fleury that she was a mature, responsible woman, she achieved her aim.

Only at the gaming table did her resolve to create a new, sober image falter. She sat down to games of *vingt-et-un* on only a few occasions, but those scenes gave the Fontainebleau letter-writers enough ammunition to last many weeks. She placed spectacularly high wagers, betting so much that only members of the royal family and a few very wealthy dukes could afford to stay the table with her. Had she lost, the efforts of a single afternoon would have bankrupted her husband, but she won so much that, it was said, she would be solvent for years to come, no matter how extravagant her tastes.

Her mission accomplished and her purse bulging, Émilie went into Paris for a visit of a week or two, opening the seldom-used Hôtel du Châtelet for the purpose. Again she was circum-spect, seeing only a few of her society friends and refusing invitations to dinner parties and the opera. Apparently she wanted no warped stories about her behavior to make their way to Berlin, where, she felt sure, Frederick and his supporters would delight in persuading Voltaire she had been unfaithful to him.

She confined herself to long talks with Maupertuis and other members of the scientific community at the Gradot, where she could now wear ladies' attire, her campaign to open the cafés to women apparently having proved successful. She also re-newed her discussions of Leibnitz and Newton with members of the Academy of Science, and in late October, 1740, at approximately the time that Voltaire was leaving The Hague for Berlin and Frederick's retreat at Potsdam, she returned to Cirey.

The silence of the isolated estate was oppressive, and although Émilie tried to bear down on her work, she needed relief from her studies and her writing. Her letters to friends at Fontainebleau and in Paris constantly reiterated a single theme: She was unutterably lonely and did not know how long she could tolerate being cut off from the rest of the world.

Friends urged her to go to Paris, and so did the Marquis du Châtelet in a brief, paternal note. But she was either afraid of the gossip or of the temptations that might cause talk, and paid no attention to the advice. In none of her correspondence did she give any explanation for her refusal to return to the city she loved.

Instead she went back to the rented house on the Rue de la Gross-Tour in Brussels, where she was closer to Voltaire in far-off Prussia. There she read interminably, conducted her never-ending physics experiments, and, on the two or three evenings each week when boredom threatened to overcome her, she dined with local members of the Austrian and Belgian aristocracies. With nothing better to occupy her, she became involved in senseless quarrels with some of her fellow blue-bloods.

The most sensational of these feuds caused repercussions throughout Europe. Princess Matilda of Thurn and Taxis was the ranking member of the Austrian aristocracy in Brussels, a haughty woman related in an obscure way to the ruling Hapsburg family. Émilie attended a dinner party at the Princess's palace one evening, and immediately took offense when Matilda announced that she would act as hostess when, at some future, unspecified time, King Frederick of Prussia visited the city.

It is probable that there was no one on the Continent whom Émilie was less anxious to entertain than the man who had, temporarily, at least, taken Voltaire from her. But everyone present knew of her relationship with the author, just as everyone knew he was visiting Berlin, so she could not allow the Princess's assertion to go unchallenged. When Frederick came to Brussels, she said, he would visit only one house, that on the Rue de la Gross-Tour.

The Princess adamantly repeated her initial claim, Émilie just as stubbornly refuted it, and soon the two women were shouting at each other. Émilie, already in a highly emotional state because of Voltaire's protracted absence, finally burst into tears and stalked out, to the delight of letter-writers everywhere, who made all they could of the incident. She and Princess Matilda did not speak again, which added fuel to the absurd fire.

When news of the quarrel reached Berlin, as it inevitably did, Frederick must have been highly amused. He knew, far better than did anyone else, that he had no intention of visiting the Belgian city, which was even drearier than his own capital.

The loss of the Émilie du Châtelet-Voltaire correspondence makes it impossible to determine how frequently the separated lovers wrote to each other, much less to guess what they said. They did correspond, to be sure. Émilie mentioned to the Duc de Richelieu that Voltaire found the climate of Berlin unbearably cold and that he disliked the rusticity of the royal retreat at Potsdam. She said to d'Argental, with some satisfaction, that the rich foods prepared by Frederick's French chef were causing Voltaire considerable gastric discomfort. She seemed to be snatching at any straw that would indicate he was miserable, homesick, and that he missed her.

Certainly Voltaire's second visit with Frederick was not as successful as the first. On the surface, to be sure, the monarch and the author thoroughly enjoyed each other's company. Frederick played the flute, and Voltaire applauded him. Frederick showed the Frenchman his collection of French paintings, and Voltaire admired them, later writing to various friends in Paris that they were poor imitations of masterpieces. Voltaire wrote some of his always-polished verses praising the King. Frederick returned the compliment in poetry so ragged that Voltaire must have winced in private.

The homosexual atmosphere of the court, which Voltaire found amusing when he first arrived, soon palled on him. He was himself too cosmopolitan and broad-minded to stand in judgment on men who had love affairs with other men, but he soon became bored by the company of the pretty, rouged young males in their female finery. He had been a gallant too long, and missed the exhilarating company of real women.

Above all, he was having trouble finding out what Frederick was planning to do in an international situation that had become tense and complicated. Late in October the Holy Roman Emperor, Charles VI, died at his Vienna palace, leaving his vast, sprawling Austrian possessions to his inexperienced daughter of twenty-three, Maria Theresa. Charles had anticipated trouble, and had reached an agreement with his fellow monarchs in which they promised to respect the rights of the young Empress. But portions of the rich realm were close at hand,

and the land-hungry rulers of Europe coveted them. Every nation was mobilizing, quietly, and Maria Theresa, who would prove to be one of the greatest queens of all history, was busily preparing her defenses.

Frederick was delighted to discuss Aristotle's *Aesthetics* with Voltaire, but merely smiled when the Frenchman brought up the subject of the superbly trained Prussian army. The King was fascinated by Newton, but looked blank when his guest mentioned the potential tactical uses of the magnificent Prussian cavalry. Frederick was delighted when he could show off his expertise in distinguishing ancient coins, but he seemed deaf when the subject of his own growing war chest was mentioned.

The official French ambassador, the British ambassador, and other diplomats accredited to the Prussian court learned nothing, either, and played a guessing game. Voltaire, aided by his knowledge of history, carefully engaged some of Frederick's leading generals in conversation, and repeatedly returned to the subject of the Holy Roman Empire whenever he thought the young King had imbibed one glass too many.

Although he found out no more than did his professional colleagues, Voltaire proved that his insights were sharper. In a letter to Cardinal Fleury, which he took care to send in the French diplomatic pouch, so it would not be opened by Frederick's spies, he ventured the opinion that Prussia intended to attack and annex the Austrian province of Silesia.

The subject of money created a certain coolness between the cash-conscious Voltaire and his penny-pinching host. Frederick had offered to pay the traveling expenses of his wealthy guest, and apparently had expected the polite gesture to be refused. But Voltaire considered himself something of a pauper when he thought of the riches locked away in the state vaults of Prussia, and eagerly accepted. Not only did he believe that a man whose health was delicate should travel in style, but it seemed eminently reasonable to him that the King should pay for the weeks he had spent in The Hague supervising the publication of the *Anti-Macchiavel.*

He submitted a detailed expense account, including the estimated cost of his return journey to France, and Frederick was shocked. The total was one thousand three hundred gold louis, a small fortune by any standards, and the young monarch remarked waspishly that his purse was not as heavy as Mme. du Châtelet's. He not only revealed ignorance of the true financial relationship of Voltaire and Émilie, but hinted, insultingly, that the author was being supported by his mistress.

Ordinarily Voltaire might have been amused by the jibe, but he never found humor in a situation wherein someone owed him money. Also, after a visit of a month, he was growing weary of the sly, stiletto-like thrusts of the homosexual court, where every cut was feline and indirect. He would reconsider the expense account and submit it again, he said, and the following day he handed a new list to Frederick. A few minor details were different, but the sum he claimed was unchanged.

Frederick grumbled but paid, having learned the hard way that the most renowned of living writers was no court jester, but a man who placed a high value on his time and on any inconveniences he was forced to suffer. His protests were very mild when Voltaire announced that he could remain no longer and that the exigencies of his own business made it necessary for him to return home.

An express courier must have brought the good news to Émilie, who received word from her lover on December 8th that he had planned to leave Berlin on December 2nd and would rejoin her in Brussels in ample time to eat Christmas dinner with her. She had won her greatest victory over the most persistent of her foes, and exulted quietly. *"M. de Voltaire is coming home sooner than I had thought, and I rejoice,"* she wrote to the Duc de Richelieu. *"He writes with care, no doubt afraid that the Prussians, like other barbarians, read his mail;*

but he makes it plain that he feels contempt for the ruler who would not be satisfied until he had exhibited the head of my beloved one upon a pike."

She was even more direct in a note to d'Argental. *"The honeymoon of the little Frederick and M. de Voltaire has come to its end, and we shall hear no more of the glorious literary exchanges His Majesty had hoped to use for the winning of his immortality."*

Europe soon learned that Frederick was thinking in other terms, and had his own ideas for the achievement of immortality. On December 12th he gave the first great ball of his reign, a splendid affair that many of the guests considered as elaborate as the grand fêtes held at Versailles on special occasions. The following morning, when those who had attended the party were groggily sipping their breakfast wine, they learned that Frederick's hard-bitten legions had crossed the Austrian border and were engaged in a full-scale invasion of Silesia. A major war had been launched, and it was inevitable that every nation in Europe would be forced to take part.

Voltaire, who heard the news on his homeward journey, was disgusted. *"The King of Prussia,"* he wrote, *"fancies himself a civilized man, but beneath the thin outer skin of the aesthete lies the hide and the soul of a butcher."*

Émilie's reaction was no less intense, but far narrower. *"What does it matter how many provinces Frederick takes,"* she asked rhetorically in a letter to Maupertuis, *"as long as he does not rob me of my happiness?"*

That happiness was postponed, however, by the worst early winter weather that Europe had known in a generation, and Émilie would know the anguish of anxious waiting before she and Voltaire would be reunited. Vicious ice storms closed every road, and heavy snow, which fell for several days thereafter, made it unlikely that any traveler could resume his journey in the near future. Mail service was disrupted, too, so Voltaire's letters telling Émilie of his frequent changes in plans were delayed for many days.

The disillusioned author was making frantic efforts to rejoin his mistress. First he tried alternate routes, but could ride only a few miles each day, and he knew that if he stayed on the road he would be certain to suffer an accident. But he found German inns lacking in every civilized comfort: the rooms were cold, the beds were hard, and the heavy food gave him severe, chronic indigestion.

Unwilling to wait indefinitely for an improvement of the roads, he conceived the idea of continuing by ships that would hug the coastline, sailing out of the Baltic through the Kattegat and Skagerrak around Denmark into the North Sea, where he would go ashore in Holland or Belgium as soon as the weather permitted.

Unfortunately, however, a series of fresh storms caused interminable delays. The tiny coastal vessels wallowed in the high seas, and Voltaire became seasick. Occasionally a vessel was forced to take temporary refuge in a cove, but there were no inns anywhere in the vicinity, and even if reasonably good accommodations had been available, the raging seas, combined with unending rain, snow, and hail, would have prevented the author from going ashore.

Voltaire did not appear in Brussels by Christmas, and there was no word from him. The days stretched into weeks, and as his silence grew longer, Émilie became convinced that he had died, or, at the very least, was lying desperately ill in some remote place, wanting her beside him yet unable to communicate with her. She became a victim of mounting hysteria, and by late January, 1741, her letters to friends in Paris were almost incoherent.

In vain the friends pointed out to her that the weather had slowed travel to a crawl and that no mail from any foreign country was being delivered. Émilie convinced herself that

Voltaire was dead, and she ordered her seamstress to make her a complete new wardrobe in black. Before she could wear it, however, Voltaire suddenly reappeared in Brussels on January 27th.

Neither he nor Émilie wrote a single letter to anyone for the next eight days.

XIV

The reunited couple traveled extensively in 1741, seldom staying in any one place for more than a few weeks. And Émilie, for the first time in her adult life, interrupted her own work schedule in order to devote virtually her entire time and attention to Voltaire. She spent a minimum of six to eight hours each day reading, to be sure, but that was a normal, natural pastime, and she neither conducted experiments nor engaged in any major writing project of her own.

After spending February and March in Brussels, during which time they made a brief journey to Cirey, Émilie and Voltaire went to Lille for the initial performances of *Mahomet,* which had never been played anywhere. There they stayed with the author's niece, Mme. Denis, with whom Voltaire was developing what Émilie called a "marvelous rapport." Had she been more perspicacious, she would not have considered this family solidarity so marvelous.

Voltaire worked hard on the presentation of *Mahomet,* with Émilie in silent attendance at the rehearsals of one of his plays for the first time. The drama was exceptionally well received, which indicated that it would be successful in Paris, but no one seeing it appeared to realize that the character of Mahomet was in reality Christ, and that Voltaire was, in effect, attacking the fundamental concepts of Roman Catholicism, an assault that would cause him great problems in France when the authorities awakened to what he was doing.

After spending a month in Lille the couple went on to Cirey, then returned to Brussels, and for several months they commuted between the two places. In the autumn they paid a brief visit to Paris, where Voltaire arranged for a production of *Mahomet* the following year, and then they returned to their travels between Cirey and Brussels.

In many ways 1741 was the least eventful year that Émilie and Voltaire spent together. There were no known explosions for either, their domestic relations were tranquil, and Voltaire managed to stay out of trouble with the authorities, which was no mean achievement. But greater excitement was in store for 1742.

Returning to Paris for the production of *Mahomet,* the couple openly took up residence together at the Palais Lambert, the magnificent home that Voltaire had purchased on the Île Saint-Louis. They had spent so many years together that it seemed absurd to go through the motions of residing apart, and by now their affair was being taken for granted by everyone from King Louis and Cardinal Fleury to the most insignificant tradesman.

But the great house was not yet furnished in the style to which they were accustomed, and neither Émilie nor Voltaire, particularly the latter, wanted to spend a fortune on the place. Paris was no longer their home, and they already had two bases of operations, Cirey and Brussels. Although Voltaire's motivation was primarily financial, other considerations undoubtedly influenced Émilie. She had returned to work with a vengeance and did not want to take the time and effort necessary to refurnish the huge mansion.

Voltaire's business acumen was as sharp as ever, and after a brief flurry of negotiations he sold the Palais Lambert for double the sum he had paid for it, thereby pocketing a handsome profit. The question of finding a new place to live arose, and neither of the lovers wanted to revert to the unsatisfactory arrangements of previous years, with Émilie reopening the Hôtel du Châtelet and Voltaire finding inexpensive lodgings near the theater.

So they began a search for a new, suitable dwelling, and soon found a small, handsome mansion in the Faubourg Saint-Honoré, which they purchased "together." The fiction of this joint purchase was a convenience they invented for the purpose of saving Émilie possible embarrassment, although it is difficult to determine why she would have become upset if anyone had accused her of living in her lover's house, which is precisely what she had been doing at the Palais Lambert.

Theoretically, she had provided half of the funds for the new house, and the myth was retained as long as she and Voltaire remained together. When Émilie died, however, no one disputed the author's sole ownership of the place, and her heirs made no claims on it.

The furnishing of the new house took only a short time, and while Émilie looked after this essentially feminine business, Voltaire created a new problem for himself, a problem unique in all of his experience. King Frederick had decided to make peace with Austria, and Voltaire, who hated all war, wrote him a hearty letter of congratulations.

A copy of the letter was made public, and the wrath of Paris descended on Voltaire.

The situation that created this reaction was simple but paradoxical. Ever since the finest legions of Louis XIV had been defeated during the War of the Spanish Succession, early in the century, by the combined armies of the English and the Austrians, the people of France had felt cheated and had hated the Austrians. Now, believing that Maria Theresa was unable to defend her realm and that France could not only obtain vengeance but enlarge her territories at small cost, people of every class were clamoring for war on the side of Frederick.

But Voltaire's stand in favor of peace played directly into

the hands of the crown, still manipulated by wily old Cardinal Fleury. The aged Cardinal loathed war, too, and was convinced that France would continue to prosper only if she remained at peace. But Voltaire provided him with a convenient whipping boy, and he was content to let the public demonstrate its anger against the author, thereby enabling the government to escape wrath while continuing to avoid war.

A military guard was posted outside the house in the Faubourg Saint-Honoré to prevent rioting and the destruction of property, and Cardinal Fleury breathed a quiet sigh of relief. Voltaire, who had expected no such public response, was astonished and dismayed. It appeared that *Mahomet* would be one of his more important successes, and he wanted nothing to jeopardize its chances, so he issued a series of vehement denials that he had written any such letter to Frederick.

There were many citizens who refused to believe the patent untruth, but the attitude adopted by Émilie proved of great help to Voltaire. Now, as always, Émilie du Châtelet was a completely apolitical woman. Her only interests in life were Voltaire, science, literature, and philosophy, and the relations between nations bored her. She saw statesmen, diplomats, and warriors as people, and she was unimpressed by any of them from Frederick to Fleury to her own husband.

Consequently she felt only contempt for the excitement engendered by Voltaire's letter. It was his right to hate war, if he wished, and to express himself accordingly. Some of the very people who had applauded his previous stands in favor of free speech were among his harshest critics now, and she correctly thought them inconsistent.

In addition, she felt deep scorn for the mob. Like so many aristocrats who were executed late in the century during the Revolution, she had led a sheltered life, knew nothing of the people, and assumed that public anger would leave her untouched. Certainly no ordinary person would dare shake his fist under the nose of the Marquise du Châtelet, wife of a general and herself a bona fide blueblood.

Undeterred by the presence of huge, threatening crowds beyond the cordon of troops stationed in the street, Émilie went about her daily business with a superb calm that could have been rooted only in ignorance. She left and reentered the house repeatedly, usually riding in a small coach, and her city routines of years were unaltered. Her head held high, she found it easy to pretend the shouting, angry citizens were misguided zealots who did not exist.

The crowds were aware only of what appeared to be Émilie's courage, and had no understanding of its cause. Everyone admired the magnificently gowned woman, and after a day or two the public began to wonder whether Voltaire might be innocent of the charges that most Parisians considered treason. After all, they reasoned, Mme. du Châtelet would not be able to maintain her tranquil air if her lover were guilty. So the crowds grew smaller, and in less than a week they disappeared. Unwittingly Émilie had helped her lover's cause.

The feeling against Voltaire reached the vanishing point by the time *Mahomet* opened, and the threats of demonstrations at the opening performance did not materialize. The play was a rousing success, one of the biggest hits Voltaire had ever enjoyed, and he settled back to collect his royalties. But, a few days after the play opened, the sharp-witted censors suddenly understood the real meaning of the play and were horrified. *Mahomet* was closed without ceremony, and permission to play it again was withdrawn.

Cardinal Fleury wisely decided not to confuse the issues by revealing the true reason for closing the play. There was continuing agitation against Voltaire because of the letter to Frederick, particularly in military and other patriotic circles, and it suited the government to let him draw the bulk of fire. So crown agents let it be known that the play had been closed because the lives of the actors might be endangered.

Voltaire and Émilie could scarcely believe the official reason for shutting down *Mahomet,* but if the author suspected the real cause, he discreetly held his tongue. Knowing the actual significance of the play itself, he had no intention of stirring up more trouble for himself.

Then Fleury unexpectedly gave him—and Émilie—something else to think about. The government was still in the dark regarding the future intentions of Prussia, but the continued enlargement of her armies made it unlikely that she would remain at peace for any protracted period. Calling the couple to his quarters at Versailles, the Cardinal said that Voltaire, more than any other man, was in a position to find out what Frederick had in mind, and with Émilie's help he could do France a great service. In September, Fleury had learned, Frederick was paying a visit to Aix-la-Chapelle, which was located a short distance across the Low Countries' border from Cirey.

It should be easy, he said, for Voltaire to obtain an invitation to visit Frederick there. Then, instead of sending official letters to the government via the diplomatic pouch, as he had done when in Prussia, he would write to no one but Mme. du Châtelet. Ostensibly he would be visiting Frederick as a private citizen and would be corresponding only with his mistress. Frederick might be thrown off guard by the maneuver and might reveal more than he intended. The letters sent to Mme. du Châtelet would be written in code, to be sure, and the Cardinal left it to the clever couple to devise their own secret code.

Voltaire, who became enthusiastic when asked to play the role of a spy, agreed vehemently. Émilie was less than enchanted, but had no real choice and was compelled to accept, too.

So the author wrote again to Frederick, saying he was returning to Cirey, and, as anticipated, Frederick promptly invited him to Aix-la-Chapelle. The King carefully refrained from mentioning travel expenses, so Voltaire subsequently obtained repayment from the French government, even though the journey was absurdly short and his expenses negligible.

The author's visit produced no results of consequence. Frederick was charming, solicitous, and pleasant, but remained close-mouthed. Voltaire worked hard on his complicated code when he wrote ostensible love-letters to Émilie, and she worked equally hard deciphering what he had penned but had no information of value to pass along to Cardinal Fleury.

Émilie discussed the visit calmly in a letter she sent d'Argental from Cirey early in October. *"M. de Voltaire did not abuse his liberty, because he left here on Monday and returned on Saturday."*

She also revealed to d'Argental that the King had offered Voltaire a fine house in Berlin and a handsome estate in the country, but her lover had refused, saying he preferred his comfortable quarters on the second floor of Mme. du Châtelet's house.

She also told d'Argental that Frederick had begged Voltaire to visit him in Berlin late in November or early in December and had followed his verbal invitation with a written one. It was clear to her by now that Voltaire was disenchanted with the Prussian monarch, and that he was drawn to Frederick only to the extent that he could not resist the occasional opportunity to show the world that he was on close personal terms with a potent ruler. Her comment to d'Argental revealed not only her awareness of the situation, but also the somewhat changed nature of her own relationship with Voltaire. *"M. de Voltaire has refused,"* she wrote, adding dryly, *"but I assure you it does not appear to me to have the merit of a sacrifice."* It seems that the blind, romantic passions of the early years had given way to the more realistic approach to life that couples who had been married for years knew well.

Life at Cirey was busy in the winter of 1742-1743. Voltaire was rewriting *Mérope,* his play about mother love, and Émilie was acting a role she seldom played, that of a loving mother.

The gossip of friends had made her alert to a situation she felt she could utilize to the benefit of her daughter. A homely, middle-aged Neapolitan nobleman who had no known virtues other than his exceptionally high rank, the Duke of Montenegro-Caraffa, was enamored of France and was in the market for a French wife. Believing himself sufficiently well situated financially to live in comfort, the Duke was not particularly interested in the size of the dowry his bride would bring with her. Émilie immediately pictured her daughter, Gabrielle-Pauline, as a duchess, and acted accordingly.

Montenegro-Caraffa was invited to Cirey, and Gabrielle was on hand, wearing a new wardrobe Voltaire bought for her. No one refused the rare opportunity to see Voltaire and Émilie in their native habitat, and the Duke accepted. The Marquis du Châtelet came home for the occasion, and although his new mistress, a ravishing, brainless creature with flaming red hair and green eyes, accompanied him to Cirey, he readily agreed to pass her off as a friend of his daughter's.

The visit was successful beyond all expectations. Émilie was charming and displayed no eccentricities. Her husband managed to stay awake long enough each evening to engage in the small talk that followed supper. His mistress faded into the background and did not respond on the few occasions that Montenegro-Caraffa flirted with her. Voltaire, who enjoyed playing a role similar to that of characters in his own comedies, put up the bland pretense that he, too, was a mere family friend. His task was a light one, since he appeared only in the evenings, when he and Émilie, as always, dominated the supper table conversation.

Émilie bore the brunt of the visit, and when Montenegro-Caraffa was sufficiently impressed to get down to business, it was she who negotiated with him, even though the Marquis sat beside her and listened. Émilie succeeded, Voltaire wrote to the lovely Duchesse de Boufflers, in obtaining a marriage agreement that contained the lowest dowry payment ever recorded, and he called her a genius.

Everyone went to Paris, where the wedding was held early in the spring. Hundreds of guests filed into Notre Dame for the ceremony, and the spectacularly gowned and jeweled mother of the bride far outshone the bride. For whatever consolation it gave Gabrielle, she now ranked higher than her mother, but it was Émilie who permitted no one to forget that she was the mother of a duchess.

Then, the wedding out of the way, everything reverted to normal. The Marquis du Châtelet returned to Lorraine, where his divisions stood on guard against the possibility of a surprise invasion by the Prussians. Frederick was an avowed Francophile, it was true, and had no quarrel with Paris, but liaison officers who had seen his troops in action had been so impressed that the French army was taking no chances.

Émilie and Voltaire moved into the little mansion on the Faubourg Saint-Honoré, which she opened after closing the Hôtel du Châtelet, and the author immediately started work on the production of *Mérope*. Apparently he sensed something out of the ordinary in the work, and was meticulous in his treatment of it; ordinarily he refused to change a play once he had written it, but he made literally hundreds of changes in *Mérope*, large and small, and was still rewriting only twenty-four hours before the tragedy opened.

Mérope was not only Voltaire's greatest success, but the biggest hit of the century. The audience applauded for more than thirty minutes after the final curtain fell, and for the first time in the history of the French theater, there were calls demanding that the author appear on the stage.

But Voltaire proved himself surprisingly modest in the presence of a large audience, and after briefly acknowledging the cheers from a box, he disappeared. Émilie, who had been sitting with him at the rear of the auditorium rather than in a box during the performance, was not seen by more than a few people, and vanished with him.

Overnight *Mérope* was established as the most popular play in the repertory of the Comédie Française. It played for months, establishing new records, and could have played for years; it was revived regularly, always playing to capacity audiences, and it made the reputations of many famous actresses through the decades.

Voltaire's wallet bulged with francs, which he did not need, and his letter of the previous year to King Frederick was forgotten. In fact, cheers greeted him when he was recognized in the streets, a novel experience.

Émilie could have shared in his glory, had she wished, but she was too hard at work. She had been interrupted far too many times in her translations of the poetry of Catullus from Latin, and was spending most of her days on the project.

Her enemies, always eager to make her appear at a disadvantage, were quick to attribute her infrequent court appearances to a jealousy of her lover's new popularity. But these claims were nonsense. Neither Émilie nor Voltaire ever sought public applause in the sense that actors or soldiers sought it, and her letters, including several long, glowing communications sent to her daughter, indicate that she felt very proud of the new triumph Voltaire had achieved.

Meanwhile France was beginning to flounder in a morass created by the sudden but not unexpected death of Cardinal Fleury in 1743. Louis XV, trying to emulate his grandfather, took the reins of state into his own hands, appointing ministers who were able technicians, but as lacking in imagination as they were in authority. The Minister of Foreign Affairs, Jean-Jacques Amelot de Chaillou, was a man of particularly limited ability, which was unfortunate at a time when the immediate future of France depended, in large part, on what Prussia intended to do.

The Duc de Richelieu, who was both a soldier and statesman, had the ear of King Louis, and it was Richelieu who invented a scheme that the enthusiastic Louis, seconded by Amelot, considered foolproof. Voltaire had failed to glean any information of value from Frederick on his previous visits to the Prussian, it was true, but Frederick had been rightly suspicious, knowing that his friend was on good terms with the French authorities. According to Richelieu's complicated plot, Voltaire would appear to be in trouble.

His play, *La Mort de César,* had been denied the right of public presentation because some of his comments on dictatorships, particularly rights of free speech, struck too close to home. Very well, in the light of the huge success achieved by *Mérope,* Voltaire would put *César* into rehearsal at the Comédie Française. A few nights before the scheduled opening, he would be denied a license and would be threatened with arrest.

Then he would disappear from Paris, and a rumor would reach Berlin, via the French ambassador, that he was fleeing from France before he could be arrested. The rumor would be followed by a long silence.

After two or three weeks Émilie du Châtelet would write a letter to Frederick, sending it from Cirey. She would beg the monarch, in the name of friendship, to give Voltaire refuge from his enemies at home. There would be no need for the King to reply to her letter, she would tell him; M. de Voltaire would be writing to him from a safe place in the immediate future.

Next, Voltaire himself would write to Frederick from Brussels. He would denounce his compatriots scathingly, give an address in The Hague where he could be reached, and would request that he be allowed to come to Berlin.

Frederick would find the lure irresistible, and would not only invite the refugee to come to him, but would, under the circumstances, be much more inclined to speak freely of his future plans.

There was one more string to Richelieu's bow. Voltaire in Berlin and Émilie at Cirey would correspond, each of them pretending the exile was real. The Prussian secret police, who would report on the correspondence to Frederick, would be convinced the story was genuine, and so would their monarch.

Richelieu presented the plan to Voltaire, who reacted like a child with a glittering new toy.

But Émilie balked, violently and vocally. She was tired of the games of international power and intrigue that men played, and thought them childish. She had no use for complicated schemes and less for the men who conceived them. Voltaire had achieved the greatest triumph of his vocational life, and deserved a rest, an opportunity to rejuvenate himself, a chance to think about the many new writing projects that were buzzing in his head. She, too, was tired, and after spending two years moving from one place to another, wanted to return to Cirey with her lover. She was longing for isolation and the opportunity to work without interruption, and she resented the strains that another separation, another mission to Prussia would impose on Voltaire and on her.

Richelieu reasoned and argued with her in vain. Émilie refused to cooperate, and when Richelieu persisted, she finally lost her temper, treating him to one of her famous tantrums. She was so furious that, for the only time in all the years of their long relationship, she stopped speaking to him, and did not become friendly with him again for a number of months.

Now it was Amelot's turn to persuade her, but the head of the Foreign Ministry was ill equipped for the task. A minor noble who felt uneasy in the presence of his social superiors, he had spent years following Cardinal Fleury's orders, and was comfortable only when analyzing a dispatch from one of his ambassadors, a task at which he excelled. He was hesitant and apologetic in his approach to Émilie, and she not only refused to listen to him but became personally insulting. Voltaire later remarked that in all probability, no woman except Amelot's wife had ever treated him with such contempt.

It became necessary for Louis XV to intervene personally,

and although he disliked direct participation in the detailed affairs of state, he had no choice. Mme. du Châtelet was summoned to Fontainebleau, and appeared in a spectacular new gown, wearing most of her jewelry. In other words, she was deliberately trying to create an atmosphere suitable for a social audience rather than an official interview, and subtly maneuvered so the King's new mistress, the Duchesse de Châteauroux, was present at the meeting.

Marie Anne de Mailly-Nesle, Duchesse de Châteauroux, was a sister of Louis's previous mistress, and happened to be a very old friend of Émilie's. Émilie assumed she could count on strong feminine support for her cause; what she either forgot or ignored was the fact that the Duchess was a niece of Richelieu's, and was strongly under his influence. What Émilie did not know was that Richelieu had enlisted the support of his niece when he had first concocted the plan, and the Duchess, enjoying her intervention in matters of state, thought of herself as co-author of the scheme.

From the outset the audience was embarrassing to everyone concerned. Louis's subjects automatically did his bidding, and he didn't know how to ask one of them for a favor, never before having found himself in this position. Mme. de Châteauroux, although an ardent advocate of the scheme, nevertheless could understand Émilie's opposition to it, and was ill at ease because of the unhappiness she was causing her friend, something that had not occurred to her when the idea had been developed.

Émilie conducted herself with aplomb, never raising her voice, never indicating the fury that raged beneath the surface. She listened to Louis, heard everything Marie Anne de Châteauroux had to say, and smiled. It was her understanding, she said, that M. de Voltaire's assignment was voluntary, and she sought confirmation.

The King assured her she was right, that the crown could not order Voltaire to undertake such a delicate mission.

Sure of her ground, Émilie said she would not presume to

advise M. de Voltaire, and under no circumstances would it be proper for her to urge him to ignore or refuse a request made by the King.

Louis may have congratulated himself, believing he had won a victory. If so, his joy was premature.

If M. de Voltaire conceived it his duty to visit Frederick in false guise for the purposes of gleaning information deemed valuable to France, she would make no attempt to persuade or influence him in any manner contrary to his duty. On the other hand, the dictates of her own conscience, combined with her lack of understanding of international affairs, made it impossible for her to be a party to any such scheme. Certainly she would not of her own volition write a falsehood to King Frederick, with whom she had corresponded for years, and whose respect and admiration she had long treasured. Further, if M. de Voltaire chose to write her letters from Prussia that did not reflect his true situation, he would be free to do so. She, however, could not force herself to write him in a similar vein.

Louis found himself trapped. It would be difficult to order Mme. du Châtelet to participate in the venture. Her reluctance would appear, almost inevitably, in her correspondence with Voltaire, and the Prussians soon would realize that the scheme was a pretense designed to win Frederick's confidence. Under the circumstances all that Louis could do was to ask her to reconsider, tell her the plan was important to France, and hint that she would earn his displeasure if she failed to comply.

There was literally nothing that Émilie wanted from the crown for herself, so it did not matter in the least if Louis should be annoyed with her. She indicated this in some subtle way that did not emerge in detail in the subsequent correspondence of others on the subject.

The audience ended on a note even stiffer than that on which it had opened. Émilie did not linger at the palace for chats with friends or even a game of cards, an indication that she herself was upset, and, perhaps, that King Louis already was making her feel somewhat less than welcome under his roof.

It would have been beneath the dignity of His Christian Majesty to take part in a conspiracy, so the Duc de Richelieu did his dirty work for him, and wrote a letter to the Marquis du Châtelet, telling his old comrade in arms that it was necessary they meet in the immediate future on a matter of urgent state business.

That meeting took place at Orléans, away from the prying eyes and listening ears of the court. Nothing could be allowed to leak out regarding the scheme, the success of which depended on its acceptance as a true development by everyone in France.

All that is known about the meeting of the Marquis and the Duke is that it took place. Richelieu undoubtedly explained the plan and certainly asked the General to cooperate. Whether he hinted that the coveted baton of a Marshal of France would not be forthcoming if the Marquis failed to enlist in the cause is a matter of conjecture.

Only a few things can be said with certainty. War, in the eighteenth century, was still a gentleman's business. Spies were employed, to be sure, but they were civilians, directed by civilians, and the honorable, professional soldier did not stain his hands by dealing in matters of espionage. So it is unlikely that a professional soldier of stature would have been willing to join in persuading his own wife, regardless of their personal relationship, to play a major role in a complicated espionage plot.

Whatever may have been said, the Marquis du Châtelet did not get in touch with his wife or try in any way to influence her. Not bothering to visit Émilie, he returned to his troops in Lorraine. It may be significant that he did not see her, since a high-ranking military man who lived most of his life in the field rarely missed an opportunity to spend a few days in Paris. But the Marquis apparently wanted nothing to do with the situation, and if he could not agree to do the King's bidding, at least he could protect himself by washing his hands of the matter.

There is no record of any correspondence between Émilie and her husband at this time, but the lack need not be significant. They seldom wrote to each other except on matters concerning the family lawsuit in Brussels, problems concerning their children, or, more rarely, questions of repairs being made at Cirey.

In any event, the burden of convincing Émilie that she should take part in the scheme now fell on Voltaire. He alone was capable of convincing her, and this he did, using methods of persuasion that only he and Émilie knew. She capitulated, but with bad grace. It was unfortunate enough that she was being forced to participate in something she considered absurd, but it was far worse that she had lost a battle. Her competitive spirit made her a bad loser.

She remained in Paris for a few days after Voltaire disappeared, and then went to Cirey, where she remained. Not until the first part of the scheme had unfolded and everyone in France believed that Voltaire again was in trouble with the authorities and had fled to Prussia did she mention the fact that he was not at Cirey with her.

Now a new situation caused her anguish. She had become a party to the deception, albeit against her own will, and therefore could not reveal the true situation to anyone, even close friends. Also, because everyone in Paris gossiped and the Prussian ambassador would be listening, she had to add fuel to the fire of the myth that Voltaire was a refugee.

Still another factor was important in her thinking, as was indicated in correspondence between Richelieu and his current mistress, Mme. de Tencin, a good friend of Émilie's, who was privy to the secret and was the one person in whom the unhappy Mme. du Châtelet could confide. Émilie lived in dread that Frederick would learn the truth, and she had a far clearer concept of the young monarch's character than did most of his contemporaries. She knew he was ruthless, cold-blooded, and vengeful, and could act without human feeling if he believed such action were dictated by his best interests.

Frederick had received Voltaire in Berlin, believing the story that the French authorities wanted to arrest him because he had attacked the dignity of the crown in *César*. What would happen if Frederick learned that the entire situation was a sham that had been conceived and executed for the purpose of fooling him? He would not take the chance of doing anything to injure the reputation he had so carefully cultivated as an intellectual and patron of the arts. But he was the undisputed master of Prussia, and Berlin was far from the French border. Therefore it was conceivable, even probable, that Voltaire would suffer a fatal "accident" after he left the Prussian court, and Émilie didn't put it past Frederick to play the role of the chief mourner.

The terrified woman, living alone at Cirey, was the victim of her own imagination, so some of the hysteria that appeared in her letters undoubtedly was genuine. She meant what she said when she cried that she was afraid she would never see Voltaire again, that she had lost him to Frederick. Her friends placed a different interpretation on the letters, to be sure, which is what she intended. Certainly she could not have believed, at this juncture, that Voltaire was enamored of life at the Berlin court or contemplated settling in Prussia.

Voltaire himself corresponded infrequently with Émilie; perhaps he did not trust her to keep up the pretense, or it may have been that his silence was a manifestation of a love beginning to wane. Whatever the cause, the lack of communications from him added to Émilie's distress. On one occasion she learned from newspapers that he was visiting Brunswick, and on another she discovered he was spending a week or two in Bayreuth. When an assistant to the French ambassador returned home, she was in touch with him at once, writing to ask whether Voltaire was presently in Berlin, how he fared, and whether he was bothered by his stomach disorders.

"I am cruelly paid for all I have done on M. de Voltaire's behalf," she wrote sadly to d'Argental. *"I feel, without desiring such a feeling, that he wishes to be rid of me, and has chosen the way of a cad and a coward to convey his sentiments to me."*

As the weeks stretched into months it appeared that Émilie was forgetting the purpose of Voltaire's visit to Prussia. Even her letters to Mme. de Tencin no longer mentioned his secret mission, nor did she bring up the subject with Richelieu after forgiving him and resuming her correspondence with him. Her grief became overwhelming, she was convinced she was a woman abandoned, and she succumbed to a sorrow that would not be assuaged.

Autumn came, and the weather was raw, but Émilie formed the habit of taking long daily walks, since she could not bear the solitude of the château. Inevitably, she caught a bad cold, and went to bed with a fever and a racking cough. Self-pity engulfed her, and, convincing herself she had a congenitally weak chest, she expressed fears she might suffer the fate of Mme. de Richelieu and die of consumption.

Meanwhile Voltaire was being entertained at banquets, opera performances, and supper parties, but was not enjoying himself. Frederick could be a charming companion, but often was busy elsewhere, and Voltaire was wearied by the constant companionship of homosexuals and sickened by the antics of the King's pretty young men. What frustrated him far beyond everything else was the wily monarch's refusal to discuss his future plans.

In October, after Voltaire had spent the better part of five months with him, Frederick suddenly launched into a discussion of foreign relations with him, and the nature of the King's observation conveyed the hint that he had not been fooled by the elaborate ruse perpetrated for his benefit. He appeared to see Voltaire as an ideal messenger who would take an accurate report of his thinking to Paris.

Prussia, Frederick declared, was reluctant to resume the war against Austria because Maria Theresa had renewed her nation's traditional alliance with England, and the young King had no desire to be caught between two foes. But France, he said, was still the most potent force on the Continent, and could neutralize England. Therefore, if the French went to war with the English, he would make a secret alliance with Louis XV and launch a new campaign against the Austrians.

Voltaire had learned all he had come to Prussia to find out, and wrote at once to Émilie, telling her he was leaving and expressing the hope that she would meet him in Brussels. When she received his note she enjoyed a miraculous improvement in health, her fears of consumption dissipated, and she hurriedly prepared for the journey to Brussels, reaching the city two days before Voltaire arrived on November 6th.

Nothing is known of their reunion, but, at the least, Émilie was relieved.

Three days later the reunited couple left for Paris, where Voltaire would submit a report on his mission, but they found time for a brief stay with M. and Mme. Denis in Lille. Voltaire awaited the royal applause that was certain to be one of his rewards, and Émilie hinted, in a note to Mme. de Tencin, that he would not be surprised by the award of a pension.

Paris, he was shocked to discover, was in a chaotic state, and affairs at Fontainebleau were worse. Amelot and Mme. de Châteauroux had been intriguing against each other, the director of the Foreign Ministry had been dismissed, and, as nearly as Voltaire could learn, the King's mistress was in charge of French foreign relations. The author's report was received with phlegmatic calm, both Louis and Richelieu already having guessed what he told them, and he was dismissed with curt thanks.

Voltaire went into seclusion, locking himself into a small suite in the Faubourg Saint-Honoré house. But Émilie visited all of her old friends, and never had she looked so radiant. She was savoring the triumph, even though it was not of her own making.

XV

Relations between Émilie and Voltaire were strained during the winter and early spring of 1744. She had not yet forgiven him for his cavalier attitude toward her, and he was still annoyed because the crown had failed to show appreciation for his efforts. Perhaps the road would have been smoother at Cirey or Brussels, but the couple had no desire to return to the dreary Belgian town, and they had good cause to stay away from the château.

The Marquis du Châtelet, enjoying his first long leave of absence from army duty in many years, had moved into Cirey with his stupid, red-haired mistress. Émilie and Voltaire did not mind spending a few days with them, but the mere idea of being compelled to tolerate their company for endless months was too dreadful to contemplate. And while it was true that Voltaire's money had rehabilitated Cirey, it was also true that the Marquis was the proprietor of the place, and therefore could not be asked to take himself and the redhead elsewhere. Émilie and Voltaire stayed in Paris.

Voltaire sulked, and Émilie, who may have been balancing the scales of self-conceived justice, had never been gayer. She left the house at noon each day to visit the salons of friends, to make appearances at Fontainebleau, and to visit the mathematicians and scientists at their café haunts. Every evening she attended dinner parties, went to the theater, and was seen frequently at the opera. Above all, she gambled.

Never had she played for such high stakes, never had she sat down more often at the *vingt-et-un* tables, and never before had she lost so consistently. Within a short time she lost sums that far exceeded the contents of her own purse, and Voltaire was forced to rescue her.

"Mme. du Châtelet's opponents," he wrote, *"do not realize she performs prodigious feats with numbers in her head, and supposedly knows what cards they hold. That they are beating her is due, one must believe, to the elements of chance."*

What he really believed, as he confided to several of his close friends, was that Émilie was punishing him for his neglect during his months in Prussia. But he paid her enormous debts, the equivalent of about forty thousand dollars today, and at last she desisted.

Neither Émilie nor Voltaire had been productive for a long time, and suddenly they went back to work. King Louis commissioned the author to write a play that would be performed at the festivities connected with the forthcoming marriage of his eldest son, the Dauphin, his manner indicating that he was conferring a favor. Voltaire, however, firmly believed he was doing the crown a favor; not for everyone would France's most famous author write a trifle on demand.

No one, including Voltaire, knew what Émilie was doing. She secreted herself in her workroom for hours each day, but she refused to discuss her project. Voltaire, knowing the creative mind, did not press.

War clouds were thickening over France, which was being drawn into Frederick of Prussia's quarrel with Austria. England and Holland were honoring their old alliances with Austria, and the battle lines were being drawn for the conflict that would be known as the War of the Austrian Succession.

Émilie had reason to rejoice, however, and Voltaire, for the first time, did not protest too vehemently against the coming of war. The Marquis du Châtelet was recalled to duty to lead his divisions, and returned to the field, taking his mistress with him. Early in April, 1744, Émilie learned that her husband had vacated Cirey, and she made the best of the happy news, arriving at the château with Voltaire ten days later.

"We are once more in charming Cirey," Émilie said in a hastily scribbled note to d'Argental. *"It is more charming than ever. Never have we known such tranquility, never has there been a more benign spring, never has the sun been brighter or warmer. Your friend appears enchanted to be here."*

Old routines were resumed, old rhythms were reestablished, and old habits became second nature again. Émilie and Voltaire spent their days apart, working furiously, then met for elegant, intellectual suppers, where they relaxed. Only one guest joined them, and they were not hampered by him. Rev. François Jacquier, a Jesuit, was a noted geometrician and philosopher who had written an analytical version of Newton's *Mathematical Principles of Natural Philosophy*, and had come to Cirey to finish a new scientific treatise. He was a welcome addition.

Voltaire labored diligently on his play, the *Princesse de Navarre*, and found that the words refused to flow as he wished. A letter to d'Argental was filled with complaints and misgivings:

"I begin to wonder if a life in Paradise is conducive to the writing of a play that will be the quality of that which is now expected of me. I am afraid it will make the Dauphin and Dauphine yawn; I know it makes me yawn. But it may amuse you, for Mme. du Châtelet likes it, and you are worthy to think as she does.

"The troubles this trifling work causes me are endless, and always I think of the couple, lacking in the wit that such as you and I savor, for whom it is being prepared. How to amuse them? How to make them laugh? Oh, that I should be writing for a royal court! I a mere jester! I am degraded. But no matter. I have accepted the assignment, and must keep my word.

"I am afraid of writing nothing but nonsense. One writes well only when one delights in the choice of a subject."

Eventually he read a draft of the play to Émilie, who enjoyed it so much that she wept copiously. Voltaire told her that her critical faculties were blunted, that she was so prejudiced in his favor she could not make a fair judgment. He himself was dissatisfied and went back to work on the play.

In the summer of 1744 Émilie finished her own work, a long philosophical essay that she called *Traité sur le Bonheur*. It was her only original work for a non-scientific readership, and in a preface she said she had not prepared it for the general public, but for people of stature, meaning those of established financial and social position.

The *Traité* was a curious document. It was not only written in the first person, but was frankly autobiographical, and the author's candor, combined with her renown, made it the equivalent of a best-seller after it was published, later in the year, in the form of a thick pamphlet.

The opening section was devoted to a discussion of gambling, which, Émilie said, provided her with great excitement because she was not wealthy and therefore could not afford to lose large sums. If money meant nothing to her, gambling would bore her.

Cards, she insisted, were one of three pleasures left to a woman when she grew old. Another was study, which gave joy at any age, provided one's brain did not deteriorate, and the third was gluttony. She hoped she would not be seen piling her plate high in the manner that so many old women piled it, but she was afraid that when she became aged, she would succumb, too.

Meanwhile gambling kept her young. The human soul was far too tranquil, and needed to be aroused by the twin, opposite passions of fear and hope. Gambling caused one to run the gamut, from extreme hope to extreme fear, and consequently kept the gambler in good health.

In a philosophically reflective mood, Émilie gave her recipe for human happiness, first explaining that most people did not discover the recipe until old age overcame them. Her recipe, she declared, was simple:

One must live virtuously.

One must rigorously rid his being of all prejudices against persons and customs.

One must retain the illusions one deemed important in childhood.

One must live sensibly in order to enjoy the blessings of good health.

One must cultivate strong tastes.

One must develop strong passions.

Obviously Émilie considered herself a virtuous woman, which surprised those who had been titillated for years by her notoriety. She did not fill out the skeleton of her recipe, and gave her readers no clues that would help them achieve some of her heights. How one went about ridding himself of prejudice went unexplained, as did the admonition to retain the illusions of childhood.

But she discussed passions at some length, in terms sufficiently cryptic to cause her readers to wonder precisely what she meant. The reader would inquire of her, she said, whether the exercise of passions do not make more people unhappy than happy. One did not know. In fact, one could not reply accurately to such a query. The reasons were simple. As the reader well knew from personal experience, it is always the unhappy people of the world who talk about themselves. But the happy people hug their happiness to themselves; no one really knows them, and often they are actually anonymous.

No one, she pointed out, ever wrote plays or operas about happy people. She defied the reader to name one play about happy individuals who remained happy. She hastened to add that she was not recommending the exercise of strong passions without restraint, because such exercise caused many people to suffer unhappiness. On the other hand the exercise of passions within reason was desirable because no individual could enjoy true pleasure without such exercise.

The single most important requirement for the enjoyment of passions, Émilie wrote, was the good health of the individual. All persons, she said blithely, were born in radiant health, just as all persons were destined by their Creator to spend a certain time on earth, provided they did not harm themselves. Too much food or too much drink could be harmful to health, she warned solemnly, as could too little sleep caused by overly late hours.

She had consoling words for those who loved to eat. Gluttony was a legitimate source of happiness, and the gourmand had no need to feel ashamed of himself, provided he did not indulge his cravings too frequently. It was possible, she said, to overeat at regular intervals without harming one's health or digestion. Unfortunately, however, one's peers were always quick to criticize one's habits, so she advised those who enjoyed overeating to observe the amenities in public and indulge in their favorite pastime only in the privacy of their own homes.

Surprisingly frank, Émilie discussed her own drinking. There was nothing she enjoyed more, she said, than a glass of strong alcohol. She was not referring to the table wines commonly in use or the watered wine one drank in the morning. Rather, she meant the distilled wines that cause a burning sensation when consumed. She herself had been forced to renounce all distilled beverages, she confessed; they made her too uncomfortable, too hot, and she spent the following morning trying in vain to find relief by drinking various elixirs. No elixirs, she added, were worth what one was forced to pay for them.

Gluttony, however, was another matter, at least in her case. Sometimes she felt ravenous, and on such occasions she ate as much as she wished. In fact, she ate until she could not touch another morsel of food. Sometimes she had been known to be ravenously hungry for days on end, and had given in to her cravings. But she issued a solemn warning to the gourmand who might wish to follow her example. It was essential to good health, she declared, to follow periods of overeating with even longer periods of very strict dieting. He who would eat too much was compelled to diet; that was one of nature's first laws, and could be transgressed only at one's peril.

The achievement of happiness, Émilie said, was possible only by defining one's goals and working without pause toward them. Too many people lived aimless lives, and wondered why they were not happy, but the cause was obvious. Too many people build and construct one day, destroy their handiwork the next —and then repent.

Émilie's view of repentance placed her in direct conflict with all organized religious groups that followed the Judeo-Christian tradition, and particularly outraged the French Roman Catholic hierarchy. Repentance, she declared, was one of the curses of mankind, a device invented by human beings for the purpose of torturing themselves, a form of breast-beating that caused misery and did no one any good.

Of all the sentiments and feelings that course through the mind and body of an individual, she said, repentance was one of the most disagreeable. In fact, the individual who found himself in the grip of despair was one of the most miserable of people, and his despair not only caused him mental anguish, but destroyed his appetite and his love of life itself. Therefore the individual needed to be on guard against himself at all times, and whenever he discovered himself feeling repentant, it was his obligation to his tranquillity to eliminate the sense of repentance.

There was a very good reason it was useless to repent, no matter what clergymen preached. A person made a mistake and repented in order to avoid making the error a second time. But nothing in life ever happened twice in precisely the same way. It was said that history repeated itself, but a noted historian of her acquaintance assured her this was not true; history merely *appeared* to repeat itself. This was true in one's personal experiences, too. There was only a semblance of repetition, not real repetition. Therefore repentance was nothing more that a useless form of self-torture.

Instead, she advised her readers, they should go forward from their present positions, never looking over their shoulders at the past. In this regard, she insisted, it was wise to reflect on agreeable matters. The disagreeable weighed down the soul, made one morose and destroyed one's ability to enjoy life. So, in effect, a person was merely hurting himself. But he would find he was endowed with a far greater capacity for enjoyment if he concentrated, always, on that which was agreeable.

The best example of the disagreeable, she declared, was death. One's demise was inevitable and unavoidable, as was that of everyone one knew, everyone to whom the individual was related. So she saw nothing to be gained by the contemplation of that which could not be altered, be it one's own death or that of another. Death was a very sad experience, and for those who loved life it was actually humiliating, so it could do no good to dwell on the subject.

Émilie had some special words of advice for her feminine readers. Women, she declared, found happiness far more difficult to achieve than did men, due to the fact that women led such restricted lives. A man could do what he pleased, live as he pleased, pursue any career he pleased. Women, however, were limited.

Joan of Arc had been a great general, it was said, but Émilie suspected the story was a myth, invented to placate women who, as little girls, had entertained the hopeless ambition of pursuing military careers. Most women were sensible, of course, and hated war, so she would not weep for the few who regretted their inability to become soldiers.

There were many women, however, who had a great gift for politics. Émilie knew of several whose understanding of the complex politics that either bound nations together or separated them was as sensitive and advanced as that of any man. But, alas! men were jealous of their prerogatives and barred women from politics, too.

So it went in many other fields of endeavor; women were barred from this profession and that. So a woman had to find happiness in her own way, which was not the same as that of a man.

Study, she declared, was the greatest of resources available to a woman. No one could prevent her from reading, from becoming the pupil of a great teacher, from doing her very own independent research into a subject that interested her. If she applied herself diligently, study enabled her to master any subject, to know more about it than any man could possibly know, and the knowledge she obtained would give her lasting satisfaction.

On a more frivolous level, she could find happiness in many small ways. Every woman, even the homeliest, loved pretty clothes. When a woman's spirits drooped, Émilie advised her to order a new gown from her seamstress; it should be a lovely gown rather than one that was merely practical, and if it made her feel attractive, her spirits would rise.

If a woman found herself in such a miserable state that a pretty gown would not lift her spirits, Émilie advised the purchase of a new piece of furniture. A gown could be worn no more often than once every three or four weeks, if one's wardrobe was limited. But one could sit in a chair, lie on a chaise, or play cards on a table every day. A new piece of furniture that was pleasing to the eye could guarantee an improvement in the spirits of even the most depressed of women.

Women could achieve happiness for themselves in other ways, too, Émilie said. The acquisition of jewelry gladdened the heart of every woman, but gems admittedly were very expensive. So a woman who could not afford diamonds and the like would be wise to limit herself to the collection of less expensive objects whose possession she enjoyed. Snuff boxes, for instance, could give one a great deal of pleasure, and Émilie said she knew from her own experience that the addition of a new snuff box to one's collection could give one intense pleasure.

A woman could also do many little things that would make life more pleasant for her and improve her serenity. Émilie advised her feminine readers to remove their shoes when their feet were pinched; this could be done, even in polite company, if one screened one's movements with discretion. Regular visits to the privy also improved one's disposition, as she knew from her own experience, and she recommended the practice. Finally, Émilie knew of no pleasure like that of keeping one's body warm in very cold weather; the mere knowledge that one was snug and warm gave a woman intense satisfaction.

The *Traité*, more than anything else that Émilie wrote, made her famous in her own time. At least six editions were published in Paris prior to her death, a remarkable number, and although no one can guess how many copies were printed and sold, she made a handsome profit, which was unusual. She translated the pamphlet into English herself, and London booksellers reported a brisk demand. A Jesuit priest who was a friend of Voltaire's prepared a Dutch translation, and a total stranger translated the work into Swedish.

The philosophy Émilie expounded in the *Traité* was anything but profound, and many of her ideas appear absurd when judged by the standards of a later age. But it must be remembered she was writing for a specific, limited readership, the individual of means, especially the lady who was burdened by few responsibilities.

In a larger sense, Émilie was creating a new type of "literature." Others, seeing her success, either imitated her or wrote similar treatises that gave the author's own formulas for achieving serenity and balance. Surely it is not an exaggeration to say that Émilie du Châtelet created the prototype of the "how to find happiness" books that would be found in profusion on bookstore shelves in a later time.

The joy that Émilie herself felt in the summer of 1744 was

due to the tranquillity of her relations with Voltaire. Never had they known such harmony, never had they quarreled so infrequently. After living together for more than a decade they were enjoying the equivalent of a second honeymoon, and their letters to friends in Paris reflected their serenity. Neither uttered a single complaint, and each repeatedly mentioned the pleasure found in the other's company.

Early in the summer Voltaire's niece, Mme. Denis, paid a brief visit to Cirey. Her husband had died, suddenly and unexpectedly, at their home in Lille. The grief of the young widow was contained, in part because she had never loved her husband, and Émilie complimented her, saying she was behaving "with much good sense." Voltaire took it upon himself to console his niece, with Émilie's approval, and during her visit he took several long walks with her in the hills. He, too, could find only good in her, and praised her at length in his letters to friends in Paris.

The social season that began in the autumn of 1744 promised to be the biggest in the history of the French court, which would make it truly spectacular. Not only were innumerable festivities planned in connection with the coming wedding of the Dauphin, but many additional functions were scheduled to celebrate the recovery of King Louis from a serious illness. Voltaire was not needed as yet for his production of *La Princesse de Navarre*, but he and Émilie had no intention of missing the gala splash of a lifetime, so they left Cirey in September and took up residence, as usual, in the house on the Faubourg Saint-Honoré.

Émilie's pamphlet was published shortly after their arrival, and the stir it created added to her luster. She found hostesses competing for her company, and was amused that many of them were women who openly disliked her. She did no work whatever, other than her daily studying, which she did not consider work, and devoted the better part of her time to the social whirl. It is not known whether she and Voltaire had reached an agreement on the subject of her gambling, but the fact of the matter is that Émilie did no card playing during the stay of almost six months in the city.

Voltaire was still dissatisfied with his play, and spent several hours of work on it each day, but he devoted himself to the good life, too, and accompanied Émilie everywhere. They were seen together at dinners and suppers, galas and performances of the opera, which he privately found boring. Émilie accompanied him to the Procope when he went there to catch up on the latest theatrical news and gossip, and he escorted her to the Gradot for her ponderous chats with scientists and mathematicians.

They were inseparable until January, when it became necessary for Voltaire to put the *Princesse de Navarre* into production. He summed up his state of mind in a letter to his friend, Cideville, in which he said: *"I beg you to pity a poor devil who is the King's fool at the age of fifty, and who is more embarrassed with musicians, decorators, comedians, singers and dancers than eight or nine electors would be in making a German Caesar. I run from Paris to Versailles, and I make verses in the post-chaise. It is necessary to praise the King highly, the Dauphine prettily, the royal family gently, please the whole court—and not displease the town."*

Richelieu, who was in charge of the celebrations, had promised that a new theater being constructed just for the one performance of the *Princesse* would be ready by February 23rd, the scheduled date. But the workmen were behind schedule, and a threatened postponement caused Voltaire to make one of his rare public scenes. He lost his temper at a rehearsal, and his rage did not abate until Richelieu doubled the work crew, restoring the play to its original schedule.

The entire royal family was present for the performance, as was the whole court. Ordinarily Émilie would have been expected to sit with relatives, it being the custom, on occasions of state, for one to refrain from parading one's romantic affiliations. But Voltaire was unique, and his play was the grand climax of the celebrations, King Louis's way of reminding Frederick and other monarchs that only the author's own liege lord could command him to write a special work for a special occasion. Émilie fitted no known mold, either, and was almost universally regarded as the most brilliant member of her sex in Europe, so she believed herself privileged, too.

She and Voltaire calmly defied convention, sitting together in a box directly opposite that of the royal family, where everyone in the theater could see them. Émilie refused to wear a wig and powdered her own hair, a trick she had learned from some of the more attractive actresses associated with the Comédie Française, and she wore so many jewels that some members of the diplomatic community, who did not know her, assumed she was a princess related to the royal family.

Voltaire paid scant attention to the performance and even less to the reactions of the audience at large. He kept close watch on the party opposite him, and his heart sank when he saw the Dauphine yawn repeatedly. At the intermission, when he crossed the theater to pay his respects to Majesties and Highnesses, the Dauphine complained that the play was lacking in humor, and his heart sank.

When he rejoined Émilie he could only mutter that a Spanish Infanta whose knowledge of French was limited obviously could not appreciate the wit directed toward a sophisticated French audience.

What caused him far greater concern was the King's attitude. Louis XV paid almost no attention to the play, but chatted with the favorites who surrounded him, read messages brought to him from time to time by special couriers, and otherwise behaved as though spending the evening in one of the many informal parlors scattered through the palace.

At the end of the performance, however, he led the applause, and insisting he was delighted, he rewarded the author with far greater generosity than anyone had anticipated. Voltaire was given the title of Historian of France, which had been created for him, and with it he was granted an annual pension, for life, of two thousand gold louis. He was also given the exclusive right to use an "apartment" at Versailles, a somewhat dubious privilege, as the quarters consisted of a tiny, dark room at the rear of the palace, only a stone's throw from the kitchens, with an unobstructed view of the royal stables. Voltaire was also told he would be appointed a Gentleman of the Chamber as soon as a vacancy occurred, and Louis kept his word the following year. This was a coveted position, since no duties were involved and the recipient of the honor was paid an additional fifteen hundred gold louis for life.

In all, the months of effort Voltaire had devoted to a very minor work had paid exceptionally handsome dividends. He had enjoyed Paris, as had Émilie, and for the first time in his adult life the secret police had not followed him, ransacked his quarters, or otherwise made life miserable for him.

The sojourn had been delightful, but Émilie wanted to go home to Cirey. The geometric intricacy of triangles had caught her fancy, and she was anxious to initiate a number of experiments that required the use of the laboratory installed in the great hall of the château. And she felt, too, that she had shared Voltaire with others for enough months; she had been generous, but now she wanted him to herself.

Voltaire surprised her by displaying reluctance to leave, which Émilie found disconcerting, but he finally admitted that he had a special reason for wanting to stay a little longer. Mme. Denis, his niece, had just returned to Paris after settling her late husband's estate in Lille, and was in the process of moving into a new house her uncle had just purchased for her. She was alone and confused, Voltaire said, so she needed his help.

Émilie readily agreed, and Voltaire absented himself for the better part of each day over the period of a month. Émilie did not stop to think that Mme. Denis had been very competent, and by no stretch of the imagination could have been called the helpless type. Nor did it seem odd that a young woman who had spent all but a few months of her life in Paris required guidance in dealing with problems that arose only in the city.

Had Voltaire showed as much devotion to any other woman, Émilie would have been violently jealous. But Mme. Denis, after all, was his niece.

XVI

In the spring of 1745 Émilie du Châtelet looked forward to a resumption of her idyllic life at Cirey with Voltaire, but her dream was shattered when she received an urgent message from Châlons, where her son was attending school. The 18-year-old boy had contracted smallpox.

A typical eighteenth-century French aristocrat might provide a doctor but not respond personally, yet Émilie went straight to her son. Voltaire had started writing his next major work, the *Précis du Siècle de Louis XV*, and Émilie urged him not to interrupt his routines, but he insisted on accompanying her. Physicians, as he wrote Cideville, were a hopeless lot, being more opinionated than attorneys, more ignorant than courtiers, and more stupid than princes and dukes.

The young patient proved to be critically ill, and, as Voltaire had predicted, three physicians who were called in proved incompetent. They quibbled over the diagnosis, quarreled violently over the right course of medication to be administered, and could agree only on the assumption that the patient's days were numbered.

Voltaire horrified Émilie by dismissing the doctors and taking charge of the case himself. But his self-confidence was not misplaced. Like all hypochondriacs, he knew a great deal about medicine, and, in an age when science was just beginning to crowd out superstition, he may have known as much as any physician. At it happened, he may have been an expert on the treatment of smallpox, having made a lifelong study of the disease. Twenty years earlier he had written a long letter of advice to Émilie's father, who had contracted a mild case of smallpox, and he was believed to be the author of a witty, practical pamphlet on the subject.

Émilie wrote to her daughter and later to d'Argental that Voltaire saved her son's life. He gave the boy laudanum, a crude opiate, to hold down his fever, and bathed him every hour in a mixture of brandy and lemon-water, which reduced the pox and helped prevent the spread of the infection. Demonstrating the stamina he always showed in times of crisis, Voltaire nursed the patient for a week, assisted only by Émilie, and the future Marquis du Châtelet recovered. His life was not threatened again until the Revolution, when he died on the scaffold for the crime of being an aristocrat.

The couple retired to Cirey, taking the boy with them to recuperate, and there they stayed for forty days in enforced isolation, forbidden to visit or receive visits from any of their friends and relatives. It was the law that anyone exposed to smallpox had to be quarantined for forty days, and King Louis, who lived in mortal fear of the disease, personally insisted that the rule be obeyed to the letter.

During this period, on May 12, 1745, the combined armies of France defeated those of England in a major engagement, the Battle of Fontenoy. Incidentally, the French commander, Maurice de Saxe, lavished praise on a subordinate, the Marquis du Châtelet, whose chances of winning a promotion to the supreme rank of Marshal of France were vastly enhanced.

The whole country rejoiced, but Voltaire lost his poise and patience. His position as Historian required him to write a complete, accurate history of the battle for posterity, which made it necessary for him to interview officers and men of all ranks on both sides, but he was forbidden to see anyone. Various friends, including Émilie's husband, wrote him letters containing long accounts of the battle, but he found them incomplete. Restless and filled with an unaccustomed patriotic fervor, Voltaire sat down and wrote a long poem, *La Bataille de Fontenoy,* which achieved overnight fame, a renown that has endured down to the present.

King Louis was delighted, as was the Marshal de Saxe, and the country responded by buying more copies of the poem than of any other work Voltaire had ever written. The author's pacifist leanings were forgotten for the moment, as were Émilie's, and they endured the last days of their isolation by estimating the size of the enormous royalties that the published version of the poem would earn.

At the end of the forty days young Châtelet went off to join his father at the front, and Voltaire made plans to leave immediately for Paris, so he could conduct his interviews with the commanders who had been summoned by the King to receive various honors for their exploits. Émilie refused to be separated from her lover, and, although a new book on Newton was beginning to take shape in her mind, she interrupted her work in order to accompany him.

It was a surprise to discover that the Marquis du Châtelet was among those who had just arrived at Fontainebleau, and Émilie was delighted. Never one to retire modestly into the background when there was a spotlight to be shared, she bathed in her husband's reflected glory by marching into the audience chamber on his arm. Voltaire was in the audience as Historian of France, and duly recorded the scene, declaring that M. de Châtelet was awarded a rich purse, a gold sword bearing the King's crest, and was granted a number of "personal privileges," which meant that, although he moved no higher in the peerage, he was granted the prerogatives of a duke. The account made no mention of Mme. du Châtelet's presence; it was an official journal, after all, so Voltaire was required to write only the essentials.

The personal privileges granted to the Marquis caused Émilie to lose her equilibrium. She had always wanted to be a duchess, her daughter had become a duchess, and now she was as good as any duchess. She was permitted to sit in the presence of the Queen, for example, and did, which was fair enough. But she made such an elaborate ceremony of the act that a number of high-ranking ladies, including the Dauphine and several genuine duchesses, became irritated.

It was the right of duchesses to accompany the Queen to Mass, and Émilie had no intention of being left out. She applied for a place in the entourage, which was assigned to her, and the following morning she drove with the others from the main building of the palace to the chapel at the opposite end of the grounds. When they emerged from the church the Queen and four duchesses entered the royal coach for the drive back to the palace, and the fireworks began.

Two other coaches waited to transport the other ladies. Émilie, who was the junior member of the group, elbowed past the duchesses, climbed into a coach, and made herself comfortable. Startled by her rudeness, the others refused to join her, and all of them crowded into the one remaining coach.

Émilie realized her mistake and tried to follow them, but they refused to admit her, insisting—probably without exaggeration—that there was no space for her. So she was forced to endure the mortification of riding back to the palace alone. She immediately offered apologies to the Queen and the various duchesses, which were accepted, but she had given the gossips a juicy new morsel, and they talked of little else for days.

A woman more sensitive to the demands of protocol would have learned her lesson, but Émilie's mind was filled with thoughts of Newton and of her own newly acquired social stature. Joining a party at dinner in the Queen's private suite, she was so anxious to move closer to the head of the table that she took a chair reserved for the Duchesse de Luynes, who held the position of Mistress of the Robes, and was head of the Queen's household.

Half of the company immediately told the offender her error, and Émilie, flushing a deep red, moved to a place farther down the table. Mme. de Luynes, an amiable woman with a lively sense of humor, was not offended, so the incident caused no additional damage. By now, however, everyone at the royal court regarded Mme. du Châtelet as an eccentric.

Émilie escaped chastisement because King Louis was anxious that nothing be said or done to offend Voltaire. Although the monarch was no intellectual, the glory of France was of primary importance to him. This fact was driven home when it was revealed that the unpredictable Voltaire had been conducting an extraordinarily friendly correspondence with the new, liberal Pope, Benedict XIV.

One day Voltaire appeared at court, proudly displaying a gold medal engraved with the Pope's likeness. Benedict had sent it to him, and when the author had complained that it was too small, the Pope had written him: *"It is the only size that has been made. We couldn't give you a larger one if you were St. Peter himself."*

This friendship shocked the members of the Roman Catholic hierarchy in France, and the consternation increased when Benedict permitted Voltaire to dedicate *Mahomet* to him. The Pope enjoyed the play, he said, and remarked that he thought it absurd to search for Christ in the character of the protagonist. *Mahomet* was a great play on its obvious, surface level, Benedict declared, and he proved himself an accurate prophet when he predicted it would endure for centuries on that level.

Almost overnight, it seemed, Voltaire had become virtually untouchable. His relationship with Pope Benedict placed him beyond the criticism of French bishops, and if Louis's secret police molested him he might embarrass France by going off to the court of Frederick of Prussia, or worse, to the enemy court of George II of England.

It might be noted that Voltaire's stature had become so great that his many enemies, who continued to damn him, but on a muted level, could no longer prevent his election to the French Academy, the highest of honors and that which he wanted more than all the rest. It was obvious to everyone who paid any attention to such matters that he would win the next seat that opened, and whenever a member fell ill, the café wits said his seat was being reupholstered for Voltaire. When a vacancy finally did occur, in the early spring of 1746, Voltaire was elected without serious opposition.

In the main, Émilie and Voltaire lived uneventful lives in 1745 and 1746. The honors won by the Marquis du Châtelet, combined with Voltaire's increased stature and his appointment as a Gentleman of the Chamber, assured them of a secure place at the royal court, which they enjoyed. They spent as much time in Paris as they did at Cirey, and traveled back and forth frequently, making the journey three times in as many months during the autumn of 1745.

Voltaire continued to provide the funds for their household, and Émilie had learned caution; her servants complained that she paid the lowest wages in the city, which may have been an exaggeration, as the servants of others said the same. Their social life was active, but they attended fewer suppers and other parties in the city, preferring to participate in the never-ending festivities at Versailles, the King's summer palace, or Fontainebleau, which he now used as his winter home.

Émilie's work was still important to her, and she claimed it was of paramount importance, but she slowed her pace, perhaps without realizing it. Clothes and cosmetics required more attention when she rode out to Versailles or Fontainebleau several times each week, and the round-trip journey itself consumed many hours. She persisted, nevertheless, in her determination to write another book on Newton, and her voluminous, ever-growing pile of notes indicated that she hoped to prepare a definitive masterpiece.

Voltaire, as always, kept innumerable irons sizzling in many fires. Plays and poems, essays and his history of the reign of Louis XV kept him at his desk for hours each day. He was so busy, in fact, that he could not always accompany Émilie to the King's court. He was less interested than she in pomp and ceremony, as he told her, and he disliked chatting with nincompoops when she sat at the card table.

Also, he had responsibilities that kept him in Paris, among them Mme. Denis. As he told Émilie, he was the last Arouet of his generation, so she had no other uncles or aunts to whom she could turn. Unlike so many members of her generation, Mme. Denis had a strong sense of family unity, and although Voltaire had made a career of scoffing at middle-class values, he frequently praised her attitude.

The young woman had purchased her own small Paris house, giving the impression to everyone, including Émilie, that she had used funds left by her husband. It seems almost inconceivable that Émilie didn't know the true financial situation: the late M. Denis had just started out in life, and had not acquired even the semblance of a modest fortune at the time of his death. Many of Voltaire's friends, among them d'Argental and Cideville, took it for granted that the author had supplied the funds for Mme. Denis's house.

But Émilie, the genius in virtually every realm of mathematics, confined her interests to the abstract. The source of money had never been of much concern to her, and she could spend it with the air of a profligate without bothering to ask how it had been acquired. So it may be that she had no idea Voltaire had bought his delightful niece a house. On the other hand, if she knew, she probably did not attach any particular significance to the gesture. Surely it was the unquestioned right of a rich, famous man who might not live many more years to indulge in a kind gesture to a favored young relative.

Louise Denis was no beauty, and even her greatest admirers did not claim that she possessed unusual physical appeal. But she was slender, which was unusual in the eighteenth century, with dark eyes and hair, and she dressed with quiet chic. Those who complimented the taste that she showed on a limited budget had no idea that generous Uncle Voltaire supplied the funds for what only the initiated were able to identify as a discreetly expensive wardrobe.

What attracted people, particularly men, to Mme. Denis were her intellect and wit. She wrote no books, composed no music, and painted no pictures, but she could converse brilliantly on the arts, as well as on matters of politics, a subject that bored Émilie. In addition, the young woman was acquiring a reputation in artistic circles for possessing a sense of humor second only to that of her uncle. In fact, there were some who preferred it because it was less sharp, and it was said that she never attacked anyone.

The charming, amusing young widow had more than a fair share of the eligible men of Paris as admirers, among them actors, composers, and members of the nobility. She treated them with delightful impartiality, never encouraging any one of them to hope for more than her friendship, so she made no enemies, an impressive feat at a time when a single careless word could start a feud.

There were some who came to the house of Louise Denis because Voltaire was a frequent caller, and they eagerly welcomed the opportunity to engage in a chat with the great man. It did no one harm to say, "You know, Voltaire made a devastating remark about so-and-so at a little salon gathering yesterday."

Two hundred years would pass before the world would learn that Voltaire's interest in Louise Denis at this time was other than avuncular. Both were so extraordinarily careful, so discreet in all they said and did, that no one suspected they had launched an affair, a relationship that would last for the better part of their long lives. Recent discoveries, including caches of their letters and other documents, are being studied by scholars, so it may be that a definitive date soon may be given for the beginning of their affair. At the time of the present writing it is still unknown, but in all probability they were going to bed together fairly frequently early in the period between the autumn of 1745 and the spring of 1747.

Voltaire's position was similar to that of the married, middle-aged man who knew his wife so well that he took her for granted; still loving her, in his fashion, he nevertheless turned to a younger woman for new excitement. Voltaire and Émilie du Châtelet were not married to each other, of course, but they had taken such pains to publicize their relationship that it would have been impossible for them to part without making themselves look very foolish in the eyes of everyone they knew. As a celebrated mid-twentieth-century literary couple have confessed, the ties that bind those who choose to live together openly are as binding as those imposed by marriage.

In Voltaire's time it was not considered an act of incest for a man to sleep with his niece or a woman with her nephew. There were many marriages, particularly in France, the Italian states, and the Low Countries, between uncles and their nieces. Most bishops in these lands did not question the right of such relatives to marry, and the very few whose diocesan laws required special permits were considered hopelessly old-fashioned.

Certainly people as advanced and iconoclastic in their thinking as Voltaire and Louise Denis did not believe they were committing incest and probably would have been shocked and angry had the accusation been made against them. Whether they considered themselves in love, at least at this juncture, is another matter. Voltaire still professed to be in love with Émilie, and lost no opportunity to proclaim his undying affection for her in his correspondence with everyone from King Frederick to his literary friends.

Unless new facts come to light, it is difficult to say what Mme. Denis felt. In later years her greed became overwhelming, and she drove Voltaire almost to distraction with the heavy, incessant financial demands she made on him. So it may be that, from the outset, she saw stacks of gold coins in front of her eyes when she looked at him. On the other hand, it is also possible that his interest flattered her, and she could have fallen in love with him. No man could exercise greater charm, and Louise was young, unsophisticated, and relatively inexperienced at the time the affair began.

Émilie, like the proverbial middle-class wives of history, had no idea that the man she loved was straying. It was true that she and Voltaire were spending much more time in Paris from 1745 to 1747 than they had done in years, but circumstances made the change in their routines seem very natural. The author was enjoying unprecedented high favor with the most important authorities in the land.

To the best of anyone's knowledge he was writing nothing seditious or libelous, and certainly he was publishing nothing that would win him the renewed ill-will of either state or Church. So the secret police had stopped breathing down the back of his neck, and he no longer had any reason to live near the frontier, with his luggage packed, ready to slip over the border if he landed in fresh trouble. Paris was still the hub of the French intellectual's universe, no matter how much he might damn its shortcomings, and both Voltaire and Émilie were delighted to be there.

What's more, they did go to Cirey frequently for long weeks of the isolated existence and unorthodox routines they had made their own. Perhaps they slept together less frequently than in bygone years—there are hints to that effect in Émilie's correspondence with the Duc de Richelieu—but a woman who had lived with a man for the better part of a decade and a half undoubtedly felt less ardor and expected less passionate devotion than did one who was starting a new marriage or affair.

Émilie had more to occupy her time and thoughts, too. She had given up none of her former activities, but now she was enjoying the prerogatives that Voltaire and her husband had won. It was a never-ending joy for a marquise to be treated like a duchess, and Émilie did not tire of her new privileges. In addition, she was enjoying the fruits of her own hard-won fame. Henry Beston, a young English scientist-philosopher, came to Cirey for the purpose of studying with her, and several young Italian priests, all of them mathematicians of promise, also appeared, eager to receive instruction from her. It was a mark of unprecedented achievement that men who called themselves scientists, mathematicians, or philosophers should, of their own volition, seek a woman as their teacher.

Émilie enjoyed her fool's paradise. She continued to make extensive notes for her new work on Newton, and Voltaire, as thoughtful, considerate, and generous as ever, spent uncounted hours helping her with her studies, conducting laboratory experiments with her and guiding her into the more advanced paths of Newtonian theories.

Her social life was all she could ask. The greatest scientists of the age continued to accept her as an equal and listened respectfully to her views in the long discussions they held at the Gradot. Thanks to Voltaire, she was a member of the innermost theatrical circle. And she had moved so high up the ladder at court that she was now a member of the very small, very select group permitted to play cards with the Queen. Émilie was so appreciative of the honor that she always took care to lose a small amount when she sat at Her Majesty's table, an attitude that Voltaire found very amusing in his letters to his English friends and Frederick.

Had Voltaire been less tender, less devoted to Émilie, she might have suspected him of infidelity, but he was as clever as a successful philanderer in one of his own comedies. And Mme. Denis contributed her full share to the deception, too.

Émilie was pleased to have found something of a kindred spirit in Louise, and enjoyed holding serious discussions with another woman. Mme. Denis was a frequent, invited guest at the house on the Faubourg Saint-Honoré, and Émilie boasted that the younger woman's wit was a major factor in enlivening her salon. At no time did she regard Louise as a competitor, however. The correspondence of a fairly large body of ladies who paid calls on Mme. du Châtelet indicates that the niece of M. de Voltaire was a perfect guest, one who never contradicted her hostess or became embroiled in an argument with her. Mme. Denis, in brief, behaved like a loving, dutiful, and helpful niece, and Émilie praised her lavishly in letter after letter, written over a period of several years.

Voltaire may have succeeded in hiding the truth from the woman who was his more-or-less "official" mistress, but the strain of the double life he was leading told on him in other ways. Late in 1745, almost overnight, he became irascible again, and his dyspepsia increased after his election to the Academy. He plunged into a half-dozen new literary quarrels, and unnecessarily renewed an old one with the discredited Abbé Desfontaines. He gratuitously insulted some of his Academy colleagues, and he wrote viciously rude criticisms of authors and philosophers who lived and worked in other countries. Only the English were spared the bite of his pen.

Many of those whom he attacked retaliated angrily, so he increased the pace of his war against them, and by the end of 1746 some of his friends, d'Argental among them, tried to calm him and extricate him from these senseless feuds. He was lowering his own dignity, hurting no one but himself, d'Argental told him in a series of stern letters.

Voltaire agreed, but seemed incapable of breaking off the quarrels.

In the midst of this already complicated situation, Émilie and her husband won the appeal of their lawsuit in Brussels. The Marquis du Châtelet, who received the good word at his field headquarters in far-off Bavaria, knew that Voltaire's intercessions with King Frederick had been responsible, and he wrote the author a letter. He was deeply grateful to Voltaire, he said, and he knew that Émilie depended on him for her happiness. So he was grateful, above all else, for the knowledge that the relationship was permanent.

Voltaire's quarrels with his colleagues became more intense and irrational.

XVII

The departure of Voltaire and Émilie from Paris was sudden, ignominious in the extreme, and strictly their own fault. Tensions that had been building for so long finally exploded in the early spring of 1747.

Voltaire had added a new burden: He was writing *Sémiramis*, later to be recognized as one of his best plays. He was always on edge when doing creative work, and apparently had been quarreling with Émilie, because she broke one of her own rules. Instead of playing cards cautiously, she gambled recklessly at the Queen's table one evening at Fontainebleau and lost a vast sum of money. Voltaire, wandering from room to room, came to the table to see how she was faring and exploded when he learned the size of the debt he would have to make good.

"You're mad," he said in a low, intense voice, addressing her in English. "Don't you know you shouldn't be playing cards with these women? Every last one of them is a cheat!"

For the only known time in her life, Émilie was unable to speak. The insult to two duchesses was bad enough. But nobody in his right mind, under any circumstances or at any time, could call Marie Catherine Sophie Félicité Leczinska, Queen of France, a cheat!

Voltaire was in grave personal danger, she knew. The insult was so direct, so offensive that not even his reputation could save him from severe punishment, and when the story became known, no other monarch in Europe would blame King Louis for throwing the offender into prison for years.

When Émilie recovered from her initial shock she saw that the expressions on the faces of Queen Marie and the two duchesses had not changed. Was it possible that Voltaire had spoken in such a low tone that they had not heard him? Or was their command of English too limited for them to have understood? On the other hand, as they were well-bred ladies, were they simply waiting until the author withdrew before telling King Louis what had happened? Scenes at court, as Émilie had learned, were avoided at almost any cost.

Voltaire was petrified, too. He had realized the enormity of his mistake as soon as he spoke, but it was too late to recall the words, and he did not want to compound the error by offering a clumsy apology.

Émilie was the first to recover. Pleading a sudden illness, she begged to be excused.

Queen Marie smilingly granted permission for the withdrawal of the Marquise du Châtelet and her companion.

Before Émilie departed, she announced that her indisposition was too severe to permit her to make the long drive back to Paris that night. Therefore she and M. de Voltaire would throw themselves on the mercy of the Duc de Richelieu and ask for a night's lodging at his château, which was located only a short distance from Fontainebleau. She made certain that the Queen and the duchesses heard every word of her supposed plans.

When she and Voltaire reached the carriage, however, she wasted no time on recriminations or explanations of her tactics. There was literally no time to lose: At any moment they might be approached by a squad of Musketeers, the household regiment, bearing a royal warrant for Voltaire's arrest. Voltaire could not return to Paris, either, she said, as a squad well might be awaiting him at their house.

Voltaire was in a state of near-hysteria, and the breakdown of the carriage made his condition even worse. The repairs seemed to take forever, and the better part of the night was gone by the time the pair resumed their journey.

Émilie kept her head and remained surprisingly calm. At first she had thought that Voltaire should go direct to Cirey, but now she had changed her mind. If the crown intended to arrest him, troops would be sent to Cirey when Voltaire failed to appear in Paris, and probably would be waiting there for him. He needed the help of someone powerful enough to offer him a safe refuge until the incident blew over. The one person who came to mind was the Duchesse de Maine.

Émilie's thought was inspired. Anne-Louise de Bourbon-Condé, herself of royal blood, was the widow of the eldest of Louis XIV's bastard sons who had been made legitimate by the Sun King's decree. A wizened, somewhat fey old lady who liked to think of herself as an intellectual, the Duchess presided over her own court at the palace of Sceaux, and she feared no one alive, including Cousin Louis.

Ordinarily Voltaire tried to avoid people like Mme. de Maine, who fawned over authors, and he disliked the frivolous, carnival-like atmosphere of her miniature court. She was a very old friend, however, and he had to admit that Émilie's idea was brilliant: the Duchess would not only take him in, but her love of intrigue was so great that she would be delighted to keep him concealed.

Voltaire left Émilie in a small village located off the main road that connected Fontainebleau and Paris, and she agreed to join him when she could, at Sceaux or elsewhere, and would bring clothes, his current manuscript, and anything else he might need. Voltaire had no attire with him other than what he was wearing, and, having paid Émilie's gambling debts before leaving Fontainebleau, he carried only a small sum of money.

Somehow he made out, as he always did. He sent a note

ahead to Mme. de Maine, telling her what had happened and asking her help. Her palace, located beside a lake in a deep forest, was only a few hours' ride from the village, but Voltaire's love of mystery and drama was so great that the journey took him two days. He changed horses frequently in order to throw possible pursuers off the scent, and thoroughly enjoyed himself, arriving at Sceaux at two o'clock in the morning, with his purse empty.

The eccentric old Duchess awaited him, and had him housed in a secret apartment at the rear of the palace. There Voltaire stayed all day, every day, and privately joined the Duchess for supper in her own apartment every night at midnight. She loved entertainment, the wittiest man on earth was her captive, and they had splendid times together.

Émilie, back in Paris, was suffering. The crown took no overt action against Voltaire, but she was afraid Louis was lying in wait until Voltaire revealed his whereabouts. So she deliberately let it be known that he had gone abroad on urgent publishing business, and told no one except d'Argental the truth. As far as is known, not even Mme. Denis knew where he was.

Émilie was afraid that if she, too, went to Sceaux, she would be followed. And under no circumstances did she dare send Voltaire a letter. Occasionally she heard that someone was leaving for a visit at Sceaux, but could not trust any member of the nobility enough to give him or her a letter, since no one knew Voltaire was there. For that matter Émilie wondered if he had ever arrived there, having received no word from him since their parting at the miserable little village.

Many weeks after Voltaire's arrival the Duchesse de Maine used sources of her own to find out his true status. Queen Marie spoke very little English, and suspected that Voltaire had made an unkind remark about her, but did not know what he had said. The duchesses claimed they hadn't heard him; perhaps they didn't want to become involved. But one fact was clear: Voltaire would not be sent to prison. He left Sceaux for Paris after giving the Duchess his solemn promise that he and Émilie would return soon for an "open" visit.

Wanting to test the atmosphere at Fontainebleau, the reunited Voltaire and Émilie went there as soon as he reached Paris, and quickly discovered the atmosphere had chilled. The Queen was cold, Louis was remote, and even his new mistress, the lovely and talented Jeanne Antoinette de Pompadour, who admired Voltaire, could not budge him. Never again, it might be noted, did Voltaire enjoy the complete confidence of the French court, and although his surface relations with Louis remained cordial, the author was held at arm's length.

The rebuff was depressing, so this seemed the best of times to repay his debt to Mme. de Maine. That, at least, is what Voltaire thought. Émilie, after her many weeks of terror and worry, wanted to retreat with him to Cirey for a long period of quiet recuperation. It may be that Voltaire, because of his new attachment to Mme. Denis, had no desire to be alone with Émilie. In any event, he insisted they go to Sceaux.

They arrived late at night, arousing the entire household, and from the start Émilie was in a foul humor. She complained because the propriety-conscious Duchess gave her quarters on one floor and housed Voltaire on another. She complained about her room, which was changed three times in four days. She complained about the quality of the bed linen, the slovenliness of the servants at the palace, and, in letters to d'Argental, Cideville, and others, about the stupidity of the other guests.

Émilie seemed determined to be an ungracious guest, and Voltaire, for whatever reasons, followed her example. They lived in accordance with their own routines when in the country: They ate breakfast and mid-day dinner in their own rooms, worked all day, and did not appear until ten o'clock at night. Then Émilie wanted to talk about Newton to people who scarcely knew his name, while Voltaire, who deemed it politic to work on his book about the reign of Louis XV, wanted to discuss military heroes at whom the pleasure-loving guests at Sceaux privately snickered.

The huge losses Émilie had suffered at *vingt-et-un* in her catastrophic game with Queen Marie had taught her a lesson, and she refused, rather rudely, to sit down at a card table. Voltaire, whose views on gambling were well known, was not asked to play.

The company at Sceaux passed the time by spending two or three evenings each week visiting the homes of some of the wealthier nobles in the neighborhood, but Émilie refused to accompany the party, stating bluntly that the good lords and ladies were so dull they weren't worth the ride. Voltaire stayed behind, too. A play was presented at the palace, and Voltaire pronounced the whole effort frightful. The play was badly written, the nobles who played the various roles were caricatures, and the direction was nonexistent.

By the end of a week only the Duchess was enjoying a warm relationship with the misbehaving guests. Voltaire, apparently deciding that he and Émilie were going too far, sat down and dashed off some of his effortless verses that praised the entire company.

A few days later the Duc de Richelieu arrived, en route to Genoa, where he was joining his troops, and everyone at Sceaux was relieved when Émilie and Voltaire left with him, intending to accompany him for a day on the road while he brought them up to date on their present state of grace at the royal court.

The Duchesse de Maine and her guests heaved a collective sigh of relief. Émilie had appropriated tables from a number of rooms to hold her books, manuscripts, and jewelry. Voltaire, it was discovered, had given strict orders regarding his diet to the housekeeper, and the kitchen staff was disrupted. The head seamstress at the palace resigned in tears because Émilie had forced her and two assistants to work all night making a new gown she wanted to wear when meeting Richelieu, and then, not approving of the women's efforts, had ripped the dress to shreds.

In spite of their boorish behavior, Émilie and Voltaire paid a return visit to Sceaux late in the year. Their reason, it developed, was to show how a play should be done, and they brought with them the script of a comedy Voltaire had just completed, the *Comte de Boursouffle*. Émilie played the leading role, and, as always, acted with great gusto. Voltaire directed, and flew into rages when the amateur performers bungled some of his dialogue. And, in an ultimate display of bad manners, he sent hundreds of formal invitations to his theatrical and literary friends in Paris, inviting them to the performance. They came, their carriages filling the long palace driveway, to the astonishment of the Duchess, who not only was unacquainted with them, but had no idea they were coming. They filled every seat in the palace theater, forcing many of the Duchess's own guests to stand, they ate and drank prodigiously, cleaning every scrap of food from the buffet tables prepared for the Duchess's friends, and they stole "souvenirs," including several valuable statuettes and other pieces of bric-a-brac as they departed.

Voltaire was delighted. Émilie's performance had been excellent, his play had been enthusiastically received by a professional audience, and he had shown the nobility how to stage a drama. The Duchesse de Maine was less than enchanted, however, and may have wished she had been less loyal to Voltaire. There was a distinct lack of warmth in the Duchess's hospitality, and Émilie and Voltaire left Sceaux two days later for Cirey. They did not return.

For the present, Émilie had won. She and Voltaire arrived at Cirey in time to celebrate the arrival of 1748 there, and she was ready to settle into the old routines. But her lover had changed, and, although she didn't know why, she realized it. According to a meticulous diary kept by Voltaire's secretary, Longchamp, who had been a member of Émilie's household staff for a time, the couple quarreled violently and incessantly.

Voltaire made a scene one night when Émilie was late for dinner and claimed she was having an assignation with Clairault, the scientist, who was a house guest. On another occasion Voltaire, gesticulating during an argument, knocked a china cup from Émilie's hand and broke it. He himself had given her the cup, and she would not be mollified until he bought her another. Then he grumbled for days because it had cost him ten times the price of the original cup.

In brief, the romance was becoming very frayed. Yet Émilie and Voltaire were still capable of becoming completely absorbed in each other and in topics that interested them. The astonished Longchamp wrote at length in his diary about the night the couple were driving home to Cirey from a visit after a very hard snowstorm. Drifts made travel hazardous as well as difficult, and finally the carriage overturned, caving in a door.

Émilie and Voltaire were extricated, the uninjured author shouting that he had been killed, or at least maimed for life. One of the coachmen had been hurt, so he was taken off to the nearest farmhouse, which was some miles away, and the other coachman set out to find some peasants who would turn the carriage right side up.

Voltaire and Émilie removed the cushions from the carriage, and sat down near the crest of a small hill, where they tucked themselves in with blankets. They brought with them the wine, cold meats, cheese, and bread they always kept with them for emergencies when on the road, and to their delight they saw the night was so clear that not one star was missing in the sky.

For the better part of the long, bitterly cold night they discussed astronomy, which in turn led to philosophical ruminations on the nature and origins of the universe. Blissfully unaware of their surroundings, they conversed learnedly, and even the eavesdropping Longchamp, who disliked both of them, had to admit they remained bouyant. Their wit, he said, was crackling.

At last the injured coachman returned, peasants of the neighborhood righted the carriage, and the journey was resumed at daybreak. Neither Émilie nor Voltaire was in the least disturbed by the night's experience, and they shared one regret: They had lacked a telescope that would have enabled them to investigate the position of the stars that night.

There were few such incidents, however; the isolated idyll at Cirey was destined to be short-lived. Three people were responsible. The first was Stanislaus Leczinski, twice King of Poland and twice deposed, who still retained the courtesy title of monarch, and now lived as Duc de Lorraine, maintaining the fiction that he was independent of France. King Stanislaus posed no danger to the French crown, to be sure; in the first place, he had no desire to rule and sought only pleasure at Lunéville, his luxurious palace. Equally important was the fact that he was the father-in-law of Louis XV.

Stanislaus's mistress, Marie-Françoise, Marquise de Boufflers, was even more important to the future of Émilie and Voltaire. One of the most beautiful, personable, and intelligent women of her age, she was also one of the least moral, which is saying a great deal. She had at least four other known lovers during the years she spent with Stanislaus, and the total number of men she welcomed into her bed during a lifetime of more than threescore years is unknown.

Mme. de Boufflers was one of the few great ladies of France who became friendly with Mme. du Châtelet at the court of France, perhaps because she was one of the very few who could rightly consider herself Émilie's equal. Her appearance was just as striking, her own social position was secure, and she was independently wealthy. In addition, her mind was just as good as Émilie's, although she had relatively little interest in scientific matters.

The third member of the triumvirate was a Jesuit priest, Father Menou, first name unknown, who was Stanislaus's confessor. In January, 1748, he arrived unexpectedly at Cirey, bringing warm invitations to the geniuses of the château, who were urged by Stanislaus to pay him an extended visit. The priest also brought with him an informal letter to Émilie from Mme. de Boufflers that repeated the invitation in even more pressing terms.

The delighted Voltaire was eager to accept without delay. Royalty was his weakness, and a hearty reception at Lunéville would compensate, at least in part, for the chill that had set in at Fontainebleau. He had another, private reason, to be sure, impelling him to leave Cirey, where he spent most of his time exclusively in the company of Émilie. His thoughts were centering on Mme. Denis, to whom he wrote occasional, cautious letters filled with double meanings. It was unlikely that Émilie would bother to read communications to his niece, but after a decade and a half of almost-married life, Voltaire was taking no chances. In any event, his relationship with his "official" mistress would be far less strained at a busy, social court than under the roof of the dwelling that was still the property of the Marquis du Châtelet.

Émilie's reaction was more complicated. She truly enjoyed the friendship of Mme. de Boufflers, and the idea of spending time in the company of a confidante she considered her equal had a considerable appeal. Also, she was smarting from the snubs at Fontainebleau, too, and would have been less than human had she failed to respond to the prospect of the glittering balm offered her as a personage and celebrity at the court of Stanislaus.

The delicate matter of the deterioration of her personal relationship with Voltaire played a part in the making of her decision, but its extent is unknown. Certainly she was aware of a change, as she told Mme. de Boufflers in a letter that was both candid and discreet:

"You, of all my friends, will know what I mean when I say that no love between a man and a woman remains forever on the same plateau. Alas! when we fall in love we scale the heights

of the highest mountain, and when we are fortunate, as I have been, we remain for many years at that peak. The fires of passion burn brightest at the summit.

"But the fuel is consumed more rapidly there, and after a time the flames rise less high, the heat becomes less intense. Thus it has been between every man and every woman since the beginning of time, and thus will it always be.

"I have read that the flames can be rekindled and leap high again, but this is the romantic posturing of poets, nothing more. When passion goes, it cannot be aroused once again to a higher pitch between that man and that woman.

"More often than not, it is the man who first displays an inability to love as intensely as does the woman. Occasionally, to be sure, it is we who begin to yawn, and when this happens it gives us a feeling of triumph; all the same, we are saddened by our own lack of constancy. From what I have observed, it is the man, however, who finds his ardor first cooling. Why this should be so, I do not know, but am certain that this is the way of life, of nature, of the metaphysical as well as the physical that distinguishes between the man and the woman. One cannot change that which is and must be, but must accept it with good grace."

There were hints, far less direct, in Émilie's correspondence with d'Argental and Richelieu, that her relationship with Voltaire was changing. There had been no diminution of the intellectual ties that bound them together, and they undoubtedly drew on the reservoir of companionship that had been built up over so many years. But Émilie would have been stupid not to notice that Voltaire was no longer eager to sleep with her, and no one ever accused her of being dense or insensitive.

Her relatively calm acceptance of the situation is surprising. Longchamp noted that she and Voltaire quarreled frequently, which was only natural in view of the strains they were undergoing. But she no longer became hysterical when she contemplated the prospect of a permanently changed relationship. She had matured emotionally, or at least had become resigned, since the days when she had gone wild at the mere thought that Voltaire might visit Frederick of Prussia without her at his side.

Voltaire was still very fond of Émilie, and his affection for her remained undiminished. That much, at least, comes through in the story he tells in his *Mémoirs:*

"*My connection with Mme. du Châtelet was never interrupted; our friendship and our love of literature were unalterable. We lived together both in town and out of town. Cirey is situated upon the borders of Lorraine, and King Stanislaus at that time kept his little agreeable court at Lunéville. Old and fanatic as he was, he still had a friendship with a lady who was neither. His affections were divided between Mme. la Marquise de Boufflers and a Jesuit, whose name was Menou—a priest the most daring, the most intriguing I have ever known.*

"*This man had drawn from King Stanislaus, by means of his Queen, whom he had governed, about a million livres— nearly 42,000 pounds—part of which was employed in building a magnificent house for himself and some Jesuits of Nancy. This house was endowed with 24,000 livres—or a thousand pounds a year—half of which supplied his table and the other half to give away to whom she pleased.*

"*The King's mistress was not by any means so well treated; she scarcely could get from his Polish majesty the wherewithal to buy her petticoats; and yet the Jesuit envied what she had, and was violently jealous of her power. They were at open war, and the poor King had enough to do when he came from Mass every day to reconcile his mistress and his confessor.*

"*Our Jesuit at last, having heard of Mme. du Châtelet, who was exceedingly well-formed and still tolerably handsome, conceived the project of substituting her for Mme. de Boufflers.*

"*Stanislaus amused himself sometimes in writing little works, which were bad enough; and Menou imagined an authoress would succeed with him as a mistress better than any other. With this fine trick in his head, he came to Cirey, cajoled Mme.*

259

du Châtelet, and told us how delighted King Stanislaus would be to have our company. He then returned to the King and informed him how ardently we desired to come and pay our court to his majesty.

"Stanislaus asked Mme. de Boufflers to bring us; and we went to pass the whole year at Lunéville. But the projects of the holy Jesuit did not succeed; the very reverse took place: we were devoted to Mme. de Boufflers, and the friendship of Mme. du Châtelet and Mme. de Boufflers was particularly keen, so Menou had two women to combat instead of one."

This tale, although dramatic, is verified by no other source, and nothing can be found to substantiate some of the supposed facts. For example, there is no record to indicate that the Marquise de Boufflers traveled to Cirey in order to conduct Émilie and Voltaire to Lunéville. It is possible that Voltaire took heavy advantage of author's license to tell a good story.

What is demonstrably true is that Émilie and Voltaire did go to Lunéville, arriving at Stanislaus's carnival-like court early in February, 1748. They did stay for a long time, and the friendship between Émilie and her hostess became firmer.

At first the visit was similar to others that the renowned couple had made elsewhere. They set their own rules, working when they wished, as well as giving vent to the other eccentricities expected of them. They gave productions of a number of Voltaire's plays, with Émilie always cast in the leading roles, and they enjoyed themselves enormously.

But life was not what it had been in the past. Voltaire missed Mme. Denis, and his lack of intimacy with Émilie caused his "official" mistress embarrassment and pain. It is not surprising that she began to look elsewhere for ego relief and, perhaps, a touch of revenge.

Almost as a footnote to the romance of Émilie and Voltaire, another man entered their lives. Jean François, Marquis de Saint-Lambert, was a nobleman with an impeccable heritage, a feeble talent as a poet and dramatist, but clever enough to win election to the Academy in his middle years. In his public life he was something of a poseur. Other gentlemen dressed elegantly, often flamboyantly, but Saint-Lambert always attired himself in somber clothes. His manner was grave, and he smiled so seldom that Voltaire swore he had no sense of humor, which was possible.

Saint-Lambert had a penchant, in his private life, for seducing the mistresses of other men. He slept with the Marquise de Boufflers for a time in 1747, but he bored her, and she terminated the affair. He was shrewd enough to remain attentive to her, which assured him a place at Lunéville as long as he wanted. In later years he stole the mistress of Jean Jacques Rousseau, and this theft, combined with his relationship with Émilie, may be responsible for posterity's low opinion of him. A man who steals the women of the two most prominent authors of the century does so at his own peril, since their views become lasting.

Tall and ruggedly handsome, the seemingly withdrawn Saint-Lambert was thirty-two years of age at the time Émilie and Voltaire came to Lunéville. They could not have avoided him at the little court, and there is nothing in the record to indicate that Émilie tried. As both were members of a tiny, select literary circle, it was inevitable that they should see each other frequently at Stanislaus's court.

The part that Mme. de Boufflers may have played in fostering the romance of Émilie and Saint-Lambert is debatable. According to some accounts, which seem flimsy, she actively sponsored their affair, pushing them toward each other. According to other stories, including her own, she was surprised when she learned they were sleeping together.

It may be that neither version is correct. Émilie was unhappy, and it would not have been strange if she confided the reasons to her dear friend, Mme. de Boufflers. Whether Saint-Lambert was already attentive to Émilie is unknown, and there is no definitive information available to indicate that Mme.

261

de Boufflers told her Saint-Lambert was a remarkably passionate man who could help her forget the humiliation she was suffering.

Although Émilie was ten years older than Saint-Lambert, he would have been blind had he found her unattractive, and he was noted for his sensitivity to lovely women. She may have been forty-two, but she looked far younger, and he made advances to her almost from the outset of her visit to Lunéville. He made no secret of his admiration for her; it was completely in the open, and everyone—including the privately delighted Voltaire and the wise Mme. de Boufflers—was amused.

Émilie did not share in that amusement. A young, virile, and handsome man found her desirable, and she leaped enthusiastically into an affair with him. Soon after the start of the affair she wrote to Richelieu that she had solved all of her problems. She would spend the rest of her life with Voltaire, her dearest friend, but she would sleep with Saint-Lambert, whom she called "the most extraordinarily passionate of lovers."

In May the new lovers were forced to part for a time. Saint-Lambert was recalled to military duty, King Stanislaus went off to Paris for a visit with his father-in-law, and Émilie returned to Cirey with Voltaire. She planned to resume her normal work routines, but found she could not concentrate, and Voltaire was no help. While she wrote long, secret, and very foolish letters to a younger man, telling him she adored him, Voltaire was busily scribbling notes with double and triple meanings to a vastly younger woman. Two infatuated, middle-aged people were behaving like adolescents.

In June Saint-Lambert's regiment was transferred to Paris, and Émilie felt the sudden need to refresh her spirits by visiting the city. Voltaire needed no persuasion, and soon was reunited with Mme. Denis. Before Émilie saw Saint-Lambert she had a gift prepared for him, a watch which, when a secret spring was pressed, revealed her portrait inside.

Saint-Lambert was delighted, writing to her that he prized

the gift because it was similar to a watch she had given Voltaire some years earlier. He was also pleased when she sent him another gift, a bottle of hair oil that would retard his rapidly increasing baldness.

Although Émilie was whirling madly, she was still a good wife, looking out for the interests of her husband. With the aid of Mme. de Boufflers she persuaded Stanislaus to give her husband a splendid honorary appointment: late in June the Marquis du Châtelet was made Grand Marshal of the non-existent armies of Lorraine in return for wages of two thousand gold louis per year. Florent-Claude was duly grateful and wrote his wife a long letter of appreciation.

In July Émilie and Voltaire returned to Lorraine, joining Stanislaus and his suite at their summer palace, Commercy. Saint-Lambert obtained a convenient leave of absence from his regiment, and Émilie became more blatant in her affair with him, probably because her suite was far removed from that of Voltaire. Mme. de Boufflers helped by assigning Saint-Lambert quarters near Émilie's, and Voltaire unwittingly cooperated by falling ill. Confined to his bed for almost two weeks, he could not appear at odd hours in Émilie's apartment.

The author's recovery was swift, however, and late one night he went to Émilie's suite, where he found Émilie in the company of Saint-Lambert under circumstances that left nothing to the imagination. His dignity and vanity bruised, the outraged author withdrew, ordering his secretary to obtain immediate transportation to Paris. Meanwhile the shocked Saint-Lambert told Émilie his honor had been tarnished and that he would challenge Voltaire the next day.

The incident jolted Émilie into temporary sanity. She followed Voltaire to his rooms, forcing Longchamp to admit her, and spent hours talking to her lover of so many years, addressing him first in English, then in French. The gist of her argument was that both of them would look absurd if he acted hastily, and Voltaire, eventually becoming calmer, realized he had lost nothing. In fact, he could show less caution hereafter in his affair with Mme. Denis, so he laughed and agreed to drop the embarrassing matter.

After handling Voltaire, it was easy for Émilie to deal with Saint-Lambert. She persuaded him to forget the proposed duel, telling him Voltaire was far too famous to indulge in such juvenile nonsense. But her peacemaking efforts were almost spoiled the following day. Voltaire, who had just written a long letter to Mme. Denis, met Saint-Lambert in the corridor of the palace and condescendingly accepted an apology that had not been offered. All Émilie's efforts as a diplomat and temptress were needed to terminate the new squabble.

Voltaire's literary affairs in Paris were becoming complicated, and by mid-autumn the author wanted to return to Paris. Émilie found one excuse after another for remaining at the court of Stanislaus. Saint-Lambert again had returned to military duty, so her dalliance made no sense to Voltaire, but at last he wormed the shocking truth from her.

Émilie confessed to him that she was pregnant.

The situation was worthy of the most trivial French farce, but it was also grim. Many years had passed since Émilie had last gone to bed with her husband, so she couldn't try to claim that the baby was legitimate. Certainly Voltaire had no intention of saying the baby was his, and Émilie faced the twin horrors of ridicule and disgrace.

Her position was even more precarious than Voltaire knew, she finally admitted to him. She had written the news to Saint-Lambert, who had not deigned to reply. Afraid he had not received the communication, she had sent him four more letters, none of which he had answered.

Voltaire pondered for a time, and then said that since the child would be unable to claim a father, it would have to be classified as one of Émilie's miscellaneous works.

Her sense of humor muted, Émilie wrote to the Marquise de Boufflers, now in Paris with Stanislaus, telling her friend the whole story and asking if she could give birth to the baby at Lunéville, as she dreaded the isolation of Cirey.

The energetic, practical Mme. de Boufflers solved the problem by laying it before King Stanislaus. He sent for Saint-Lambert, who was at the front in Flanders, and had a long talk with the young Marquis behind closed doors. By the end of the session Saint-Lambert agreed not only to acknowledge the paternity of the child but to stand beside Émilie during her ordeal. Stanislaus occupied no throne, but knew how to use the power he possessed, and he was a man of high ethical standards.

Émilie and Voltaire went to Cirey, where they broke the news to the Marquis du Châtelet. Émilie's husband accepted the inevitable, perhaps because he had no choice, but no one could blame him for escaping the mess by cutting short his visit and hurriedly rejoining his troops.

Voltaire's kindness to Émilie during the months of her trial demonstrated, as nothing else could have done, the depth of his devotion to her. King Frederick chose just this time to request that the author pay him a visit in the immediate future, and the French authorities exerted pressure of their own on behalf of their gallant ally. But Voltaire, telling no one his reason, insisted that nothing would or could persuade him to leave Émilie's side. Even Mme. Denis had to get along as best she could without him; he wrote to her that he would not see her again until an event of which both were cognizant took place.

Stanislaus returned to Lorraine, and granted Émilie permission to have her baby on any property he owned. She and Voltaire rejoined his suite at Lunéville in the late spring of 1749, then went on with the party to Commercy. Both geniuses buried themselves in work. Voltaire was writing a new, untitled tragedy and was adding new chapters to his history of Louis XV's reign. Émilie was making a translation of the complete works of Newton, a project that would take many years to complete, and her old friend, Clairault, came to Lorraine so she could study abstract theories of mathematics with him.

In mid-summer, when Émilie's time approached, she and Voltaire preceded Stanislaus and his court to Lunéville. There Saint-Lambert joined them, in August, but the three were spared the embarrassment of being forced to share each other's company by the return of Stanislaus, Mme. de Boufflers, and their company. Saint-Lambert, still in disfavor, was housed in a building located a mile and a half from the palace, but he made it his business to call on Émilie several times each day.

She admitted him to her quarters, but her infatuation had come to an end. Voltaire was still her dear friend, to be sure, but she saw him only at supper, which they ate in private. She spent the rest of her time concentrating on her work, which preserved her sanity.

On September 1, 1749, the forty-three-year-old Émilie du Châtelet gave birth to a daughter while sitting at her desk translating Newton. Voltaire immediately sent word to friends in Paris, and had to make up a dramatic story. Émilie, he said, was writing out a Newtonian equation, and was so absorbed in her work that she didn't realize she was in the throes of childbirth until the baby appeared. Not knowing what to do with the infant until she could summon her maid, she placed it temporarily on a quarto volume of geometry. Then, because it was expected of her, she had gone to bed.

Stanislaus, Mme. de Boufflers, and the whole court rejoiced, and Émilie's suite was filled with visitors. Voltaire, who was in constant attendance, privately complained to Mme. Denis that he was losing valuable work time. And Émilie's rooms were so crowded that Saint-Lambert often was compelled to cool his heels in the corridor outside.

On September 5th Émilie felt pangs of what she considered to be indigestion, but they weren't severe enough to curtail the party atmosphere in her suite. The next day she felt somewhat worse, and physicians were summoned. They diagnosed her ailment as a stomach upset caused by a particularly rich dish

Stanislaus's chef had made to celebrate the birth of the baby.

On September 7th Voltaire and Saint-Lambert were summoned to Émilie's apartment. She was either asleep or in a coma, and Mme. de Boufflers, who arrived with the two men, tried in vain to arouse her friend by holding a handkerchief soaked in vinegar under her nose. All at once Émilie stopped breathing, and the physicians arrived to pronounce her dead. The Marquis du Châtelet, who had arrived at Lunéville the preceding day, came into the suite just in time to hear that his wife was gone.

Voltaire completely lost his equilibrium, and, weeping copiously, dashed out of the apartment. He stumbled, lost his balance and struck his head against a post, which caused him to tumble down a flight of stairs. Saint-Lambert, who had been close behind him, hastened to pick him up, and Voltaire, although badly shaken, did not lose his sense of the dramatic. "My friend," he said in a loud, clear voice, "my death, too, lies at your door." Then he cursed at the unfortunate Saint-Lambert before being led away to his own suite.

In his *Mémoirs* he dealt with the matter succinctly: *"Mme. du Châtelet died in the palace of Stanislaus after two days' illness; and we were so affected that not one of us ever remembered to send for priest, Jesuit or any of the seven sacraments. It was we, and not Mme. du Châtelet, who felt the horror of death."*

At the time his grief overwhelmed him. He spent twenty-four hours in his chambers, alone, and then sent a brief letter to Mme. du Deffand, in which he blamed himself for the joking tone he had used when writing to his friends about the birth of the baby:

"If anything could increase the horrible condition in which I am, it would be that of having taken with gaiety an adventure of which the conclusion will render the remainder of my life miserable. They are taking me to Cirey with M. du Châtelet.

From there I shall return to Paris without knowing what will become of me, and hoping soon to rejoin her."

Neither he nor anyone else demonstrated the least interest in the infant, which soon followed her mother to the grave.

Before leaving Lunéville, Voltaire also wrote to d'Argental: *"I have not lost merely a mistress, I have lost the half of myself —a soul for which mine was made, a friend whom I saw born. The most tender father does not love his only daughter more truly."*

Stanislaus gave Émilie a state funeral worthy of a queen, delaying it until the arrival of her son, now the deputy commander of a regiment. The following day the Marquis du Châtelet, his son, and Voltaire went to Cirey. There the author wrote to King Frederick:

"She was a great man whose only fault was in being a woman. A woman who translated and explained Newton, and who made a free translation of Virgil, without letting it appear in conversation that she had done these wonders; a woman who never spoke evil of anyone, and who never told a lie; a friend attentive and courageous in friendship—in one word, a very great man whom ordinary women knew only by her diamonds—that is the one whom you cannot hinder me from mourning all of my life."

The atmosphere of Cirey, where Voltaire had spent so many years with Émilie, weighed on his soul, and he said that every moment he spent there was a torture. Thoughtfully packing all of his belongings, including many cartons of books, he also took most of Émilie's personal furniture, and sent off a wagon train to Paris. He followed a day or two later, taking up his residence in the house on the Faubourg Saint-Honoré, but spending most of his evenings with Mme. Denis, who gave him the consolation he needed.

Émilie's death was the sensation of Europe, and thoughtful men everywhere mourned the most intellectual woman of the era. Society reacted to the news in its own way, and at Versailles the nobles tried to compete with each other in writing witty epigrams and jokes. One of these, its author unknown, survived longer than any of the others: *"It is to be hoped that this is the last of Mme. du Châtelet's airs. To die in childbirth at her age is to wish to be singular, and to have pretensions to do nothing like other people."*

Principal Bibliography

Assé, Eugène. *Lettres de la Marquise du Châtelet.* Paris, 1806.

Bestermann, Theodore. *Studies on Voltaire and the Eighteenth Century.* 2 vols. London, 1956.

Desnoiresterres, M. *Voltaire et la société française.* Paris, 1867.

Espinasse, F. *Voltaire.* Paris, 1882.

Hamel, Frank. *An Eighteenth Century Marquise.* New York, 1911.

Longchamp. *Memoires sur Voltaire.* Paris, 1826.

Mitford, Nancy. *Voltaire in Love.* New York, Harper, 1958.

Morley, Lord. *Voltaire.* London, 1872.

Noyes, Alfred. *Voltaire.* London, 1936.

Robertson, J. M. *Voltaire.* London, 1922.

Stern, Jean. *Voltaire et sa nièce Madame Denis,* Paris, 1957.

Voltaire. *Correspondence.* 11 vols. Paris, 1881–1897.

INDEX